THE EXTRAORDINARY WORKPLACE

THE

Extraordinary Workplace

Replacing Fear with Trust and Compassion

✳   ✳   ✳

Danna Beal, M.Ed.

SENTIENT PUBLICATIONS

First Sentient Publications edition 2010
Copyright © 2010 by Danna Beal

A paperback original

Cover design by Kim Johansen, Black Dog Design
Book design by Timm Bryson

Printed in the United States of America

Library of Congress Cataloging-in-Publication Data
Beal, Danna.
 The extraordinary workplace : replacing fear with trust and
compassion /
Danna Beal. -- 1st ed.
    p. cm.
 ISBN 978-1-59181-105-3 (pbk.)
 1. Work environment. 2. Interpersonal communication. 3. Quality
of work
life. 4. Corporate culture. I. Title.
 HD7261.B36 2010
 658.3'8--dc22
                            2010032039
10 9 8 7 6 5 4 3 2 1

SENTIENT PUBLICATIONS

A Limited Liability Company
1113 Spruce Street
Boulder, CO 80302
www.sentientpublications.com

*In memory of my father, Daniel "Bud" Gates,
and Rodney Edward Gannon, an enlightened leader.*

*Dedicated to my mother, Margaret "Peggy" Meenach Gates
And to my son and daughter, Kyle and Stephanie,
for their ever-abiding love, faith, and trust in me.*

Never doubt that a small group of thoughtfully committed citizens can change the world; indeed, it is the only thing that ever has.

—Margaret Mead

CONTENTS

10. EMANCIPATION   211

EPILOGUE: PERSONAL FREEDOM AND GLOBAL ONENESS   243

PURPOSE

This book is about rebuilding relationships in the workplace by honoring the spirit in ourselves and in others that resides beneath our self-created identities, which battle and compete for power and validation. This shallow interpretation of ourselves, a shabby imitation we have come to believe is true, belies our incredible authentic power. One day, when fear can be replaced with trust and compassion for one another, there will be a shift in consciousness. People everywhere will be restored to their true identities, their inner spiritual greatness intended by the Creator. To that end, this book is dedicated.

ACKNOWLEDGEMENTS

I humbly acknowledge those people whose roles in my life have profoundly touched me and taught me who I am:

My sisters, Nancy Martin, Cindy McMahon, Deb Prouty, and Tammy Von Steuben, and my brother, Dan Gates, for their loving support for a lifetime.

My supportive friends Pat Keas, Robin Houston, Kris Lundberg, Ronna Lynch, Pat Carey, Mikki Bieber, Pat McNamara, and Colleen Anderson with whom I shared spiritual evolution, laughter, and tears, all of which were invaluable to this work.

My spiritual brothers John Pilley, Bob Beale, Leonard Szymczak, and Brante C'Evan for helping me with my destiny of sharing this message in the workplace.

To my agent, Bill Gladstone, Waterside Productions, and my publisher, Connie Shaw, Sentient Publications, for bringing this book to fruition and out to the world.

You have all contributed to my life's work.

INTRODUCTION

Something was wrong. As a business consultant and speaker throughout the United States and Canada, I had worked closely with leaders and employees in a wide variety of businesses, organizations, and industries, including hospitals, physician practices, CPA firms, law firms, auto dealerships, banks, restaurants, museums, retirement centers, retail stores, non-profit agencies, school districts, insurance agencies, government agencies, construction companies, chambers of commerce, and numerous small businesses. I was very concerned.

These experiences provided a bird's eye view of the internal workings of so many diverse entities. Although these wide-ranging businesses and organizations had various services and products, they all had one thing in common—an underlying theme that was very disconcerting.

Sadly, I came to realize that most workplaces are filled with misunderstood relationships, emotional turmoil, internal competition, and reactionary dynamics. The complexity of most organizations is escalating; the water is heating up, so to speak. Now more than ever, people feel uncertainty, trepidation, and deep anxiety about their future.

The present workplace environment is fraught with fears and envy, egos competing for validation and attention, managers disempowering employees, co-workers hurting and sabotaging one another, and most insidious of all, an underlying fear permeating the atmosphere with insecurity and indecision.

Do you think this is an exaggeration? It is not. The pressure resulting from the high demands in an ever-competitive business environment can be seen in the faces and heard in the words of employees on any given day in any business. The pain and high levels of stress are reflected in numerous national and international studies of employee satisfaction, employee engagement, loyalty, and retention. The work environment has never been more combative and filled with emotional turbulence. It is almost amazing that any work is accomplished, considering all the distractions. I am going to suggest that most business productivity and achievement is motivated by fear rather than inspiration.

Suspend your judgment and consider the possibilities for new levels of business success and advancement if we had an environment of compassion, respect, and freedom. Instead of wasting energy and time with negative emotions, individuals could contribute from their full potential with eagerness and enthusiasm.

More than ever before, businesses and organizations need the energy and synergism that comes from good relationships, teamwork, creativity, and productivity among leaders and employees. Developing the potential of everyone, and allowing their full expression and talent in the roles that they play, is essential for a company's success. To rise above the clamor in such a declining market, and to navigate during the lean times, companies must understand the power of honor, respect, and group engagement. Enlightened leaders who recognize that they must release the powerful energy and intelligence of the people in their organizations will build extraordinary workplaces and achieve high levels of business success. But in reality, most leaders do not maximize performance, and instead unwittingly deplete the energy of those they need to drive their financial goals.

Businesses have followed a model of managing, measuring, and distributing financial capital as a basis for increasing profitability. What this old model doesn't recognize are the resources that create capital: people, relationships, and the innate ingenuity of the employees within the organization, often the frontline workers. This potential is being suppressed in businesses everywhere.

Measurements and metrics that don't address the underlying issue of managing people and relationships will produce limited results. They could be likened to a football game in which demands are made to increase the scores on the scoreboard without consideration of the team members who must play the game and make the touchdowns. Metrics are simply the reflection of the activities, services, and relationships of people, not the other way around.

Top-down directives do not allow for possibilities coming from the human capital, which could, in fact, increase market success, create new business opportunities, and ultimately drive profitability. The old model is obsolete and new steps are necessary to stop the tidal wave of events threatening businesses all across the country. Blind faith in dogmatic, rigid systems has led to enterprises that are imploding. Downsizing is increasing and unemployment is rising, with predictions of more layoffs.

Enlightened leaders recognize the value of human capital and the importance of relationships within the company and with customers. Creating an environment of trust that capitalizes on all people in the organization will produce a competitive advantage. The business will also be a happier place to work, a driver for loyalty, retention, and commitment. The new model will produce cooperation instead of competition as leaders respect and honor the spirit in those they lead. I am suggesting that within every human being is an invisible, inner spirit that is connected to the power that sustains all life, as well as to one another. Whether we are aware of it or not, this internal spirit resides beneath the ego roles and is eternal.

While working with many different organizations, I have observed the results of the old business model. I have seen prejudices, harassment, political and territorial battles, selfishness, grandiosity, betrayal, and suffering—all consequences of disempowered human beings trying to elevate themselves at the expense of others. Gossip by both men and women is rampant, and power struggles between individuals and groups occur at all levels—from the CEOs down. Gossip provides temporary relief from pain by giving a sense of power to those engaged in it and by allowing them to share their misery. Even as it appears to temporarily relieve some pain in individuals, gossip does so at the cost of adding more negativity and uncertainty to the work environment.

Some people are energized by a competitive environment. This, however, is only temporary because fear and mistrust always accompany the cutthroat atmosphere. Deception and suspicion are prevalent, and the ever-present shadow of anxiety lurks in the background. Emotions are suppressed and people are psychologically and energetically out of balance.

The workplace has become an emotional combat zone where people suffer from stress and insecurity in the very place they rely on for their financial security. And so great is the fear of losing job security, many people cannot readily admit, even to themselves, that the situation is this traumatic. Finally, leadership rarely recognizes or is willing to acknowledge these problems, even though they are felt throughout the organization. So the anxiety resides beneath the surface, because addressing it is too frightening and filled with unknown consequences for those who dare.

Why is all this turbulence in the workplace occurring?

It is the result of the ego's efforts to overcome its own sense of powerlessness in the face of fear and uncertainty. Large financial business failures, problems in the national and global economies, and rapid changes in the local and worldwide business environment have created a new level of anxiety and apprehension. In addition, the need to learn new technologies, the "personal hell" created by email, a 24/7 work week powered by mobile and electronic technology, and a workaholic theme that permeates businesses today have all added to the sense of exhaustion and helplessness. People feel they cannot keep up with the demands yet they must continue to produce and to maintain their jobs. And as the economy drops and the downsizing increases, numerous employees are working with the sense of a hatchet hanging over their heads.

People everywhere have a sense of being lost in the storm, and feel insignificant and vulnerable. The inner sense of authentic power and confidence required to withstand this pressure is obscured by fear, fatigue, and the need to cope with the ever-present cutthroat attitude of bosses and co-workers. Some leave the employment environment in favor of self-employment or entrepreneurship. Those options require the courage to take risks, which include the loss of healthcare and other retirement benefits, and uncertain income. Those are difficult choices when one is supporting a family. So most employees feel trapped in their workplaces, where they are disengaged, not working at their full potential, emotionally suppressed, and secretly looking for a new job.

This harried and impersonal environment has resulted in a variety of behaviors by people attempting to cope and to reduce fear. These are methods to disguise and prevent pain. The projection, blame, gossip, back stabbing, manipulation, and other dysfunctional behaviors are all attempts by the ego to deny the deep lack of self-worth. These attempts to bolster the ego are futile strategies to mask insecurity and alleviate anxiety. Unfortunately, the pressure to perform leads to sacrifice, compromise, and abandonment of values at all levels within the organization. The corruption and greed of leaders in many organizations are starting to surface and be revealed in the news on a daily basis.

The current model is a fractured system of falsities and misalignments. Elaborate schemes to protect the power and wealth of the dominant few have made business and government systems very complex, with many layers of protection. These structures need to be weakened, broken, and eliminated to allow a new system to take their place—one that honors and respects the privacy and rights of everyone. The more people who understand the way out of this massive delusion, the faster we can escape it.

The response from both leaders and employees of various organizations throughout the country is a resounding "yes," confirming that the situation has, indeed, reached critical proportions. The crisis doesn't exist in just a few organizations and businesses, but occurs to some degree in nearly every single business throughout the country. Today, people cry out for a solution and anxiously pray for some relief from this dilemma.

People are spiritually hungry and emotionally depleted. They do not know how to escape from the misery experienced in the very place where they spend three-fourths of their waking hours. It is a double-edged sword: they feel they depend on the organization to provide their economic security, and yet staying in the organization causes them enormous levels of anxiety and apprehension. Many people feel immobilized. Counselors and physicians are seeing a growing number of desperate and unhealthy people who suffer from job stress. In addition, because of their desire to be loved and appreciated, people are slaves to a rigid system of rivalry and dysfunction.

Rebuilding relationships with trust, honor, and respect is the only way businesses will survive. I will share a new method for understanding and breaking through the intense drama. Those engaged in it are unable to discern the underlying causes of the confusion and resentment. The solution is simple but very abstruse. Those on the stage are too deeply involved to see the whole picture. In fact, it is nearly impossible for an individual to come out of the depths of the drama without a helping hand to lift, support, and show a way out.

This book will share with you a framework that illuminates and simplifies the complexity of the web of reacting and counter-reacting egos. The model will help you discover a way to operate from authentic power rather than from the fragile power of the ego. It is then a process of practicing and demonstrating this new way to interact with the people with whom you work. You must do the suggested steps (not just read the book) to truly rise out of the dissension and confusion, and thus have the power to create change for yourself and others. The results will be the proof. The positive outcome will be recognized and perpetuated. It will cause a domino effect in the workplace, and it will be self-rewarding to those who commit to and practice this unique approach.

The good news is the workplace can provide many opportunities for learning and evolution because life lessons are presented in relationships. Because of the repeated interactions in the workplace, egos are often hooked in, resulting in suffering, anger, projection, and self-doubt. Frequent interaction with the same people results in intensified emotions and reactions. When you can respond to conflicts with self-reflection, confrontations and painful experiences will provide portals for personal evolution and realizations. It is our life purpose to become restored to our inner greatness, our true selves, and our inherent joy. As they bring up pain and anxiety within us, relationships can also lead us to discover the source of the problem, so we can release it and become free.

However, it is not easy to give up the demands of the ego, because we will do anything to protect its false identity. We find it personally humiliating to let go of our need to be in control because we fear doing so will diminish the image we have of ourselves. Our ego is dependent upon the reactions of others to validate and to reinforce its identity; we do not give up this emotional turmoil easily, even when it causes immense suffering.

This book is intended to help create a transformation in business leaders that will then make it safer for employees to also begin the process. Although anyone can stop playing their automatic part in the scenes played out by others in the workplace, it is generally more impactful when the practice is initiated by those in leadership positions, because of their perceived authority.

Through this model, it will become clear that the only path to genuine success, inner peace, and ultimate happiness comes from facing and then challenging the ego. The book is intended to help people step off the stage of the long-running drama in the workplace and find personal freedom.

GETTING TO THE SOURCE OF THE POWER STRUGGLES

How does this change come about in the tightly woven drama of intertwined egos? The aim is to shed light on the core causes and fundamental reasons for power struggles, territorial battles, and lack of camaraderie.

Leaders, business managers, and owners can most easily begin taking steps to unravel the closely-knit mesh of egos in the workplace. Those they lead are often too disempowered and wounded to initiate the process. However, we are all endowed with the same authentic power, in spite of the temporary roles we play in our workplace. If you can see beyond the hierarchy, you can be a light for others as you relax and operate from your inner source rather than from the fear of loss and the need to placate. You will add a positive stream of energy, helping to uplift those around you.

This book is not a simple how-to course on the steps to become a good leader. I have found most courses and books on leadership are instructions on how to change behavior and how to act like a leader. Any real, long-lasting change comes from discovering the underlying belief systems that limit decisions and opportunities. This book teaches you to realize and release barriers that prevent inner qualities of authentic and enlightened leadership from emerging.

Most leaders in all sizes of organizations operate from the ego, rather than from authentic power. The ego blocks true creativity and energy that could be unleashed in the workplace. Egoic leadership also constrains the abilities and possibilities of its followers, which impacts the bottom line.

Some symptoms of an ego-driven management style include the following:

- Personal agendas rather than the common good of the organization are the order of the day.
- Conditioning from past mistakes and disappointments is the basis for decisions.
- External validation such as money, status, and power are the motivators.
- Projection and blame, rather than ownership and personal responsibility, are the norm.
- Fear is the underlying factor for all action.
- Rivalry and internal competition block true teamwork and alliance.
- Lip service and inauthentic communication are common.
- Rigidity and high control are the underlying structure.
- Disregard of employees' needs or feelings is normal and usually rationalized.
- Discrimination (age, race, gender, weight, sexual orientation, religion, etc.), though denied, is occurring.

Moving away from the ego-driven, top-down management style is critical for companies to grow, to attract and retain competent employees, to increase employee engagement, to gain loyalty and respect, and to build cooperation and contribution.

What does it take for leaders to make this transformation?

A restoration to authenticity requires the courage and willingness of leaders to look with an unflinching eye at their own inadequacies and fears. It means looking within and seeing errors, misjudgments, and false claims of righteousness. Honest and deep reflection will allow strength of character, integrity, and true leadership to arise.

This book will aid in finding freedom from the ego, the self-created identity and source of the endless battles in almost every business. Becoming an enlightened business leader will require disengaging from the insane drama and creating an environment of harmony, trust, and compassion.

Because of ego-driven management, millions in the workplace feel as though they are in prison, with little freedom of expression or ability to perform and contribute at their highest level. Learning to face the ego and becoming an enlightened leader are meaningful and necessary goals. Business leaders who begin to personally transform and become restored to their true selves will free employees to work creatively and productively within an environment that fosters their true potential.

As leaders give up the need for superiority, employees will lay down the defenses and complaints of the downtrodden. People will learn to give up blaming others for their circumstances and take back their own destinies. As leaders elevate their own understanding, they will be models for those they lead. Those they guide will find liberation and discover their own inner authority. People who are free will perform better.

The ability to transcend murky waters and complex interactions can come about only when one connects with the inner spirit residing in each of us. Then we acknowledge the same spirit in others. Giving up ego demands, however, is very difficult and will take commitment and determination. The ego's goal is to keep fear below the surface and to convince you and others it is invincible. Getting someone to give up the demands of the ego is like taking a favorite toy away from a child who grasps it tightly. We do not let go of our demanding ego without a fight.

The real conflict becomes ego versus spirit. It is a most formidable battle because the ego is relentless and shrewd in its desire to remain in charge. But as you persevere, the grip of the ego will diminish and spiritual strength will begin to replace the artificial power of the ego.

Like anything new, it will take practice, and you will have some trials and errors in the workplace. But gradually, the results will become apparent. People will begin to communicate on a deeply honest and respectful level when they feel trust and integrity in the environment. Gossip and sabotage will become a thing of the past as people begin this process of changing internally and accepting personal responsibility. They will enjoy coming to work, sharing mutual goals, and feeling the satisfaction of a job well done.

Businesses will reach new, extraordinary levels of success as the synergy of teamwork is allowed to emerge in an environment where optimism and compassion prevail. Employees will start to feel loyalty once again, and organizations will attract and retain the kind of people they desire. Cooperation without suspicion will return to the workplace. When everyone no longer expends energy in battles with one another, new vigor and vitality will become available for positive production and success. This positive force of human dynamics has been so restricted in the current environment.

I invite you to join me in the worthwhile endeavor of rebuilding relationships in the workplace so businesses can become extraordinary and people everywhere can have a better quality of life. The workplace is where millions of people come face to face with the issues within themselves that need healing. Let us use the opportunity to rediscover who we are and be restored to our inner, spiritual greatness. Discovering our strength by recognizing and letting go of fear will lead to genuine happiness and deep fulfillment. As the workplace atmosphere becomes peaceful, our families, communities, social structures, governments, and future generations will be affected. We will begin to experience the joy, tranquility, and vitality we desire and deserve.

So to be very clear, the goals of this book are two-fold: short term—heal the pain; long term—heal the soul. As we each do our part to awaken to our authentic selves, we contribute to the collective consciousness and we create an extraordinary workplace.

CHAPTER 1

The Current Workplace Environment

✳   ✳   ✳

PEOPLE ARE SUFFERING

This book is about a restoration process—the restoration of you to your authentic self and the restoration of the workplace to an environment of trust and compassion. These are grave times. Sadly, people suffer everywhere in businesses and organizations because they operate from wounded egos in environments of fear, rather than of respect and cooperation. Leaders under pressure to perform and employees under the fear of job loss feel fatigue and emotional depletion.

However, acceptance of what is an unhappy atmosphere perpetuates the situation because without acknowledgement, no correction or improvement can be made. Only when it is recognized that we do not have to live this way can we agree to resolve it. Dan Dana, Ph.D., international speaker, author, and founder of Mediation Works, states, "Unmanaged conflict is the largest reducible cost in organizations today, and the least recognized."

Below the surface of most workplaces lurks an undercurrent pulling people down. Although the surface appears calm and the undercurrent is not visible to outsiders, those who work in this environment become exhausted from using so much energy to navigate through it. Some swim on top, furiously trying to stay ahead of the current, many tread water, others backpedal, and some are drowning.

Speaking at national and international conventions throughout the United States and Canada, I have asked the audiences of all sizes and industries to describe the current workplace environment and what they perceive to be the barriers to an extraordinary workplace. These participants are leaders and managers from a wide variety of businesses, organizations, and government offices.

Here are the words these people from different levels of management, in cities both large and small, use to describe the workplace environment:

- Paranoia
- Egos
- Fear
- Blame
- One-upsmanship
- Lack of trust
- Cliques and power structures
- Turf protection
- Gossip
- Insecurity
- Lack of appreciation
- Power struggles
- Secretiveness
- Sabotaging
- Withholding information
- Hidden and personal agendas
- Intimidation
- Sucking up

- Unpredictability
- Workaholism
- Lack of open communication
- All kinds of discrimination (sexual preference, gender, race, religion, etc.)

Does that sound like a wonderful place to spend eight to twelve hours a day, five to six days a week—or more?

Keep in mind: The above comments are from leaders and managers from around the country. However, employees and lower-level staff have the same complaints—only amplified, as they have less power to bring about change. Some CEOs claim politics are not allowed, which only keeps the problems below the surface and certainly doesn't solve the problem or get to its source.

As a consultant to businesses, I begin new engagements by conducting an information-gathering session with each member of the organization's management and staff. These sessions are confidential so I can assess the organization, its culture, its needs, and its goals from a variety of viewpoints.

Individuals who are in pain often reveal to me, the outside consultant, what they will not share with the leadership in the organization, even through anonymous surveys and exit interviews, for fear of reprisal. Repeatedly, I have heard men and women, managers and staff, individually describe to me the stress and suffering of working in their current environment.

It is not the job or work they dislike. In fact, most people enjoy work itself, and people inherently do want to do a good job. The problems are the politics, undercurrents of biases and power struggles, fear, insecurity, internal competition, and lack of trust in the environment.

In general, employees express feeling unappreciated, left out of decisions, suspicious of fellow employees, and exhausted from being unable to meet workload demand.

In addition, they convey little loyalty, as they often feel the management does not care about them. They describe management as interested in them only as a tool to make more money for the owners, shareholders, or senior-level managers. They often feel their job could be eliminated and management has no loyalty toward them.

The managers are distrustful of other managers and wary of those they manage. Fear of others outperforming and replacing them is very common, although not easily admitted. Individuals at all levels state a desire for improvement in the environment, a need for teamwork, and hope for relief from stress.

However, most people indicate a feeling of resignation, a sense of despair and cynicism about the possibility that anything could change. They communicate an attitude of "that's just the way it is and it probably won't change." Many individuals admit they are keeping their eye out for another job opportunity somewhere else where they believe they would find a better environment. According to a study by consultants Towers Perrin, 55 percent of US employees are passively looking for new jobs. This means they are not engaged at work and are vulnerable to other offers. It shows a vast reserve of available employee performance potential that could drive better financial results if only companies could tap into this reserve.

Unfortunately, when people depart from an organization they will usually discover the same scenario wherever they go. Real change starts when we look within for choice. Otherwise, the new workplace will be a continuation of the same issues, with different people. We are really looking for self-worth and significance, and we want to make a contribution.

EMPLOYEES' PERCEPTION OF THE WORKPLACE

Let's look more closely at the workplace from the perspective of employees. The world of an employee in a company where spirit and compassion are not present in the leadership looks like the following. (This is a composite of comments made to me by employees with whom I've consulted.)

> On Sunday, I am often depressed, thinking of returning to the harshness of yet another day at a workplace that I find uncertain and unsatisfying at best, miserable and intolerable at worst. I try to deny this because I am dependent upon the job to financially survive. I convince myself and others that my job is tolerable.

At work, I am unaware of the company's mission. And if there is a mission, I had no input into it, so why should I have any personal commitment to it? [Research has shown that employee input into the company's mission or seeing the benefit for them in it is an important component to job satisfaction.] I don't feel in the know. Communication from management is incomplete and inconsistent, and there is often a sense of secrecy. There is an unspoken agreement that many issues and topics are not open to discussion.

There is some camaraderie and there are efforts to appreciate others, demonstrated by celebrations, employee recognition events, picnics, birthdays, etc., but they are often tinged with a sense of tension and a lack of authenticity.

And lying under the surface is the actual lack of trust felt toward management, as well as each other, which creates a constant uneasiness and unrest. Most everyone feels an undercurrent of rivalry, although it is rarely admitted or addressed.

I may be a very high performer, but my accomplishments are often the result of my fear of being replaced or overlooked, rather than of positive motivation. However, I feel unappreciated. I'm rarely acknowledged for a job well done. [This is the most common complaint about the work environment.]

I'm expected to provide outstanding service for the company, and yet I feel there is no integrity about this. I'm obligated to project something outward that is not practiced from within my company. I feel like a hypocrite, trying to represent a standard that is not operating internally. I wonder why management doesn't practice what they preach.

Because I feel I really have no voice, after my initial phase of employment I gave up trying to express concerns or make a difference in my workplace. Besides, issues addressing employee happiness and internal consistency are rarely acknowledged. Even if they are, little is done to speak to them and nothing really changes. I have become resigned to how things are and have stopped trying to contribute when my work is not recognized or received with good intention.

My viewpoint of management is that the company is out to just make money, create personal power, and look after its own interests. As a result, I have very little allegiance to its leadership. When another opportunity for me opens up elsewhere, I will be gone in a flash, leaving everyone surprised because of my unexpressed misery.

Of course, not wanting to burn bridges, I probably will not express my true feelings about the workplace or the reason for leaving. Management doesn't really care, and if anything, will assume it's not the company's fault. They will quickly move on to hire my replacement, never examining what lesson might have been learned or what could have been done differently to have kept me.

On the other hand, perhaps the management will hold it against me for leaving—a simple case of projection of the problem onto anyone but itself.

Meanwhile, in this depressing environment I leave at the end of the day exhausted and unsatisfied with the work completed, but happy the day has ended. Hump day (Wednesday) I embrace with enthusiasm, as I look forward to Friday and relief from the exhausting, endless grind of my job. The weekend flies by and Sunday is upon me once again, almost ruined at some point in the day when I begin to think of returning to work on Monday.

Does this sound like you? Or could this be someone you manage? This perception of being a victim comes from the wounded ego who cannot see its participation in this insufferable situation. Employees often feel they have no voice and therefore believe nothing can be done to alter the situation. Because of their perceived lack of power, they are usually not able to make significant differences, so they resort to other methods to cope in the unhappy workplace.

Since employees have little influence to make structural change, any significant transformation in the culture usually must be initiated by the company leaders. However, individuals who are not officially designated leaders sometimes wield influence because they operate from strength of character and integrity. They command respect from others based on their inner traits of courage and honesty. They stand up in the workplace and refuse to be hooked into the company's ongoing power struggles. They have authentic power.

Often employees do see the truth—the powerlessness of egos running the company. They may be able to see the Emperor Wears No Clothes scenario, but are usually too frightened of repercussions to try to impact the dynamics of management. They joke with each other in an attempt to minimize their own anxiety and elevate their sense of confidence. Complaining or kidding about the gloomy situation may relieve some tension but doesn't solve the real problems.

When those in charge of organizations focus on their own personal development and seek to reach their inner core of truth, they impact the whole organization. Challenging the dictates of the ego is the only gateway to genuine personal growth, as both a person and a leader.

UNDERSTANDING THE EGO

An understanding of the ego, in the sense I am using it, is important here. Enlightened leadership requires freedom from some of the constraints of the ego mind. The ego is a self-created identity, which is a small portion of who we are destined to become. It is a role we project into the world to create an image we think is desirable. It helps us cope in uncertain situations, get what we think we need, and keep safe.

It is not real, but merely a way to define who we are that we believe will get us through life with as little bruising and suffering as possible. The ego unconsciously knows it is really very small and does not want this discovered by the self or others. It is very insecure and looks outside itself to find security and support for its role in the world. Most of all, our ego wants to present an image of confidence to cover our fear. When I ask my audiences what they really fear, I always get the same answers, regardless of the industry or level of employment:

- Rejection
- Humiliation
- Lack of acceptance

- Failure
- Appearing stupid
- Pain
- Lack of respect
- Vulnerability
- Abandonment

Our false image requires us to have a countenance of confidence and self-assuredness that is an artificial cover for our deepest fear: we are not needed or wanted. Mother Teresa once said, "The biggest disease today is not leprosy or tuberculosis, but rather the feeling of being unwanted." But to reveal this, even to ourselves, we believe would be an act of weakness.

The powerlessness of the ego is difficult to recognize because the ego is such a good actor. It offers relief but it secretly travels in pain. Unfortunately, the path of the ego is the way to inevitable torment and always leads to the same conclusion. However, the ego's denial is so strong and impenetrable we usually won't believe it is leading us astray until the pain reaches intolerable levels. The collapse of financial institutions and large industry leaders' business failures are pushing people to new heights of pain. Relying on our artificial power and plotting strategies will not continue to work for us.

The ego has run our lives so long, though, it is difficult to even discover it is not who we are. As we progress in the book, we will look at ways we can begin to undo the grip the ego holds on us, but for our purposes now, it is necessary to understand five things:

- The ego operates from fear.
- The ego has no internal self-worth.
- The ego needs external stimuli to validate itself.
- The ego lives in the past and a projected future.
- The ego is not real.

It is important to note that the ego is not bad or evil. It is necessary in our lives, just as we need a body to navigate through life. We have many life skills and personality traits that arise out of the ego and they are a pleasant part of our life experience. But often our ego is childish because we first started to develop it in childhood. And like a child, it sometimes needs the discipline of a wise and loving adult—your authentic self.

STRATEGIES FOR COPING IN THE WORKPLACE

Let's look at how both leaders and employees who operate from their egos currently cope with the politics, pain, and misery in businesses. The ego's strategies are created to avoid feeling fear and lack of self-worth.

IDENTIFICATION

Identification occurs because the ego has no authentic power or self-worth, so it must create roles and identities it believes are worthy. These false identities are like characters in a movie with certain characteristics that define their role in any situation. They rely on the drama to keep their false identity in place. Creating a lot of fervor substantiates the character or role, and continues to keep the ego alive.

Peace and quiet would cause the identity to dissolve, so the individual must keep the atmosphere stirred up by playing out these roles and dramatic episodes. The drama surrounding the ego is self-sustaining and persistent. The cause of the drama is unconscious, and therefore it is hard to identify the need for drama in oneself.

In addition, the complexity of the drama makes it difficult to discern the source and one's part in creating it. It has a certain momentum that tends to draw in other players, which then validates the chosen roles and perpetuates the drama.

But under the drama, which feeds on itself, is a huge *fear* of exposure by each of the people playing out the other roles. This nagging trepidation ultimately depresses and exhausts the very people who originated the drama. Ultimately, self-worth will never be found in perpetuating the drama.

BLAME

When we feel fear and want to expel the pain, blaming someone else is the most common method we use. We believe it exonerates us. People carry shame and guilt from their childhood that they project onto others. Creating enemies on whom we can blame our suffering takes us off the hook and keeps us from feelings of disgrace and inadequacy, we believe. However, when we blame others, we push them into a corner, which creates a reaction to which we then counter-react.

Sabotage is a technique employed by the ego in the workplace to attempt to disempower others through an attack on the person or persons perceived as a threat to the ego's identity. Gossiping is an attempt to be superior to those we are afraid could hurt us, and is a very common form of sabotage. Gossip and backbiting are strategies to briefly elevate the status of those engaged in them, but at the cost of adding further negativity to the environment.

Other methods of sabotage can range from the subtlest comments designed to cause doubt about the credibility of a person, to body language (i.e. rolling eyes, scowling), to out-and-out verbal, and occasionally, even physical attacks. Other examples of sabotage in the workplace are harassment and discrimination based on perceived differences, such as sexual orientation, gender, race, religion, economic groups, age, weight, etc.

SELF-RIGHTOUSNESS

Self-righteousness is a tactic that appears to be the opposite of blame and projection. But self-righteousness and blame are two sides of the same coin. Self-righteousness asserts that oneself is good while the other person is evil. It is a false accusation that claims innocence while holding another responsible for your pain and suffering. The false claim is very insidious, and in almost any conflict you will find both sides maintain self-righteousness.

In other words, when you are the self-righteous victim, you are saying you are blameless. This can only mean the other is the cause of your feelings. And this is never true. And now you are blaming them! So who is the victim?

James P. Carse, in his book *Finite and Infinite Games,* says, "Evil is never intended as evil. Indeed, the contradiction inherent in all evil is that it originates in the desire to eliminate evil." We need only look at recent history to see wars initiated in the name of eliminating evil. This kind of logic and moral justification can end only as we see it in ourselves, and it takes courage to look within to see your own accountability. Responsibility, honesty, and authenticity are rarely seen these days.

RESISTANCE

Resistance is a shield that prevents awareness of fears and insecurities from coming to the surface. The belief system of the ego is so small it cannot stand the challenge from a higher source. The ego is ever alert and vigilant to defend itself against anything it perceives as a threat. Whatever is resisted continues to persist and becomes even more powerful and vexing to the ego.

Resistance is really just a defense, but only the ego needs defending. Honor stands on its own and needs no defense. A defensive posture in yourself or another is really a mask of fear. When you know this, you will begin to give up your own defenses and see past the defenses of others.

You can also begin to see that when you attack others or corner people in some way, you provoke their ego, so they become more defensive. The more you push, the more others will need to defend their position and prove they are right.

Facing the denied dread beneath the defense is usually seen as insulting to the ego, but the very act of examining what the ego believes it must defend can set us free. Challenging the trepidation would lead to liberation. But the ego will project the fear onto another rather than look behind its own mask!

GRANDIOSITY

Grandiosity is the ego's shallow attempt to persuade itself and others that it is powerful. It supports this belief with other people and uses external things to help validate the image it has created—an image it doesn't really have faith in itself. The ego's role is fraught with anxiety because of our fear of being found out and exposed as a fraud.

The companion to grandiosity and self-boasting is pride. Pride, unlike authentic power, is the demonstration to others of a sense of superiority, or one-upmanship. This technique seeks fame and personal glory to help elevate the ego's image. We have all seen cockiness in business leaders, government heads, and CEOs who have later fallen from their self-serving pedestals and experienced public disgrace.

The ego is very fragile and always seeks ways to fortify itself, but fails to look within, where the only true power resides. Authentic power needs no such claim, but often receives the recognition and admiration from others that the ego desires but cannot generate. The energy felt when in the presence of someone who is authentic is comfortable and free flowing.

MANIPULATION

Manipulation is a method employed by the ego to control others, circumstances, and outcomes. This is based on the belief that the individual is not safe—therefore, the ego must calculatingly manipulate others to do and be what it needs to survive. This menacing form of control of others is often difficult to recognize, but is always felt by those being manipulated.

Manipulation is not an example of power, as the ego believes, but rather the opposite, a demonstration of weakness and fear of the future.

Control is seen as strength by the ego.

Other forms of control include hyper-vigilant structure and routine. The mind believes that tightening the framework insures the outcome and creates security. However, it is a false sense of protection.

The world of control and manipulation is like living in a very small house with tiny windows and doors, keeping people and opportunities out. It is a small world, lacking in spontaneity and freedom. It limits the authentic self from expanding and keeps the ego in an artificial world of safety.

ALLIANCES

Alliances are ways individuals in the workplace join with others to strengthen their positions. Seeking evidence and allies to support your case gives a sense of power and relief but is usually followed by an unconscious sense of guilt. Wanting to be part of a particular group that offers prestige or a sense of entitlement is very prevalent.

Sometimes alliances can occur in political groups, bargaining groups, or any group of individuals joined together for the purpose of overcoming another group. They occur as a cause—usually with a mighty mission—

but result in polarity. A true armistice occurs by reconciliation of ideas, not by commitment to the unyielding position that the ego demands.

This is not to be confused with taking a stand for or making a commitment to a valuable purpose or higher principle that contributes to the common good. Aligning yourself with a universal principle or a platform that benefits others is a way to your own enlightenment. Aligning with a special interest group and fulfilling personal agendas are what's seen most often in the workplace.

Alliances to promote peace in the world can create a powerful force of group will that can catapult action into higher levels. However, alliances to overcome other groups of people or nations are examples of group ego dynamics.

The key is to ask yourself when joining with others for any purpose, "Who benefits from this alliance?" If it is for a special interest group, a select few trying to gain power, it is an alliance of the ego, trying to strengthen itself.

DISASSOCIATION

Disassociation is the ego's final attempt to thwart any attack on its identity with the position "It's not me, it's them." Sometimes this belief results in ignoring or trying not to be engaged in the dynamics. Another option is to leave the workplace and find a more welcoming and accepting environment where the individual will be truly appreciated. However, since this technique is yet another outward projection of the problem with no change from within, the new environment will soon prove to be just as threatening and emotionally turbulent.

The new environment is often more intense. The drama escalates. The ego goes from a local stage to Broadway theater.

COST OF FEAR IN THE WORKPLACE CULTURE

Countless young people enter the work force with enthusiasm, spirit, and fresh ideas to contribute to their organizations. Then they are gradually beaten down and indoctrinated, and finally become like the other egos, defending and pretending in an effort to survive with minimum damage.

These people's inherent potential and talents, which could be utilized in growing businesses, are wasted. The employees begin to look around for another company or career, either because their family is complaining or their doctor orders a change to alleviate their stress.

What is the energy force that drives companies? Is it not the energy of its people?

This depletion of energy and creative power goes unrecognized by businesses as they analyze every other element of their operations to determine how to increase profitability, reduce costs, and increase productivity. It is as though someone puts holes in their gas tank and wonders why they get poor mileage.

It is time for leaders and managers to become aware that they shoot themselves in the foot when they allow this ego-driven management, which operates from insecurity, to permeate the business. The costs are estimated to be in the billions in terms of loyalty, retention, corporate memory, retraining, customer service, and business potential. Many researchers are finding widespread employee disengagement, which obviously affects productivity, creativity, and profitability.

Lateral violence is a term used to describe backbiting, infighting, and condescension in workplace relationships. The financial impact goes uncalculated by administrators and leaders. The turnover of registered nurses in hospitals is reported by various studies to be anywhere between 30-60 percent because of lateral violence. And this is in a profession that is supposed to be based on compassion!

This high turnover rate of nurses is estimated to cost $22,000-$64,000 per nurse. Other studies indicate that replacing one employee in most industries can cost up to 25-200 percent of the annual salary. Those expenses impact the bottom line. And yet changing the environment and creating a new, respectful kind of leadership to reduce these costs are rarely considered.

What's more, according to market information group TNS and The Conference Board, managers are not prepared to effectively meet major challenges presented by the future American workforce and remain globally competitive. Drawing on results from recent surveys and data from the U.S. Bureau of Labor Statistics, they argue the new American workforce will be one of polarized skill levels, diversity, and disengagement.

Some ego-driven managers bring their people to their knees, and people on their knees are not productive. Many companies would be better off to eliminate some of their management positions and just allow people to work on their own! Individuals would at least not be under the kind of pressure that wounds and depresses their vigor and life force.

Leadership today is escalating its top-down, machine-like attitude. But people are not machines that can simply be plugged in and expected to work. Measurements and detailed spreadsheets may give a sense of control but they don't solve the relationship and leadership problems. Too many tracking reports and compliance activities may be a hindrance. Time may be wasted on doing reports that could be better used to execute the work the reports are intended to measure. Spreadsheets are simply a reflection of the relationships and activities between employees, customers, vendors, and management. One reason for over-proliferation of reports, meetings, and restrictions is they help substantiate the jobs of those managers requiring them, even as they limit the actual performance.

These conditions result in high stress, health and safety issues, lower productivity, and distress. Ever-increasing demands, unrealistic goals, attempts to extract every ounce of energy from people, and impersonal and uncaring attitudes all impact the morale of everyone in the organization.

A revolutionary new model of honor, respect, and unity—a replacement for the current internal competition—is the enlightened answer for the future growth of companies. Without a change in the strict structure that dominates most businesses, employees will not feel dedication, inspiration, or commitment, and the level of work will be mediocre. Disregard for employees' feelings and compounding pressure to produce have dire consequences. Egos in leadership positions damage the core of their organization, their most valuable resource—the human potential that is the fuel driving the company.

Annette was a very successful field representative for a national company, calling on business clinics in her region. A highly motivated and dedicated sales person, she consistently threw herself into her job. One year, she exceeded all her sales goals, won the MVP player award, and was invited into the President's Club, winning a trip to Hawaii. She was proud, happy, and enthusiastic about her job. Management asked her to be a speaker at the national and regional training meetings and often sent new employees from others states to ride with her and gain training on making successful sales calls.

But then things began to change. A new, highly analytic man took over sales from the corporate office. The daily tracking, the number of conference calls, the meetings, and the direction from the top all increased. In addition, Annette's territory was cut in half, even as her target goals increased. Her reward for a job well done was to make her job more difficult and reduce her income. The detailed reports and written narration and analysis of every client required by her boss soon took several hours every evening. She was beginning to feel discouraged and defeated. And she now had to travel farther with fewer offices and potential clients on whom she could call. She watched her numbers and commissions fall, and her ranking as a top producer dropped.

Frequent conference calls also took up time, often with little purpose for the meeting. Sometimes reasons were conjured up to sound valid, such as discussing an article they were all told to read. Sales reps on the call took turns saying things intended to make them look smart, each reiterating the same point while trying to make it sound different. "Dovetailing with that idea, I think...," or "Let me add to that thought" were the comments usually made. No one dared mention that this time would be better spent in the field because it might suggest that the leadership didn't have better things to do.

Annette continued striving to increase her sales, while giving feedback that she would like a bigger territory. She was hopeful they would recognize a top producer like her would be better utilized for the company with a lot more opportunities to close sales. Her suggestions were unheeded.

Unbeknownst to the company, Annette has been sought out by headhunters and now has two new job opportunities to choose from, both with higher base salaries, bigger commissions, and greater options. Like several others under the new leadership, Annette is leaving the company.

The cost of replacing them won't be considered and the leadership is unlikely to take responsibility for losing some of their most outstanding employees. Unfortunately, the leaders are afraid too, and they believe if they work harder, add more accountability, and increase the demands, they will be more profitable.

Other results of this style of management and culture include:

- Poor customer service and increased customer complaints
- Lower work performance from employees
- Increased errors and accidents
- Higher levels of absenteeism due to stress and health issues

A sad repercussion of this destructive attitude is it ultimately affects the quality of life in our country as dispirited people go home to their families in a state of exhaustion and distress. But insecurity and a need for financial stability keep most people silent.

A common complaint from management is that it is hard to find good employees, and many employees are negative and unappreciative. This projection onto employees solves nothing, and the question for those leaders or managers is: "Would employees not be more positive in a happier environment? And aren't happy people more productive?"

Although many leaders fail to recognize the value of respect and employee satisfaction, some leaders do acknowledge that teamwork is important and the environment should be harmonious. But they often complain and criticize employees even as they spout platitudes. They want to be right, not recognizing it ultimately hurts everyone.

So who is responsible for bringing about a change? It appears to be a Catch-22 or chicken-or-egg situation. But the truth is that the culture starts at the top and permeates down. Owners and managers are accountable for the work environment. For any real change to occur leaders must understand and then give up the egotistical form of management. In return, organizations will reap the rewards of creating an extraordinary workplace where people work together using their minds and their hearts. Leaders are the ones to initiate needed changes, or the suffering and political discord will continue to rise.

Lack of trust and respect leads to dissatisfaction and discouragement for everyone involved. Projection, blame, and resistance are escalating, and it is time to come face to face with this critical dilemma. It is an overdue journey. We must practice a new kind of leadership, one that creates an environment of compassion and trust that rewards everyone, not just those at the top.

Leaders need to address their own inadequacies and discover the personal path to authenticity and integrity, rather than being driven by insatiable egos. Relationships need to be rebuilt, and genuine communication needs to become the basis of operating within organizations. Leaders who operate from a foundation of integrity and strength make it safe for those they lead to do the same.

In the next chapter, we will look at enlightened leadership and distinguish it from the ego-driven style so commonly in practice, not only in the workplace, but also in governments throughout the world.

This book is a restoration process. It is the restoration of you to your authentic self and inner spiritual greatness. It is a course on discovering and releasing the barriers that prevent you from awakening to your highest self.

The gradual process of awakening to your true self can be hastened through exercises that provide another way to see the world, situations, and people. We need to change perception. The ego's habitual way of viewing the world has been reinforced in endless ways. But the good news is that a new infusion of energy has entered the environment and people are beginning to shift in dramatic ways. The rigid business structure of the past two hundred years is weakening. Inevitable disruptions and climactic collapses are the predecessors to a new enlightened model for leadership.

At the end of each chapter are suggested exercises to practice in your workplace. The ways we operate in the world can be so ingrained that we can be tempted to return to the ego's reactions to situations and people. The more you demonstrate to yourself and others the beauty of relating in a new way, the more the payoff will be self-evident.

You will be reinforced in every way, and as you apply your understandings you will experience a new kind of peace and satisfaction that has been absent in your life. However, the deep learning and shift in you comes in the doing—not just the reading or listening. So commit to awaken out of the ego world swiftly, by courageously acknowledging the mass delusion of contention and giving up your own diatribes and false accusations.

I also recommend you start and end each day with at least ten minutes of quiet, meditative relaxation. Allow your mind to relax and just watch your stream of thoughts. Don't try to stop them but do try to stay undisturbed for at least that amount of time—more if you can. Before you end, take a moment to think of the people and things for which you are grateful in your life. Get in the habit of remembering the good in your life each day. Not only is it uplifting, but the universe seems to have a way of giving more of the same to a grateful heart.

As time goes by, you will find you can remain in quiet meditation longer. It is sometimes helpful to focus on something, such as your breath. Many meditation books and teachers can help you learn about the practice. Just begin to commit the time and you will find it can be of great assistance to you for many reasons.

According to Andrew Newberg, M.D., in *Measuring the Immeasurable,* "Many preliminary studies suggest that meditation may have a number of health benefits, helping people achieve a state of restful alertness with improved reaction time, creativity, and comprehension; decreasing anxiety, depression, irritability and moodiness; and improving learning ability, memory, self-actualization, feelings of vitality and rejuvenation, and emotional stability. ...It may also provide acute and chronic support for patients with hypertension, psoriasis, irritable bowel disease, anxiety, and depression. There is also evidence that meditation can improve chronic pain, such as that of fibromyalgia. Moreover, in several studies meditators had better lung and heart function than non-meditators. There is even some evidence that it might help with cholesterol levels."

PERSONAL RESTORATION PLAN TO PRACTICE IN YOUR WORKPLACE

As you progress through your day, notice when others in your workplace are utilizing a strategy to cope with the dynamics in your office or business. Simply observe any of the following methods:

- Identification
- Blame
- Self-righteousness
- Resistance
- Grandiosity
- Manipulation
- Alliances
- Disassociation

In the evening, or when it is quiet, ask yourself:

- Can I see this person is only trying to protect him/herself?
- Do I ever utilize a similar tactic?
- Can I start to recognize when I am using an ego strategy?
- Can I look beyond others' strategies and see their spirit instead?

As you progress through future days, become aware of times when you use an above method to cope in your workplace. Can you stop yourself at the source? For example, can you notice if you start to gossip or form an alliance with someone based on the need to feel superior?

Finally, I recommend you keep a journal to write down your insights. It will help you integrate your learning and will provide inspiration in the future if you reread experiences that led to new understandings.

CHAPTER TWO

What Is Enlightened Leadership?

*   *   *

THE ENLIGHTENED LEADER

What does enlightened leadership look like?

True leadership is the process in which the spirit within the leader recognizes the same spiritual essence in those he leads. This recognition provides a conduit or channel of energy that propels everyone involved toward the dedication and action necessary to achieve a goal.

This approach to leadership is rarely understood or practiced in today's workplace. But if it were, it would make a significant difference in the work environment, as well as the way we conduct business. Leadership that comes from authenticity, that honors employees and demonstrates respect for them, will reap the rewards of commitment, alliance, and loyalty. Those attitudes translate to the bottom line.

An enlightened leader is self-reflective and understands that to lead others one must first know one's own heart. This requires the leader to: 1) direct the focus on characteristics, needs, and actions stemming from their own ego, 2) recognize these behaviors are barriers to their own deeper self, and 3) understand that without releasing the blocks in oneself, one cannot attract the respect, allegiance, and trust needed to guide others. Restoration of trust in business, government, and even religious organizations is drastically needed in today's world.

The artificial roles of superiority, a mistaken strategy, prevent true leadership from being expressed. When a person in a leadership role is willing to challenge directions from the ego, authentic internal power emerges. Reliance on strength from the inner spirit, instead of the mind and mental constructs, is the source of great leadership. To be an enlightened leader, pretentions must be given up and fear released. Unraveling the drama in your own mind precedes unwinding the complex reactive environment in the workplace.

In addition, a great leader recognizes the contributions and abilities within each person in his group. Through caring guidance, an enlightened leader acknowledges the inherent power of every individual to transcend their ego state and expand their potential. Enlightened leaders instill faith and hope by speaking to the hearts and minds of those they lead. They inspire, they motivate, and they touch the souls of everyone, without judgment or exclusion. This energy is sometimes described as charisma, but don't confuse it with a personality trait. The influential leaders who have united people and inspired them into action have been as varied as the people we see every day. But they all have certain inner qualities and traits.

When I was a young girl I was given an assignment in language arts to write about Thomas Jefferson, the primary author of the Declaration of Independence. The assignment was not a simple biography but a description of how we thought ordinary men were able to write such a magnificent and powerful document, which inspires us to this day.

I went home and asked my dad for help on this project. My dad had been a B-17 fighter pilot in World War II and had been shot down on a mission over Germany. He was captured and taken to Stalag Luft 1, where he was held in the prison camp for nine months. Since he was a former POW who strongly valued freedom and peace, I knew he would be able to help me with this homework.

My dad sat down and began describing what he believed inspired Thomas Jefferson's passion and compelling vision to write this influential and inspiring document. I can vividly remember writing down my dad's words and ideas that day. I understood on some level that the extraordinary qualities needed to compose the Declaration of Independence came from a higher source than the ordinary thinking of the common man. I somehow knew, even at a young age, how timeless and enduring the values and characteristics he cited were. Based on my dad's list and other life experiences, I suggest that the following traits are possessed by truly great leaders throughout time:

- Vision
- Courage
- Humility
- Integrity
- Compassion
- Trust
- Defenselessness / Non-resistance
- Affinity
- Patience
- Acceptance

These qualities are not possessed by most of today's business and government leaders. When leadership can come from an open and genuine heart, we will begin to see the needed transformation—possibly even a revolution. But relationships need rebuilding, and that starts from the top. Until we see a change in the way businesses are led, the drama and pain in the workplace will continue to soar.

Enlightened leadership comes from a compassionate heart and cannot be feigned. The leader must be genuine, or the energy exchange between the leader and group members will not foster growth and inspiration.

Artificial leaders abound and though they may look powerful, they are deceiving themselves and others.

Leading other people requires giving up personal goals in exchange for group decisions. It also includes seeing the brilliance and uniqueness in each individual. The level reached in enlightened leadership is determined by the commitment and willingness of the leader to give up the ego's needs. It is easier in theory than in practice because the ego mind is so obstinate. Challenging the artificial image means you must:

- Give up the need to know all the answers
- Give up an attachment to the outcome
- Give up the need to be superior
- Be able to say you are wrong
- Listen instead of talk

Our ego does not allow us to do any of the above well, and therefore blocks the free flow of creative energy from the group process. The unenlightened leader has a difficult time seeing that the ego identifies with the outcome and that it desires a predetermined one. This kind of leader does not realize that imaginative input and positive contributions from the group process will be missing if he has the ending already completely defined.

Leaders who are motivated by artificial power believe that vision and goals are something to be imparted to the group, and then somehow, as excellent leaders, they can convince and persuade the team to buy into it. People are not motivated by goals that benefit only those at the top. This is a misperception of the ego and is the biggest obstacle to teamwork. Leaders who use dominance to control their employees cause suppression of emotions, which results in internal competition and lack of cooperation.

THE IMPOSTER SYNDROME—IDENTIFYING EIGHT EGO-DRIVEN LEADERS

To identify the powerful qualities of an enlightened leader it is sometimes helpful to look at what is *not* leadership. The following are some common roles and actions demonstrated by the ego-driven leader. In contrast to the potent ability of an enlightened leader to promote creativity, energize, and incite action through honor and respect, the ego-driven manager operates from the impotence of fear.

The enlightened leader creates an environment of synergism in which all members of a group align with a higher purpose, and together develop passion and commitment to achieve the goal. The ego-driven leader does not.

This positive group dynamic in the enlightened leader's workplace occurs quite naturally when the barriers of the ego don't block the flow of energy. A free flow of exchange can be felt by all members and enhances the ability of each person to give to the group process.

Ego-driven leaders, in their effort to strengthen their illusion of themselves, create static, or interference of free flowing ideas in the workplace. This interference affects those they lead and hinders the creative stream of consciousness.

Let's look carefully at the qualities of a leader who operates from this egoic thought system. This leader has many talents and abilities, but does not really believe he does. Ego-driven leaders have incredible doubts and fears. They rely on their self-created image rather than the inner strength, power, and wisdom that are available when they are aligned with spirit.

Deep down inside, ego-driven leaders do not believe they are worthy of the position they hold! This belief leads to the unbearable fear that the truth will be discovered and they will be exposed as an imposter. This imposter syndrome is so prevalent it has become the norm. The practice of pretending to be a leader has become the current model of management for many companies and organizations.

What does the ego-driven leader do to protect the secret and avoid exposure?

Like all people in the workplace, ego-driven leaders have certain techniques to ensure their position and their so-called security. It is especially harmful when leaders operate from false identities because they hold institutional power. Thus it is very difficult to challenge or to not be controlled by these techniques if you are one of those they lead.

The following techniques are used by the ego to cast itself as a leader. Although many subordinates are beguiled and make efforts to please artificial leaders, many others recognize these charlatans and are aware of how disingenuous their words and actions are. But because of the apparent power of the leaders and the vulnerabilities of those they lead, this is rarely addressed.

These techniques are unconscious to those who use them since the techniques provide a sense of power, albeit false, to the egos playing these roles. Like all things created by the egoic thought system, however, this feeling of power is temporary, as fear always lurks beneath the surface.

THE DICTATOR / BULLY

This leader uses intimidation and fear to get people to do what the ego believes is needed to accomplish goals. The ego has a hidden motive as well: validation that it is all-powerful.

This false leader has no ability to feel compassion for others. The dictator's need to strengthen their small self-image precludes any awareness of others or the willingness to look outside of the self. The ego's greatest fear in this role is it will be discovered it is powerless.

STAR-OF-THE-TEAM LEADER / KNOW-IT-ALL LEADER

Playing this role allows the ego to stay in place by creating the appearance of being the champion, the rescuer of those less capable. The know-it-all leader has to be right to maintain the ego's sense of superiority, which is believed to be necessary for leadership.

Ironically, knowing everything prevents this leader from learning anything and blocks all flowing creativity from those in the organization. His ego's greatest fear is that one of the people he leads may be the understudy, waiting to replace him. But since the leader already knows everything, the employees cannot contribute anything anyway.

THE FAULT-FINDING, BLAMING LEADER

The blaming technique employed by this ego-driven leader is an attempt to direct attention away from herself, so her actual fear and doubt will not be exposed.

Those she leads are in a defensive posture because she always looks for what is wrong. This stifles any creativity and confidence in people who might otherwise contribute in an outstanding manner. The employee's focus becomes trying not to make a mistake, rather than working positively and productively and taking creative risks.

THE DISCOUNTING LEADER

This method renders employees impotent by pointing out their inferiority. Rather than acknowledge and praise his employees, the discounting leader uses his people to elevate himself and strengthen what he believes is his power position.

This ego-driven leader rarely gives others credit because it would threaten his position. The ego finds that the weak are less intimidating to its own fragile sense of power. Employees never feel appreciated and become apathetic toward any purposeful activity.

THE EMPIRE-BUILDING LEADER

Gaining territorial, political, financial, or competitive advantage over others is the method this leader uses to ensure the false image of authority, which is a demonstration of a deep lack of worth. The deeper the sense of worthlessness, the larger the empire needed to demonstrate the false power.

This person is never satisfied and will continue to attempt to build a greater empire. But it is an endless, fruitless endeavor. The acquisition of symbols of supremacy is the driving force behind this ego-driven leader.

THE PATRONIZING, PLACATING LEADER

Coming from a desperate fear of not being admired or needed, this leader appears at first to be compassionate and caring. He seems to agree with subordinates' ideas and provides positive communication. When the action is not commensurate with the words, the lack of authenticity is demonstrated.

The patronizing leader believes he has no power and therefore cannot step up to the plate, except in a subversive manner. He instills no confidence, respect, or trust in employees.

THE MICRO-MANAGER

This leader maintains all sense of identity and security by controlling the situation and others in it. To prevent anything from going wrong and the ego being held accountable, this leader exerts a microscopic vigilance over people and events of the day. The sense of superiority and feeling of safety she achieves with these actions reinforce the behavior.

The people she leads feel like they are being held in a cage, allowed to move but only in a tiny arena. Micro-managers are afraid of losing face and believe this high control will keep them protected.

THE MARTYR / SELF-RIGHTEOUS LEADER

The martyr appears selfless and benevolent. This leader seems to have the best interests of everyone at heart, but he has a hidden, underlying motive. Though unconscious, this person makes apparent sacrifices while secretly keeping score. He works relentlessly, putting in endless hours, to demonstrate his great dedication. No one can keep up with him, so employees feel guilty and believe they have to exhibit this same workaholism to keep their jobs. And sooner or later the self-righteous leader uses this strategy to make others feel guilty.

These examples of various ego methods of leadership are not all-inclusive. Variations and overlapping do occur. It is important to understand that these roles are not taken on consciously. They are simply the ego's way to cope in an environment where fear and insecurity are present. The tragedy is these ego-defined roles compound the pain and suffering for everyone who is subject to them.

Recognizing these roles is usually fairly easy when looking at others. The difficulty and denial arises in seeing them in oneself. Denial is a powerful technique to avoid dealing with the ego's dysfunctional issues, methods, and actions. It takes unrelenting commitment to the goal of transformation to overcome the denial that seeks to keep the ego in place.

Beneath the surface of a leader's ego is the trepidation that one or more of those she leads would like to sabotage her rule and her ideas. This fear reinforces in her the need for further defensiveness, which is a barrier to synergism and group will. This underlying mistrust of employees increases the complexity of the situation, adds new layers of confusion, and reduces the chances for any real communication.

The leader's mask of overt confidence is a hindrance to the work process and prevents opportunities for group expansion and purpose. But the leader is almost always unaware it is a disguise because the ego is so shrewd. Our ego prevents us from looking behind our charade because of the dread that we will find out we are weak and unworthy. So we lie to ourselves, continue on our journey, and hope our countenance will cover our insecurity.

The ego continues its attempts to validate itself at the expense of others, giving itself the illusion of authority. And when the title on the door is authoritative, the impact on those who must work with the ego-driven leader can have devastating consequences—not only for the employees but for the organization as well.

Brent was a man with an MBA who took rapid career steps that brought him to a high position at a young age. He was hired as the Vice President of Operations for an organization that based its decision on his resume and the interview process. He appeared charming, self-effacing, genuine, and very intelligent. In the early months of his employment, he joked with employees and appeased the senior administrators and board members.

Gradually, some of Brent's ego-driven leader traits began to emerge— for example, the empire builder. He added new furniture to his corner office and liked to sit at the head of the boardroom table with a look of superiority as he reigned over meetings. He would smile as he tricked someone into looking inferior in public. He played the blaming leader, questioning the integrity of people by asking questions meant to undermine their security and cause them to feel defensive. He made offhand remarks to women that were difficult to interpret but often bordered on harassment.

He gave appreciative comments to people in private, but for the board and in reports he basically took credit for anything that was a valuable contribution. He delegated with disregard to the impact it had on the people assigned to the work, and if someone tried to push back he answered with something like, "I don't buy that."

Brent started to make changes in the employee base, either letting people go or so intimidating them that they felt compelled to quit. He seemed to get along well with the board members and other administrators, playing golf, going to dinners, etc. No one seemed to notice his aberrant behavior with employees, except those who reported to him. And he appeared so contented with himself, so puffed up and important. But employees were no longer contributing; meetings were silent except for compulsory statements or innocuous comments by those who intended to stay under the radar. Brent's lack of trust began to extend down through the organization. People gossiped and become paranoid, wondering who would be next and would it be them.

How did this deplorable situation last so long? Even in the exit interviews, very few people complained about Brent, for fear it could hurt them in future job interviews. But after a year had passed and numerous formerly loyal employees had been fired or quit, his mistakes started to hit the bottom line. The other leaders began to focus on Brent. After some months with a coach and deep conversations among the other leaders in the organization, management finally recognized Brent as the charlatan that he was. He was invited to leave with a hefty severance package.

How often do unenlightened leaders operate like this? How many people have lost jobs or given up in exhaustion when the workplace was painful? This kind of artificial leadership takes an enormous toll on people and impacts relationships within and outside the business, including customers and families of employees. Yet, I suggest it happens to some degree or another in businesses everywhere.

Brent, an example of many false leaders, reacts from conditioning and pain he had as a child, and as an adult plays out his family issues to gain acceptance and recognition. These strong requirements for validation originated in a family of high achievers with a father who was dismissive and demeaning. In his elevated position, Brent was so focused on his own need to emerge as a respected, powerful leader that he didn't even feel or consider the pain he caused. The redeeming part of the story is that everyone who participated in the drama had the opportunity to awaken to higher levels of awareness—adversity holds many possibilities for personal growth.

TRUE ALIGNMENT

In contrast to the ego-driven leader, an authentic leader reaches beyond the voracious needs of the small self. Through honoring the spirit in himself and in others, the genuine leader helps release the full potential and abilities of those in the group. This mutual engagement and reciprocal exchange of energy can occur only in a trusting and respectful environment, where equality and affinity for one another are present.

In addition, focused attention and action are attained only when the goal is worthy of the energy needed to achieve it. The average person may not want to lead, but does want to feel her input is important and significant. True teamwork occurs naturally when there is an alignment to a common purpose—one that benefits everyone, not just those at the top. Leaders who create an environment of mutual support and regard for one another will find that commitment and loyalty are voluntary—not a demand by those in higher positions.

Group will is a synergistic force that occurs when two or more people work together to produce a result not obtainable by any one person independently. Leaders who ignore the basic needs of the individuals in the group rob the organization of the energy and new ideas derived from the remarkable process of group participation, mutual engagement, and group will.

So much activity in the workplace is inefficient, misdirected, and unfulfilling. People often spend endless time on mindless activities and trivia that do not satisfy the soul or spirit. Meetings and activities in the workplace are often a waste of time, acting like a gigantic procrastination game that prevents people from experiencing the real intention of work and life. The valid purpose of the organization is compromised by these senseless and mind numbing activities. Opportunities to use the power of teamwork to accomplish purposeful and meaningful work are so hindered by the jockeying for positions, posturing, and redundant work.

Everyone has talents and gifts meant to be expressed, which result in personal satisfaction and joy. This is the true labor of love, the rewarding experience of contributing and creating from one's soul. This labor of love is demonstrated in the work of artists, authors, composers, dancers, and anyone who expresses from their true being.

In a compassionate culture, projects are taken on with enthusiasm, based on the natural desire to create, innovate, and improve. People who work in groups of shared respect and responsibility have a greater sense of belonging and a stronger desire to reach common, beneficial goals. Positive relationships and friendships ensure involvement and reinforcement for innovative group processes. Individuals in any organization have the natural gift to generate from the inner source and wellspring of creativity, but unfortunately it is stifled in most organizations by power struggles and conflicting attitudes and activities.

All the busy work and unnecessary activity of the workplace is wasted time for the company, and it is a tragedy in terms of the individual's fulfillment and spiritual evolution. An environment that does not provide opportunities for meaningful expression causes individuals to become lethargic, dispirited, and depressed rather than invigorated and inspired. Energy is used to fight the battles and resist the attacks, rather than to pursue new levels of achievement and new possibilities for business success.

Tim, a thirty-eight-year-old husband and father, was a manager with a large computer consulting firm. He held two degrees and had immense experience in both the technical and business arenas. When I first met Tim, I was impressed with his confidence and creativity. In addition to his business acumen, he had great marketing skills. He was outgoing and a good networker in the community. He was a natural public speaker, and often spoke to various associations and meeting groups. His enthusiasm and high energy were very remarkable.

A year later, I saw Tim and he seemed dramatically different. He was quiet. His usual sense of humor was sadly absent. As I worked with his company, he seemed reticent to contribute. I even began to wonder if I had offended him in some way. A couple of months later, he announced he was leaving the firm. I finally talked with him and discovered the source of the problem.

A new senior partner had taken over Tim's department and had redefined the goals of the division. This man was Tim's boss for the past year, and he managed his people in a highly critical manner. He was the classic fault-finding, blaming leader, always looking for mistakes in everyone's work.

He thought he was helping his team by pointing out what they did wrong. This management style was his attempt to generate a high level of production in his people, but the process was intimidating and energy-deflating.

All those managed under this leadership style began to look over their shoulders and spent most of their time worrying about making mistakes, rather than finding new ways to increase business opportunities. The manager's demeaning behavior resulted in limiting the skills and productivity of everyone on his team.

Tim became extremely dispirited. As a result, his actual production went down. His once effervescent personality changed to one of quiet desperation and discouragement. He finally found a position with another organization after his doctor warned him about his high blood pressure and his wife became concerned about his depression. Unfortunately, Tim had suffered immense pressure and strain for almost a year before leaving. So the company lost an outstanding employee and never knew why.

Interestingly enough, I ran into Tim in an airport recently. He looked great and seemed happy and genuinely confident. He said it took a long time to overcome his sense of doubt and suspicion after the demeaning experience with his former manager. He also said he had done a lot of soul-searching and realized in some ways he had allowed himself to become a victim. He believed he would not play out the role again, and incidentally had learned how not to manage others.

The scenario Tim experienced occurs quite often as managers fail to provide an environment that brings out the best in people. This inadvertently reduces the success of the company, but more important, it causes undue hardship and emotional anxiety for those who work under such managers.

Other owners or managers in the company are often ignorant of the lack of compassion of a particular partner or manager. They are unaware that another manager is causing so much confusion, resulting in loss of productivity and even employees. And employees rarely tell management about their concerns or complaints because they fear recrimination.

Patricia was a partner in a very successful professional firm. Interns often sought opportunities to be part of this firm, and the company recently had an exchange student from a European country working as an intern. Patricia inadvertently heard some people from some cubicles down the hall say it was too bad the intern had gone back to her home country after a disappointing and stressful experience at the firm.

Patricia, a very compassionate leader, asked the individuals to come down to her office to tell her honestly what had happened. The younger colleagues were reticent to discuss the matter but finally told her one of the partners in the firm had so berated and criticized the intern she had been reduced to tears. They then confessed that most everyone who reported to him was afraid and some were considering leaving.

When she asked why they hadn't said anything before they said they didn't know if they would be believed and they feared reprisal from him. It turned out everyone beneath the partner level was aware of this unhappy situation but were too fearful to say anything.

Patricia and the partner group had dealt with this particular partner in the past and had required him to attend anger management training. He had shown improvement, and although a few issues had come up, they seemed to be resolved. He had an aggressive behavior in meetings but appeared to be controlling it now. Somehow, they believed he had changed and they were unaware of the problems he still caused for employees. His intimidating behavior was hurting people, and undoubtedly impacting revenues.

Though it was difficult to admit, the partner group realized their denial had allowed his behavior to continue until now. It was clear they must make a change and confront the whole situation with honesty. Through a series of conversations with him, they made an exit plan and restored their workplace environment to one of trust. She said the partner relieved of his responsibilities seemed thankful as he departed and prepared to go into private practice.

Even though this firm had many human resource practices in place and the partners thought they provided a good working environment, they now found new opportunities to lead with openness and authenticity. Their willingness to address the problems and support the employees changed the atmosphere to a place of compassion and cooperation. The response from the staff has been enthusiasm and commitment.

Without confrontation and honest communication, leaders who are not aware they operate from the ego continue to create an unstable environment. They don't understand that when they unconsciously side with the ego, they are attempting to circumvent the inevitable journey of waking up from the drama in the workplace.

The path to our inner spirit is everyone's ultimate destiny. Some people actively pursue the journey, some stumble on obstacles and trip their way through it, and others actively resist it. Many people would rather remain numb and not do the work it takes to come out of the mass delusion.

For some, the fear of the unknown is even more threatening than the current situation. Therefore, these individuals choose to remain a victim in the whirlpool of politics and opinions, rather than face the real battle—the conflict with the ego self. Much like the spouse in an abusive relationship, they find staying with the current job less threatening than leaving or choosing inner strength. Leaders or managers in this state of mind are most detrimental to the workplace.

If leaders of a group, organization, or country begin to recognize the traps of their own egos, they can then begin to bring about a remarkable change for those they lead. Leaders will discover ways to better guide the group process so the flow continues, unhampered by the constraints of their own limiting thoughts or by the egos of the others in the group.

Teamwork relies on the leader transcending the needs of her false self and allowing others to participate and give from their talents and abilities. This kind of alignment creates a potent opportunity for the common good of the organization.

A CLOSER LOOK AT THE QUALITIES OF ENLIGHTENED LEADERSHIP

The emergence of the qualities of enlightened leadership comes through the process of identifying and removing the obstacles and limited belief systems created in the past by the ego.

The ego cannot practice the qualities of leadership I describe because it is only an actor. True leadership comes from the higher self—not the small self.

Let's look more closely at the qualities of enlightened leadership.

VISION

Vision is the ability to see an expanded possibility or mental picture of the future from an elevated viewpoint in the present. This picture stretches the imagination, stirs the emotions, and inspires others to action and commitment. The leader acknowledges the creative force and potential of each individual as necessary to the attainment of the vision.

Holding a clear image, the leader is not deterred by obstacles but sees the vision as a future certainty. The vision is a magnificent opportunity that motivates those on the team, and ultimately is a goal that benefits everyone as it comes to pass.

COURAGE

Courage is an inner strength to face the challenges that arise in the self and that come from external conditions. Courage stands on conviction and character and does not back down in the face of criticism and judgment. Courage is getting back up when it seems it is hopeless. The strength of courage provides the persistence to attain the vision and lead others safely to the destination. Courage is willing to be the cause and take the consequences, no matter what transpires.

HUMILITY

Humility is the quality all truly great leaders possess. Humility is strength of character and gentleness of heart. Leaders with humility recognize the truth—we all are created equal. They understand that the ability to lead others is a precious gift and an honor. People feel the energy of respect that emanates from this authentic leader. In contrast, the arrogant leader is concerned with his own image, rather than seeing the spiritual essence in others.

INTEGRITY

Integrity is wholeness and consistency. Integrity is unwavering and steadfast. Integrity is an inner core that does not bend and is not shaped by outside influences. One with integrity does not give into temptation or sacrifice their values, regardless of the situation. A person with integrity can always be trusted to keep their word—not from an obligation, but from a freely given commitment with an unswerving promise to fulfill it.

COMPASSION

Compassion is seeing the world from another's point of view. Compassion is not sympathy or pity; it is knowing another's heart as one's own. It is having deep regard for others' feelings and welfare. True compassion is extended to all people and all living things. One with compassion provides reassurance, gentle support, and the powerful energy of universal love.

TRUST

People everywhere are looking for leaders they can trust. A leader who instills trust automatically and powerfully attracts others to contribute, create, and commit to a higher goal or worthy cause. Trust is reciprocal. It is a belief in each person's inherent abilities, without judgment, restriction, or control. Trust in others helps them release their own potential and soar to new heights. Trust is also reliance on the group process, not just individual goals. It is recognizing the input and participation of everyone as necessary components of the group will—*the will of the people.* Leading with trust and compassion is needed in the workplace and the world.

DEFENSELESSNESS / NON-RESISTANCE

Defenselessness or non-resistance is the recognition there is nothing to defend. Honor stands on its own. Only the ego needs a defense to protect itself from facing the fears it does not want revealed. Defense and resistance are symptoms of insecurity that alienate others. Defenselessness and non-resistance are qualities of authentic strength that attract others to be authentic as well.

AFFINITY

One with affinity sees the interconnection of all people and has gratitude for others. One who has true affinity does not judge or harm others. One with affinity understands peace is a function of people cooperating on a level of respect and honor for one another. This cannot be achieved when triumph over others is the goal.

PATIENCE

Patience is the knowledge there is a time and a season for all things. Patience with self and others is a foundation of leadership. It requires faith in the destination, regardless of setbacks. Patience is being content with not knowing, so waiting does not cause anxiety or doubt. Patience is the ultimate confidence that the energy expended will produce the desired results.

ACCEPTANCE

Acceptance is the recognition we are all equal and we originate from the same source. Acceptance does not distinguish others on the basis of religion, race, gender, economic status, nationality, or any other conditions. Acceptance extends understanding, not separation, and builds unity, not divisiveness. Acceptance embraces diversity and honors the spirit in all people. We cannot be free as long as oppression exists or we control the rights of others. Leaders who operate from acceptance know:

- Hatred does not bring about love.
- Evil does not eliminate evil.
- War does not bring peace.

These inner qualities of true leadership cannot be learned but they can be discovered within. They are a result of courageously giving up the demands of the tenacious ego and confronting the false beliefs from the past. Relationships bring up emotions and resistance and can be the portals to discovering the inner, powerful self. Relinquishment of the dictates from our small self, however, is not effortless, because the ego has been in control for so long.

Most people in the world today believe power is demonstrated with external sources and material wealth. But authentic power cannot be bought, acquired, learned, or even emulated. It must arise from the inner core of one's being, the true self. It can then never be taken away.

Deep within you is the source of joy and peace. This source is obscured when you listen to your mind's interpretations and fears. But as you clear the confusion and disconnect from the insane beliefs currently creating our world, your inner, spiritual greatness can arise. This power will allow you to fulfill your heart's deepest desire, which is your purpose in life. And as a leader, you will help others reach this same possibility.

FAILURE OF LEADERSHIP AND THE BREAKDOWN OF THE TEAM

Today's businesses recognize teamwork is desirable for creating and meeting goals of the organization. But ego-driven business leaders are not aware that the alignment of the team is dependent on the participation of all team members. They try to sell their vision to employees. Since the vision has no meaning for the employees, it is impossible to create genuine motivation to pursue goals.

CEOs, presidents, and managers complain that employees are not committed to the company's mission and goals. Often, however, the company either has no clear mission or it exists only in the leaders' own minds. But the most common situation is the mission statement is not a true reflection of the leadership's vision, and leaders don't demonstrate the values they profess in the statement. An extreme example is Enron's mission statement, which included the values Respect, Integrity, Communication, and Excellence.

Since the mission is often a cliché or worse yet, a hypocritical statement, how could employees possibly be committed to it? Honestly, in most organizations with which I have worked, very few people even know what the mission statement is.

Leaders also grumble that employees do not work hard enough and are not loyal. They say it's hard to get good employees, fully projecting the problem on their staff rather than looking at themselves. Of course, hiring and retaining the right people is always the best practice, but then complaining about their commitment level is a bit like parents saying their children are rebellious and unloving. Family harmony starts with a loving home and caring parents.

There are three reasons for these problems in the workplace:

1. The employees have no participation in the goal-setting process.
2. The goals only serve the owners, shareholders, or senior management.
3. Even when employees have input, the underlying power struggles between people prevent individuals from working as a team.

A good comparison is a family planning a vacation. If the children are not involved in the decisions, it is difficult to convince them it is a desirable destination. They want to go to Disneyland, for example, and the trip is planned for visiting Aunt Martha and the Smithsonian. The children didn't get to help choose and have input, therefore, they will likely be resistant to the trip itself.

Planning together will bring forth goals and activities to which everyone can commit. It becomes an exciting and enjoyable prospect. If you plan the family vacation together, you will find the children helping in every way to make the trip a success. They will generate ideas for finding someone to care for the yard, take the pets, and bring in the mail, and they will even pack their own clothes. Their inner enthusiasm will produce energy and motivation to carry out the necessary actions for the vacation and make it fun for everyone.

In large organizations it takes more time and processes for sharing and getting feedback and ideas from the workforce. But the more leadership listens to the front lines and the employees throughout the organization, the better commitment and participation they will receive, not to mention the great ideas and inspirations that will come from the entire workforce. And then it is important to recognize and respond to the feedback so it is not perceived as an exercise to deceive the employees. In fact, very few employees are really ever fooled by artificial leadership, at least not for long.

Ego-driven leaders do not understand the true value of this process of including employees in their goals and decisions. They are afraid to take their hands off the wheel, believing they must be in control of the vehicle.

The ego is fearful of losing control because it believes it must direct the outcome. This very attitude is what prevents the full spectrum of creativity and passion to be expressed when a group comes together.

Ego-driven leaders cast themselves in a role of superiority to others, rather than acknowledging the same fundamental nature in everyone in the group. The need to be greater than others restricts, if not blocks, the contribution from others. The synergistic power and ingenuity coming from alignment and working toward a common goal are unavailable to the group.

When people are denied freedom of expression, power struggles result. These internal battles become one more block in the free exchange of energy. The failure of the leader becomes the collapse of the team.

An egotistical leader provokes the egos of the members of the group. Some people feel they must challenge the leader. Some use other nonproductive techniques to cope. Individuals then blame one another for the lack of progress. Teams become a battleground or a stalemate, rather than a progressive opportunity for moving the company forward.

To make progress, you must distinguish the reactions and counterreactions of the others in the workplace and then unhook from them.

PERSONAL RESTORATION PLAN
TO PRACTICE IN YOUR WORKPLACE

This exercise is about looking behind the mask of artificial leaders. Read the list of the ego-driven leaders discussed in this chapter. Ask yourself the following questions about each of the roles:

- What is the fear behind this role? (i.e. fear of appearing weak, not smart enough)
- What is the benefit to this person? (i.e. feeling important, smart)
- What are the costs to the employees and the organization under this leadership?

Ego-driven roles:

- The Dictator / Bully
- Star-of-the-Team Leader / Know-It-All Leader
- The Fault-Finding, Blaming Leader
- The Discounting Leader
- The Empire-Builder Leader
- The Patronizing, Placating Leader
- The Micro-Manager
- The Martyr / Self-Righteous Leader

Now ask yourself, "Can I see myself in any of these roles? Which ones, and how does this affect my relationships?"

Think about leaders you have respected or admired in the world and in history. Look at the traits of true leadership below and notice which ones they seemed to exhibit. Also, think about these qualities in yourself. Finally, think about the people with whom you work who possess these traits and notice how it feels to interact with them:

- Vision
- Courage
- Humility
- Integrity
- Compassion
- Trust
- Defenselessness / Non-resistance
- Affinity
- Patience
- Acceptance

Continue doing your quiet, relaxed meditations, ending with the thoughts of gratitude. Playing meditative music can be helpful in relaxing. Notice your breathing and how it helps you unwind and let go of tension. Write down any insights you may have from your exercises.

CHAPTER THREE

Drama in the Workplace

* * *

ILLUMINATING THE WORKPLACE STAGE

John and I emerged from the theater among a happy crowd of people who had clearly enjoyed the movie we had just seen. This particular movie appealed to both genders and had many interesting characters who struggled with various universal themes. One moment we were brought to tears and the next, elevated to laughter. We cheered as the hero won his battle, suffered when a main character died, and rejoiced when true love conquered all.

I said, referring to one of the characters in the movie, "What about Robert? What will become of him now that everyone else left?"

John answered wisely, "Robert is getting his just deserts. It's justice being played out."

Then we looked at each other and laughed.

For a moment, even after leaving the theater, we were so involved in the drama, we had forgotten it was only a movie. Robert is just a role played by an actor. For a few seconds, however, we were so drawn into this movie we had forgotten it was not real. We felt the emotions as though we were a part of the movie.

The human dynamics and emotional drama in the workplace are much like those interactions we see in the theater. However, drama in the workplace causes real emotional problems and physical symptoms. How can we bring a clearer perception to the underlying causes of the conflicting relationships so people can be free?

I would like to suggest that complicated relationships in the workplace are much like a literary drama, and we can learn from a theater metaphor how we create and enable the drama to continue. We each see our own version of the workplace we believe to be true, but we fail to recognize our own part in producing it.

Let's look at the following comparison as a way to illuminate our understanding of the dynamics in today's workplace.

THE STAGE

An actor needs a stage. He then needs a compelling drama in which he can develop his character and play out the scenes with passion. He also needs other actors and actresses to be cast in the drama—characters whom he can challenge, compete with, and overcome; characters who support his drama of victory, defeat, love, loss, and even death.

The ego is also an actor—a false identity playing a role we believe is real. Its stage is the workplace, and its drama far too often is a tragedy— complete with pain, suffering, triumph, and loss.

This tragedy is a real-life experience as long as we exist here on the physical plane. We cannot go home and be thankful it was only a movie or stage play.

It is our life.

When we view the workplace as the stage where a drama is being played out, we can see it has all the components of any play or movie we might go see for entertainment. This can be very useful in bringing insight to the source of our pain and anguish in the workplace.

First, however, we must look at how the ego developed and became the actor it is.

Second, we will look at the elements of drama. Understanding these basic principles, we will gain some new insights into the workplace performance.

This comparison to a literary drama can turn the spotlight on the degrading human dynamics occurring on any given businesses day on any business stage. The light will assist you in coming out of the fog. Finding clarity will open you to new ways to respond to old patterns that can bring relief from the recurring tragedy. It will assist you in your perception by illuminating the interactions and revealing the thought systems fueling them.

It takes courage to challenge your own image of yourself, and certainly more honesty to identify the dramatic role you are playing in real life on the stage we know as the workplace. You are the one who will reap the rewards for this brave journey.

THE EGO—A SELF-CREATED ACTOR

The ego is the image we have come to believe is who we are. It is not bad, and in fact we could not function without an ego. The personality, an aspect of the ego, is necessary as we travel on our journey through life.

It is like a costume or a role we play, which functions for us in various situations. We send out an actor in our place—a proxy—an inadequate, small version of ourselves. Then we complain about the performance.

The problem occurs because we are disconnected from our eternal, spiritual source and rely only on the ego to carry out our intentions. The ego is only a portion of who we really are. When we feel separate from our source and from each other, we are much like small boats who have drifted away from our mother ship and our fellow passengers.

Because we feel isolated, we look for other ways to build our sense of security. We want to belong and to feel needed, accepted, and loved. But what we are looking for is significance: a way to overcome our sense of unworthiness.

The ego bases its identity on external validation and operates from fear of discovery that we are not valuable. The ego does not rely on its internal strength but seeks it outside itself. The ego wants to protect its secret—it is powerless. So it creates an identity that is worthy and appears strong.

The ego is an actor who wears a mask so others cannot see that we do not know who we are. If we recognized our inner spiritual greatness, our ego would not have to work so hard to act out a role to convince ourselves and others we are valuable. It takes great energy to create an identity and try to contain ourselves in it.

The ego first begins its development at some time in early childhood when the innocent and free little child discovers just being is not enough in the physical world. The child begins to develop a self-concept, mainly from the influence and interactions of family and friends. The child learns to define its identity based on outside feedback it receives from significant authority figures and other early influencers.

Positive reactions from family and friends support the child's identity as it develops. The self-created ego then gets further reinforcement from the outside world as it continues in life. Identity grows stronger.

For example, a comment such as, "She's such a nice little girl" or "He's such a strong little boy" motivates the child to continue exhibiting behavior that elicits a positive response. The world continues to impact the child's decision to be an identity. This conditioning process and labeling from others strengthens the self-developing role.

Somewhere along the way, some kind of pain occurs. So the child makes an unconscious decision to create a way to cope with future pains and situations. The painful experience could be anything from a reprimand to a full-scale attack by someone. A powerful event in a young child's life is one that causes them to feel shame. Experiences that threaten security cause the child to begin a protective process. The child creates another portion of the ego identity to ensure safety and to defend itself from pain or loss of love.

The more negativity the child encounters, the stronger the need to build up defenses and rely on the ego identity to protect itself. The child is well on his way in a lifelong process of pretending to be the role, which gets positive reinforcement and therefore encourages the ego to build defenses against anything perceived as threatening. This pretending and defending becomes the identity and the way of being for the child on into adulthood.

Unintentionally, even the educational process shapes and conditions the ego for coping and achieving in school. Children begin comparing themselves to others. When they fail to succeed in one area, they then compensate in other ways. And if they don't feel validation for their efforts in a subject, unfortunately they often carry this feeling and lack of confidence into other areas. If, for example, a child has reading difficulties, he may label himself as not as smart as the other children. The sense of inadequacy the ego is trying to protect, the fear of being unworthy, is often reinforced in school because of the competitive environment.

The impact of comparing oneself to others in school is demonstrated when my adult audiences are visibly relieved to hear no correlation exists between intelligence and the ability to spell. Many hold throughout their lives the message "you can't spell" as a sign they are seriously flawed and not very bright.

Throughout the years all kinds of methods for survival and protection are developed as a part of the identity. With time, the self-defined identity becomes so strong the individual believes it is really who she or he is.

But more than anything else, pretending to be what you are not is exhausting. And you are forced to defend the ego's definition of you and to try to embody this fictional role. Protecting this limited view of yourself takes great defense.

If you don't believe the ego relies on external symbols and people to authenticate itself and reinforce its identity, ask yourself any or all of the following questions:

- Who would I be if I were not someone's father, mother, brother, sister, husband, wife, boyfriend, girlfriend, child, etc.?
- Who would I be if I did not have this position, title, or role in my job?
- Who would I be if I suddenly had no money?
- Who would I be if I had no home?
- What does my choice of automobile say about me?

- What do my choices of clothes and hairstyle say about me?
- Who would I be if I belonged to no organizations?
- What do my choices of jewelry, toys, sports teams, recreational sports, and entertainment activities say about me?
- Who would I be if I did not live in this community, region, and country?
- What does my choice of music, television programs, and books say about me?
- Who would I be without my social groups and friends?
- Who would I be if I were never invited to anything, i.e. parties, weddings, events?
- Who would I be if I had no heritage?
- Who would I be if I had no church or religion?
- Who would I be if I had no name (or nobody knew my name)?
- Who would I be if I had no education or degrees?

Can you see how all the descriptions define you by outside circumstances, situations, possessions and people? Most of us get much of our identity from these sources in our past and present. The breakthrough comes when we realize we are far more than the acquired objects and recognitions in our lives.

The spirit within us is greater than all the external factors we have been accumulating our entire lives. When we understand and know that our soul is interconnected to our source and to all others on a much deeper level, we find relief and freedom. We are not alone. We can give up the search to find validation outside ourselves. We can relax and find our strength where it has always been: within us—unchanging and eternal.

But until we make this realization, we continue on the path of the ego, looking for outside reinforcement. To complicate matters, we even use other people to sustain our drama and our role. Although it's hard to recognize and admit, even to ourselves, we use other people to carry out our drama and define who we are. Without our relationships to others, we cannot see either our ego or our real self. Ultimately, relationships are the way to be restored to our authentic selves because other people are the mirror to our souls.

The material possessions, titles, teams, social groups, affiliations, and money are often simply symbols to show we are important and have significance. They have no intrinsic value—only that which we assign them.

The ego is never at rest, because it requires time and energy to play out the role it has designed for itself. It must convince others of its validity and stir up drama to keep reinforcing itself. It must be ever alert and vigilante to outside threats. This causes us to be uptight and anxious, unable to give up the ever-watchful position. Our fear of being diminished by someone else keeps us from knowing our true self.

You can recognize when the ego is in control when you find yourself doing any of the following things. They are not bad behaviors to be stamped out and rejected, but they are signals you are afraid. And instead of gaining recognition and admiration from others, these mechanisms block energy and keep others from knowing who you are. They do not allow others to be close to you.

- Defending
- Attempting to be superior
- Controlling others or situations
- Creating drama
- Feeling like a victim
- Gossiping
- Blaming and attacking
- Claiming to be right
- Creating enemies
- Withholding feelings
- Being unwilling to take responsibility
- Boasting
- Interrupting
- Being self-righteous
- Exhibiting addictive behavior
- Being the first to speak

- Having the last word
- Denying that you are afraid

The ego has a primary drive to create a sense of superiority within itself and toward others. This one-upmanship permeates the ego world, especially in businesses and organizations. It is based on the false belief if "I'm smarter, richer, prettier, nicer..." (or any number of ways of appearing better) "then you can't hurt me or make me small."

However, creating this feeling of supremacy produces exactly the opposite of the desired result—it alienates others. But the temporary fix the ego receives for appearing greater and having authority over others is very strong. It produces a powerful surge that reinforces the ego's need for dominance, but, of course, the fix is only temporary.

The ego's plan for sustaining itself is a complex matter, lying beneath the surface but needing constant attention. The gigantic performance and all its interactions go on worldwide and are so believable. Breaking through the illusion is terribly difficult. It is as though we are hypnotized to continue playing our roles and repeat the lines again and again.

Sadly, it often takes a crisis, a lot of pain, or a difficult situation to temporarily wake a person up. These moments, when they do occur, can lead to freedom from the ego, if one chooses it. Even then, it is rare when a person can achieve it for a long period of time—so powerful is the collective consciousness. It takes commitment and courage to continue challenging the dictates of the ego. But it is our destiny to evolve beyond this small description of ourselves.

As a consultant, again and again I have watched people break down and cry as they describe their life at work. Many people are at the brink. They are sucked into a giant mudslide and as the economic downturn continues, they sink deeper and deeper, feeling more desperate and helpless to stop it. And even then, with pain so close to the surface, they continue on because their economic security depends on the job. You may know exactly what I am talking about or you may have a loved one enduring this dilemma.

One by one, as people awaken and begin to see a new, freer way to live in peace and harmony, stemming from the powerful inner self, a change of consciousness will occur. First, it will happen within individuals, then groups, and then in the collective consciousness. A tipping point will be reached and awareness of who we really are will occur. The planetary evolution of humanity is dependent only on shifting our perspective and seeing our oneness with our fellow human beings. And each one of us has a significant purpose and plan for helping bring about this necessary shift.

Finally, this change in consciousness, which has already begun, will impact the world and how we experience it. It is an amazing transformation that will bring harmony and peace, instead of tragedy and wars. And it begins with each one of us, right now, where we are, in the environments in which we work and play.

LITERARY ELEMENTS OF DRAMA

Understanding the drama and its components requires seeing your ego is an actor playing out its story with intensity and conviction, believing it all to be real. The story is one of suffering in an ever-escalating play as human beings interact with each other on the workplace stage.

The performance intensifies as the characters react and counter-react to one another. The interactions cause emotional distress and insecurity. What we don't understand is that the pain is coming from inside ourselves, not from others. We experience pain and anxiety because of our resistance to looking within. Our protections prevent us from seeing the truth: fear is already in us and is not caused by others!

Your ego believes the other characters cause your emotions and responses. This is not true. Whenever your ego is provoked by another person, you are reliving past scenes originated in childhood. You then act out a response, based on a role from the conditioning you received early in your development. The deeper the intensity of the emotion, the greater the fear you attempt to disguise and project on another.

So we could say that little children dressed as adults are playing out the dramas and running the businesses and governments of the world. Without giving up the false pretentions of the ego, leaders masquerading as adults will continue to wreak havoc in the environment.

To bring clarity to the situation, let's take a close look at various literary elements and see how they illuminate what is happening in the workplace.

THEME

The ego's true theme is "I am not worthy."

We must cover the shameful secret with tactics and strategies to convince ourselves and the audience that the ego image we present is real. One of our greatest fears is that we will not be convincing and others will see through our act. We will be exposed as a charlatan and our weaknesses will be revealed. We play out the identity we made up for ourselves from years of experience in learning to pretend. Our theme is a pattern originated in the past but continually refined and perfected. The theme is so unconscious we don't even notice it is our recurring theme. We will later look at how each individual develops a unique theme, based on experiences from childhood, and we will learn how it has been running our lives. Sadly, the underlying, common theme operating in most workplaces is attack and overcome.

STAR / PROTAGONIST

The star of your drama is you—the hero or heroine of the drama.

Since each of you in your workplace perceives yourself to be the star, the difficulty occurs when other co-workers do not play out their roles as cast by you. They have done their own casting, and in their plays you are the minor character and *they* are the stars! Being the star of your drama keeps your focus on you, while the other characters on the stage do not know they are cast as bit players in your show. They believe they are the stars and fail to see your significance and certainly do not see the stage from your viewpoint. Understanding the various perspectives, you can laugh at the absurdity. However, when embroiled in clashes, it is anything but funny. You are so convincing in your role it is even believable to you. The ego will defend its role with vehemence and passion and therein lies the problem.

Your starring role leads you to act out your theme, plot, and motives every day as you return to your workplace stage. Because it is so unconscious, you don't even recognize you've played this performance before.

SCRIPT

Your script has been written by your ego and makes perfect sense to you. Most of your lines have been memorized from years of repetition in similar scenes on different stages. Have you ever noticed yourself reciting words you have said before and recognized a dilemma you are having now is similar to a previous experience? In addition, the workplace has its own cultural script and language with certain vernaculars.

The confusion and lack of communication in your work environment comes about when the other players do not have your script. They don't know their lines as assigned by you. (Imagine your dismay if you were acting in a play and the other actors began improvising their lines!)

PLOT

The plot is the story line or action that results from each individual's motives. The motives are unconscious, but they are designed to get a response from the other players, which will satisfy your need to relive the past.

But of course, this required and expected response doesn't happen exactly the way you want, so the plot thickens and the drama intensifies. An actor may change stages, but the plot never varies until the source of the drama is discovered.

MOTIVE

Motives are the unconscious goals and expectations we hold, based on our own personal history. Unresolved issues fuel our motives and cause us to reenact them with our co-workers.

We always search out and find evidence to support our personal story line, and the ego will take us down the path to the consequences its plot demands, even if it is painful or disappointing on a conscious level. The ego would rather be right than happy. Seeking evidence and allies to prove we are right are the ways we bolster our egos.

Because we are unaware of our motives, it is difficult to change the action of the drama, so we continue to play it out in the same fashion.

We may start wondering, "Why does this always happen to me?" or "This isn't fair. Why are people so ____?" You may fill in the blank because the belief system for each individual is unique and we see the world in our own way based on our perception of our personal experiences.

As long as we have unconscious motives operating from beneath our awareness, we will find difficulty in setting new conscious intentions. Our new positive goals will be hindered by the negative expectations of hidden motives. Clearing the interference stemming from unconscious motives frees us to attract new life experiences.

DIRECTOR

It is helpful to become aware of the director of your life. Since the ego created the plot and cast the characters, based on its own motives from the past, only the ego could direct the performance. The ego is the only one who knows the desired ending.

The director is usually experienced as an inner voice instructing us how to carry out the role with adequate passion, agony, or heartfelt emotion. The goal of the director is to help the ego turn in an Academy Award winning performance.

The director knows what behaviors worked in the past in scenes of victory and defeat so the director will continue to instruct the actor to carry out the same performance. The director in you does not have another way to direct the scenes or your reactions except from previous events with other people in similar roles.

CAMERA

Judgment is the automatic viewpoint, the lens and filter of the camera through which we see the world and the workplace. It is based on a limited view from our small corner of the world. This opinion comes from our starring role and it is ours alone. But we believe it is true. We operate from this personal perspective, never questioning if it is the real world. The fact is, our viewpoint is only a reflection of our own belief system. We don't recognize we are the creator of our world. We believe it lies outside of us. We don't understand we see what we believe, not the other way around.

Others have their own cameras and filters, and they do not see the performance in any other perspective but their own. The others with whom you interact do not see relationships, circumstances, or other people through your eyes. They have their own opinions, arising out of their belief system and expectations. We may even believe we know someone very well, but we cannot truly know another when we have our own judgments stemming from the ego.

However, it gets very complex because we usually continue to see and hear what we expect, regardless of what is really said or done. Our expectations are so strong we filter and block any other options. We witness the world through the lens of judgment, even though it is very clouded and distorted.

Judging is so pervasive in the workplace and in the world that we are not aware we are doing it every moment of the day. We judge not only each other, but situations, and most harshly, ourselves. We relentlessly beat ourselves up based on our own expectations and consequent judgments. We find ourselves falling short of the self-defined rules and then torment ourselves with recriminations. We deplete our own energy and suffer more self-doubt and personal abasement, never recognizing it is all come from our ego. What an agonizing and self-defeating game we play.

ACTION

The action occurs each day as the ego enters the stage and carries out its plot. The ego's driving force is control, so we expend incredible energy attempting to control our self, others, and situations, believing this will protect us and keep our secret fears safe and hidden.

The action is exhausting because it is being motivated by fear and trepidation.

It is like a gigantic chess game of moving, waiting, watching, and being ever vigilant of the terrible claim, "Checkmate!"

ENEMY / ANTAGONIST

No play would be complete without the role of at least one enemy, and there are usually several. To substantiate our self, there must be others to participate in heated action and conflict. We sometimes feel most alive in combat, even though the aftermath is guilt and depression.

The enemies provide varying degrees of intensity in the drama. The most interesting thing to observe is that the enemy is different for different people. The enemy is the person or situation perceived to be a threat to you. So casting of the enemies is based on whom or what you believe could hurt, expose, or overcome you. The enemy often changes throughout the drama, depending on who you consider to be the most threatening.

Your ego, believing the enemy to be the source of your pain or envy, carries out a battle to overcome or prevent being overcome. This battle usually causes very strong emotions.

The rival has appeared in other dramas with you, but the face was different. The enemy continues to be unrecognized by your ego as the same adversary it has battled in the past.

Having a common enemy can bring former rivals together. This shared fear creates a strong bond with others who are afraid of the same enemy. In the workplace, this is usually called politics, or more aptly, gossip. The bond is tentative and will break easily as scenes change and different characters enter the stage.

CONSPIRACY

Conspiracy is alive and well in businesses, government, and other organizations. People conspire for a single reason: supporting each other's false identities. The secret plan is necessary because if exposed, the egos would be condemned to their ultimate destiny—destruction.

These subversive alliances are attempts fortify the egos and prevent exposure. Elaborate schemes designed to protect the participants in the conspiracy add further emotional fervor with temporary excitement. These alliances are based on personal agendas and ultimately fail, often with disgrace.

THE CONFLICT

The star of the drama has a conflict to resolve over the course of the story. Throughout the performance, the star believes the conflict is with the other characters, particularly the people cast as enemies. This belief is a great misperception of the ego and keeps you isolated and blind to the truth: *all battles are with the self.* This book explores gentle ways to help the ego put down its guard and discover the path of inner peace.

THE CLIMAX

This is the high point in the drama, when the emotion has reached its peak. It is at this point the hero must make a decision. It is a critical choice, with the possibility of changing the direction of the main character—you.

The decision is always between two options: (1) "Should I follow the familiar path of pain and suffering offered by the ego?" or (2) "Should I choose the path of my inner spirit, which leads to authentic power?"

The ego is tenacious and wants you to follow its road of never-ending misery. You are so deeply ingrained in your ego's patterns that choosing spirit over ego causes an enormous conflict.

Most often, you follow the well-worn path of the ego. The ego then leads you into another drama, often on a different stage, even with different characters. The plot never varies, nor do the motives. All of them stem from your personal past experiences. Therefore, the drama is recreated but the outcome remains the same. Only the names and faces change on a new stage of endless episodes of your continuing drama.

Not until the ego finally surrenders can the authentic, spiritual self emerge to reclaim the present. Then and only then is the ego freed from the self-imposed prison of an ongoing soap opera. But until there is an internal shift and realization, the outer ever-persistent journey will continue with the same results.

As you see, your ego is directing this drama and it will never lead you to a happy ending. You must be ready to see a new view—looking behind the mask of the ego.

First, we must acknowledge and recognize the problem in businesses today. Without this recognition, no change can be initiated. This drama is not only detrimental to business success but, more important, to the very health and vitality of the people within the businesses.

Secondly, we must make a decision to be accountable and responsible for our own actions and reactions and start to extricate ourselves from the intertwined egos. It means making the necessary changes by committing to take purposeful action to awaken.

Are you willing to recognize the blocks thrown out by your ego? Are you willing to look within?

When you are, you will discover a new, calm way of responding from your inner spirit. You will no longer feel like a puppet on a stage, dependent on others for your identity and purpose. This is where true inner peace lies.

To accomplish this worthwhile journey you will need to practice challenging the ego's drama. This takes conscious attention and a commitment to yourself.

IMPACT OF DRAMA IN THE WORKPLACE

What does this entanglement of egos in the ongoing framework of complex relationships do to the workplace? The emotional drama feeds on hidden frailties and insecurities of the individuals in your workplace. The suffering continues to grow. The play-acting goes on, making it all very difficult to discern the truth.

Ray was a national accounts manager for a touted industry leader, calling on major retail outlets throughout the country. His business acumen was outstanding and his client relationships strong and fruitful. However, through various mergers, his position grew more demanding and intense with more stores to call on and fewer people to manage the national accounts. Leadership above him changed, positions were being eliminated, and job functions were outsourced more frequently. He breathed a sigh of relief each year as he survived another string of layoffs and downsizing. But the national team was reduced and his responsibilities increased until he was covering an area that was once handled by three people.

Having a family, a mortgage, and children in college, Ray worked harder and harder to fulfill the escalating requirements of his job. As the competition got stiffer and the market got tighter his job became increasingly stressful and exhausting. However, as he was in his early fifties, he felt he had no choice but to endure the pressure and mounting demands for higher performance because he thought his age would make a job search difficult.

He was recently called to the corporate office in a major city. His colleagues were also called, and the rumor was another layoff was about to occur. Ray described sitting in the outer office in the corporate headquarters with people whom he had worked with for two decades. One by one they were called into the office to be told if they were staying or being eliminated. They watched each other come out with a smile or a heartsick look on their faces.

Ray's position was not eliminated, but the lack of sensitivity toward these long term employees was shocking. The experience was similar to a firing line (literally), and the executioners were the top management to whom these national managers had been so loyal. The morale of those left behind, not to mention those eliminated, impacts not only the business but all relationships in and out of the company. This lack of regard for one another occurs in all kinds of businesses of all sizes.

Even in the face of downsizing, there are better ways of treating people. The old model of business is starting to crumble. The framework that has held it up is beginning to collapse. Leaders operating from authenticity can bring about a change. The need for approval and financial security by employees during this economic recession makes it more difficult for them to initiate the change of unraveling the interlocking elements and layers of complexity in the workplace, but if you are an employee rather than a manager, and you are sufficiently motivated, you can begin by changing yourself.

The literary model I am presenting can bring new insights for people learning personal responsibility. Managers and leaders can create positive changes in their own workplace when they themselves become responsible for their own dramas.

Fortunately, the workplace provides infinite possibilities to awaken from the delusion. As leaders, when you begin freeing yourself from the death grip of the ego, you will discover your authentic power—an unlimited power.

This framework of the theater can illustrate a way to create a new form of leadership, as well as a better way to relate in the workplace. As a leader, you will have the capacity to change the atmosphere at work to one of kindness and compassion. As you restore these elements to the workplace, people will respond in kind, and business will grow to new levels.

Begin to notice how the drama occurs at your workplace and in the world. Stop throughout the day and notice how anxious and guarded people are. Look at the expressions on their faces. Look in their eyes and notice the effort they make to appear significant and nonchalant. See past their various attempts for recognition and see how they are just like you, with a different script and theme, but the same desire for acceptance.

Then look without judgment at your own inner thoughts and actions. Try to be honest with yourself and acknowledge your own need to succeed and be triumphant. Notice how your mind can take over and run its old replays from the past. Initially, just paying attention to how the old patterns arise will be the opening to your authentic self.

As you address your issues, you will be able to calmly unhook from the ego drama, releasing others to do the same. As you are willing to take your own personal path, you will become an enlightened leader who inspires people to higher levels of success and happiness. You will experience a deep satisfaction as you enrich the lives of others by freeing them to express their true beings.

You are deeply entrenched in the way you operate in your life, so you will be tempted to return to the ego's old ways of reacting to situations and people. However, the more you demonstrate to yourself and others the beauty of relating in the new way, the more the results will become perceptible and reinforcing.

At times, the ego will entice you to use old strategies that worked before. Or you may be hooked into reacting to another's ego. For this reason, it is important to take the time to implement and practice the steps in this book on a continual and daily basis in order to strengthen your enlightened behavior. It is foolish to think just reading this will bring about a change. It takes courage, consistency, and practice in the workplace and in all relationships.

This new way of leading and communicating will be well worth the effort. Your organization will thrive and grow as it never has before. You will create a team of people coming together with the synergism and power of a shared vision, which can never occur in the ego-drama world of individual plots and schemes.

Learning to recognize the spiritual essence in yourself and others is the key to enlightened leadership. It is the only path to long-term success for an organization. Leading an organization to higher levels is impossible when you view the world and others through the eyes of judgment.

As a leader, you will be the key to changing the drama, the plot, and the on-going scenes on the stage of the workplace. The energy expelled on all the old politics and relentless disruptions will be replaced with a calm and influential way of being with others. Doubt and fear will come along the way, but your commitment and dedication will be rewarded if you dare to look behind the face of the ego.

As you get a glimpse of how truly awesome you are, it will be hard to go back completely. It is harder to lie to yourself once you have had a moment of seeing the truth behind your mask.

Who would choose the tiny, artificial power of the ego, even if for only a moment, once the authentic power of spirit has been recognized?

PERSONAL RESTORATION PLAN
TO PRACTICE IN YOUR WORKPLACE

1. Pay attention to your reactions this next week whenever you're in a meeting or interacting in a group. Try to detect your own role in the workplace by recognizing the various literary elements of a drama. We will look at some of these principles more fully in the next chapters, but become aware of some of these components:

- Theme - Is there a common theme in some of the more intense moments at your workplace? Can you see yourself enacting a theme from the past? (e.g., suffering, battling evil, winning the contest)
- Star - What character do you play as the star? (e.g., Scarlett O'Hara, Superman)
- Script - Have you heard yourself say these lines before? Listen to yourself at work.
- Plot and Motive - What do you get out of some of your conflicts or interactions?
  - Director - Whose voice(s) do you hear in your head? (e.g., mother, spouse)
  - Enemy and Conflict - Notice who hooks you or who you want to blame. What kinds of difficult situations have you faced?
  - Climax - Try to pay attention to times when you have an opportunity to find wisdom, compassion, and trust.

2. Start looking for opportunities to bring people together. Listen to others and make an effort to exhibit patience, respect, and trust, whether one on one or in groups. At the end of the day, write down any insights you may have had or actions you took that built trust with co-workers.

CHAPTER 4

The Star and Its Themes

✳   ✳   ✳

It is almost impossible not to be part of the prevailing culture of your workplace—even if it is toxic. In fact, much like a movie containing high drama, emotional intensity in the workplace can inexplicably draw you in. Because you are part of the interacting relationships, your perception is skewed and probably reflects the thoughts and ideas of significant people in your organization.

It is difficult to have an outsider's perspective when you are an insider. Because of the many layers of reactions and protections, it can be complex and difficult to discern what is really happening. Our individual viewpoint comes from our part in the organization as one player engaged with all the others.

Using the metaphor of the workplace as a stage on which a significant drama is being played out can help you see it is not real; it is an illusion. However, as long as you participate in it and play your part, it will seem real. And as in watching a movie, while you are in it—it is your reality!

What if you could withdraw your attention and step off the stage, so to speak? What if you could become an observer as well as an interactive participant? I am going to suggest a process that will shed light on the relationships at work. You will find a fresh perspective and a sense of clarity in your workplace. This new perception will enable you to operate from authenticity.

Recognizing that we created the script and continue to direct our starring role can be a huge advancement in our evolution of healing our pain and becoming free. Ultimately, it will heal our souls.

Healing requires identifying the behavior and companion emotions keeping you locked in reenactment of the same scenes. As you do this it will bring about a new understanding of yourself, your main theme, and your starring role. Seeing the continuing behavior will allow you to escape the endless trap of pain and suffering based on a false belief system, constructed from the past. This will be of great usefulness because you will begin to see how you are controlled by your ego and the egos of others.

If you have hidden agendas, designed by the ego, your progress will be limited. You must be willing to look at them and eventually, laugh at them. When you do, you will see the agendas of the ego are meaningless and are not helping you become who you were created to be.

Waking up requires strong focus and intent to reach your essence. This means bringing clarity to not only yourself but the people with whom you have relationships. No man is an island and life is made up of relationships. We need each other.

Remember the movie *Castaway,* starring Tom Hanks? It was very poignant and illustrative of a person's need for companionship. Because of his isolation and loneliness, he made a Wilson volley ball the object of his affection. He drew a face on it, talked to it, and called it "Wilson." His emotion was so real the audience was moved to sadness when his ball drifted away at sea.

The model of a dramatic performance can help you see how relationships are intertwined and continued, and how we often sacrifice a part of ourselves to be a suitable player in the action. Discovering how you react and counter-react in the web of interactions will aid you in coming home to your true self. It will assist you to step out of the fictional tale and into reality.

Let us take a more detailed look at the performance occurring in almost every business in the country, and discover how you willingly, but blindly, partake and define yourself in it.

Like all of us, you have created an identity and starring role in your life and you take this identity into your place of work. The workplace is an environment where millions of people spend so much of their time, resulting in frequent interactions with co-workers. These many exchanges with other people provide multiple opportunities to discover your true character—your higher self.

Most people derive much of their identity as a person from the position, title, recognition, salary, and financial security from their job. So the work environment is very crucial to our level of happiness and how we experience our lives. Of course, some of the daily scenes get replayed at home with your family and you probably have starring roles on other stages in your life, such as social groups, political groups, etc.

But the workplace is a primary stage for most people. You spend eight or more hours of each workday there, not even including all the outside time spent working on or worrying about your job. It is a major stage. It is here you gain your professional status, create a sense of identity in the world, provide for your family's financial security, and create an economic lifestyle. The first question people ask when they meet you at a party is "What do you do?" Your job defines you in the eyes of the world.

This stage cannot be taken lightly.

PROTAGONIST

Since the ego is an actor created to cope and operate in a world of other actors, it would naturally be the central character in the drama in which it acts.

The protagonist in a literary drama is the dynamic character who faces the challenges and conflicts of the story line. The story revolves around the protagonist's actions, words, thoughts, and reactions as the main character meets up and interacts with other characters who also help create our interest in the whole story.

To understand the protagonist in literature or a movie, we must know about its background, its appearance, its personality, its motivations, its relationships, its conflicts, and its changes as the character progresses through the challenges and new episodes of the story.

Many kinds of heroes populate the epic dramas and tragedies we see in the theater. The journey of the hero is usually one of suffering and despair, leading to triumph and victory in some form. A tragedy, on the other hand, shows the downfall of a noble or outstanding person who has a character weakness. The person is not all good or all bad, so when we read or watch a tragedy, we usually feel mixed emotions. Sacrifice is often a central theme in the experience of a tragic hero and may end in death.

Playing out the role of the victim or martyr is a phase many heroes must pass through. Slaying dragons and discovering internal power finally leads to resolution of some kind in the happy ending dramas. A tragedy occurs when the hero is overcome, even after fighting valiantly.

Many universal themes throughout history are portrayed in the books we read, television shows we watch, and movies and theater we attend. We don't realize our own real lives are cast and played out when we unconsciously follow one or more of these universal themes.

Discovering the source of inner strength and then changing the direction of your own starring role and script can be the way to enlightenment and self-transformation.

The star of your recurring scenes follows the theme depicting you as a hero on a journey of trials and tribulations, challenges and conflicts. The ego believes you will ultimately find a happy and dramatic ending as you overcome the hurdles thrust before you. However, the real purpose of your journey is, unknowingly, a plan to awaken you from the re-creation of the past. The belief system you developed in the past keeps you asleep and unaware of your current life opportunities.

The path of awakening is often one of tragedy and pain, until you surrender the ego's performance in favor of the road back to your authentic self. This does not mean struggles will end, but you will face them with an attitude of strength and optimism rather than fear and defeatism.

M. Scott Peck, in his enduring book *The Road Less Traveled,* says, "Once we truly know that life is difficult—once we truly understand and accept it—then life is no longer difficult." The surrendering of the ego is the way to relinquish the pain of struggling. You can't change the struggle but you can reveal the source of pain and begin to move through your life with new respect and an understanding of your journey. You can begin to enjoy your challenges rather than experiencing them as a burden.

THEMES

To appreciate your own process, let's take a look at how universal themes play out and become the source of ongoing dilemmas and predicaments—sometimes leading to self-revelation, other times to tragic endings.

Individuals throughout time, both fictional and real, have followed paths of self-discovery through an array of conflict, sacrifice, pain, and difficulties, which ultimately lead to either a resolution or an unresolved ending.

Recognizing your theme and your starring role can be of great assistance to you in uncovering your inner motives and discovering your true self, if you choose to learn the lessons presented. Unfortunately, it often takes repetition of the same experience in our lives to get our attention, usually occurring with more intensity each time.

Some of the themes in books and movies are very familiar in life as well. We see long periods of suffering, such as in *Terms of Endearment, Million Dollar Baby,* and most soap operas. The shattered-illusion-and-destruction-of-the-hero theme shows up in *Death of a Salesman* and many of Shakespeare's tragedies, such as *Hamlet.*

The Cinderella story is a recurring theme in such movies as *Pretty Woman* and *My Fair Lady.* Rags to riches stories are very popular, as in *Slumdog Millionaire, Oliver,* and *Annie.* Joan of Arc, Gandhi, and Christ depict the theme of great sacrifice for the good of humanity. *Rocky* and many other books and movies portray the story of the underdog becoming the victor through perseverance. Star-crossed lovers are the basis for dramas such as *Romeo and Juliet* and *West Side Story.*

Hero/warrior stories are very common—the hero fights the dragons and wins the kingdom. This theme is seen in war stories, westerns, cop shows, epic adventures, and science fiction, to name a few. Indiana Jones and James Bond are examples of the superhero who inspires our desire to rise above the mundane. We settle for mediocrity and smallness of the ego in our lives, but we go to the movies to dream of power and greatness.

Goodness and morality prevailing over evil and greed is the theme of a timeless movie watched every year by millions of people for decades—*It's a Wonderful Life*. We cry as everyone comes to the support of Jimmy Stewart's character for his heroic commitment to honesty and humanity when challenged by the greediness of the town bully.

There are many other universal themes, such as martyrdom, good versus evil, man's search for meaning, fighting oppression, rebellion and defiance, the strength of the human spirit, moral choices, destiny versus free will, unrequited love, the love triangle, man's struggle to fulfill his duty, betrayal and loss, good boy versus bad boy, and numerous others.

We identify with the hero and the struggle because we relate to the theme in our own real lives. As the center of your universe you find the obstacles and relationships needed to fulfill your journey and create opportunities to awaken, even though it is unconscious. It seems like it is happening to you. But that is not the case.

You are attracting the experiences and characters to you. The experiences, as you interact with other characters, are determined and driven by your past scenes of similar encounters. Chance meetings that appear to be coincidental are the result of interacting energy that draws people to each other. Synchronicity brings people and experiences to you based on your energy field.

Identifying your theme and starring role will help you see how you do attract situations and circumstance into your life. Be aware that you have more than one theme: one major theme and many other minor melodies accompany the main composition. However, we are often blind to our own underlying story.

One way to help you discover your leading role and theme is to recall movies or books to which you related or by which you were inspired. If it is difficult to recognize yourself in these roles, just think of movies you have really enjoyed in the past. Which ones stand out? Do they have a theme that resonates with you or a main character by which you feel moved or motivated?

The important thing to understand is the theme leads the character to the places in his soul that need healing. Other characters in the story are a mirror, a reflection showing the main character—you—the issues and struggles you cannot see in yourself. Interacting with others brings your own issues to the surface.

Much in the way that a sound wave needs to impact an object to resonate the sound, you need other characters to see yourself. You unconsciously seek out those people who will help reveal you to yourself.

Until the source is discovered, you repeatedly act out your theme. It began in childhood and is carried throughout your adulthood, even though it has been disguised to you. It will continue to run your life until something happens to get your attention. A crisis or some great discomfort is usually what it takes, but why wait for a disruption or tragedy?

Recognizing your theme and role in your own life can be a shortcut to see how you involuntarily participate in the web of egos in the workplace. Uncovering your theme can give you the freedom of choice in how your story ends, rather than letting it elevate to a critical state. Revealing to yourself the secret residing beneath your motives provides an opportunity to get off the elevator on the upper floor, rather than waiting until it hits bottom. Deep probing and a willingness to give up some of the pride of the ego will aid you in this self-discovery process. You can wake up now and break out of the repeated pattern rather than crashing and burning.

Pediatrician Dr. Michael Jones discovered his theme was "suffering is noble." His father had abused him as a child, breaking Michael's arm when he was five years old because he couldn't tie his shoes. He was also locked outside in the dark and suffered innumerable beatings. Michael's experience became his way of life.

But his theme also brought more suffering into his life. He had been mistreated and emotionally or economically abused by his wife, his stockbroker, his tenants, and others. His realization that he was a frequent victim in keeping with his theme caused a huge breakthrough.

Michael hadn't realized he was attracting the experiences of exploitation to himself because of his anguished victim identity. He thought this was happening to him because that is just the way life is. When he broke through this illusion, his life changed.

He took charge of his life and began taking a stand for himself. He no longer needed to endure the pain of mistreatment when he recognized it was just a belief system from his past that he kept replaying. His theme was not real.

Some good came from his theme and his starring role: he was motivated to help children by being a caring and dedicated doctor. But now he contributes to the world from a powerful position, not one of a wounded child.

George was an influential businessman who unconsciously employed the dictator/bully method of leadership. He was demanding of his employees and very intimidating to everyone who dealt with him at work and elsewhere.

George realized his theme of being the dictator/ bully originated in his past. He had been very overweight as a child and was never good in sports. He was rarely chosen for any teams, and the girls seldom liked him. He began fighting back by being the smartest and the toughest in his class.

He told about a time when he was a teen-ager and he had bought a used car. Suddenly he became popular with kids who wanted him to drive them to the beach. This became a weekly Saturday event. George secretly knew he was being used, but so desperate was he for friends and socialization, he closed his eyes to the truth.

One weekend, another kid in the group offered to drive. They were all waiting on the corner to be picked up, but when the boy arrived, he was driving a very small car. It was obvious they wouldn't all fit in the car. George, being the largest, was the one who would take up the most room. They all looked at him with expressions of embarrassment, clearly suggesting he should be the one to drop out. He told the group he had to mow the lawn anyway, and for them to go along without him.

Crushed by the rejection, that was the day he decided no one was ever going to hurt or overpower him again. He unconsciously solidified his theme of power and strength through intimidation, believing this pretention would protect him and keep him safe from rejection.

George recognized that although his theme gave him an illusion of safety, it was also preventing him from having love in his life.

As he gave up following his familiar theme, his business became even more prosperous, with employees who were happier and more productive, and his personal life changed as well, to include new friends, activities, and a better marriage. The change in his life was dramatic.

The interesting thing about the starring role and theme is that the star is not usually aware of the way others perceive him or her.

George was quite surprised to discover people didn't like him and were very fearful of him. He thought they respected him and their actions were a demonstration of their admiration. He was hurt and then transformed as he challenged his theme and his leading role as an intimidator. The inner journey of looking behind his protective shield led him to become a man of compassion instead.

When you see the ego's theme and recognize how you keep going down the same path, you will then begin to find out the true and worthwhile goal of the soul: discovering who you really are.

It is a tall order because you have been operating from the ego identity all your life, but as you begin realizing this role is artificial, you will also see your true destiny. You will feel a new sense of peace and serenity; your passion, energy and purpose will return.

If you want to know what your greatest lessons are, look at what hurts you, what you fear, and what causes you to feel resistant. Become aware of pain beneath the surface, hidden and disguised, even from yourself.

What are you hiding?

Nourishing your inner spirit is essential to a fulfilling and purposeful life. Facing your ego and challenging the force of its tightly held grip on you will lead to a truly expansive experience. You will discern the majestic hero you really are—a soul of great dimension and power, capable of going far beyond the tiny expectations and imagination of the ego.

You will see the ego is afraid and uncertain. Your ego cowers in the face of your immortal and true self that resides beneath the small role in which you are starring.

UNLOCKING THE CLOSED DOOR

As you begin to notice how you are acting out your role, you will start the process of unlocking the door to peace of mind and inner joy. The more you observe your repeated performances, the greater the opportunity for you to give up the role.

It is tempting to persist in believing your theme, even as you watch yourself playing it out. It feels so natural. But if you can understand that it never leads to the consequence you desire, you can start to relinquish the grasp of your ego, little by little. Old habits are not easily extinguished, but as you keep confronting the triggers to them, you will see them diminish.

When you open your eyes, even for a moment, you can expand your scope and see from an upper elevation. From a higher place, you can distinguish how traveling down your soul's true path will help you become whole and complete.

Your ego will resist the truth, however, because the ego does not want you to become your authentic self—for if you do, it will be the end of the ego. Being false, it cannot exist in the face of truth.

If you are unable to identify your starring role and theme, you can ask other people how they see you. Tell them you want them to be very candid and describe to you the character from a movie or book they think most resembles you. Ask them to describe characteristics they observe in you.

Using a favorite movie or book, or asking someone else for their more objective viewpoint can assist you. We have trouble seeing our own wants, fears, needs, and roles because we are so deeply steeped in our own drama.

Detecting these unconscious goals and needs in your life will help you identify the automatic behavior and unvarying role in which you cast yourself. Finding your *modus operandi* can help unravel the mystery of your confusion and suffering.

Cynthia was a sales rep for a pharmaceutical company. Because of a change in the drug line carried by the company, numerous employees were laid off, including Cynthia. Although Cynthia's identity was bruised, she determinedly began searching for a new job.

She was very excited when she heard about an opening with a similar company, in the same territory in which she already had good relationships with the doctors and staff. She had secured an interview and was preparing for it when a former fellow co-worker called her and said she was applying for the same job.

Cynthia immediately felt deflated and reverted to an unconscious theme of being the underdog. She described how disappointed she was and how she now believed she had no chance. She cited her friend's years of experience, spunky personality, overt confidence and persistence. She just knew the other person would get the job.

This voluntary self-dispiriting behavior was Cynthia's default mode. It felt familiar to her and she even said, "Here we are again." When reminded of her own talents and skills she immediately threw up reasons why those weren't enough to get this job and the odds were slim for her to get the position now. I finally asked her to listen to herself. I knew she was a very authentic, dedicated employee and had done an excellent job for her previous employer. How could she possibly find a new job if she thought so little of herself and had such a defeatist attitude?

She said in reality she knew she was smart and recognized her own abilities and intelligence. But it seemed she somehow always saw a hurdle that made her feel small and inadequate when confronting a new situation. So I asked her the big question.

"What do you get out of this underdog theme?"

To her credit, she admitted she got several things out of this story. She protected herself because if she didn't get the job, then she wasn't so disappointed. She also got her family and friends' sympathy and concern for her upcoming struggle. Having others worry about her and offer support was gratifying and validating. And, finally, if she did get the job or achieve the goal, it was an amazing feat and everybody was so excited for her!

So essentially, she created this whole story around a theme of the underdog who is finally victorious. As she looked into her past, she realized how her theme developed. She could recall as a child she was able to get her parent's attention when she appeared helpless and fearful. And when she succeeded in spite of the obstacles, they rejoiced with her. This way of obtaining a sense of love and self-worth developed into a recurring theme that was now becoming apparent to her.

We all develop patterns in our own lives, with our own story line, including remarkable episodes. They are different but they are all concocted by us and we accept them as true. But we waste a lot of energy on the emotional roller coaster that could be better spent toward moving forward in our lives. We expend energy and then reach a conclusion that is a celebration, a rationalization, or more suffering. Then we repeat it, hoping for a different outcome.

It is difficult to be congruent and in alignment with our true purpose of self-realization when we are distracted with our emotional ups and downs. These can occur within ourselves or in group dynamics when the culture is reactive and counter-reactive. I have seen many dysfunctional organizations create havoc with their frenetic energy, rapid decisions, and lack of honest communication.

In Cynthia's case, she realized going on an interview with this underlying, unconscious attitude was not the way to get the job. And as she was so brutally honest with herself, she discovered she could no longer lie to herself. Instead, she could honor her true self and use her vitality and spirit to meet her life's challenges and goals with optimism. Her positive energy will attract the best opportunities and a job she truly desires.

The walls, situations, and enemies that we believe are outside ourselves are defined by us, based on comparable circumstances occurring long ago.

When we can start to recognize our role as the star is not real, however benign it appears, we will begin to find our authentic selves that lie beneath the roles. Although our character is not bad, replaying the theme does prevent us from realizing our full power, our natural inheritance, and our ability to be all we choose. In many ways, the stories we create from past experiences are the shackles keeping us locked in a rerun, with different characters and situations, but replays none the less. Old stories keep us reliving the ancient past and stop us from being in the present moment.

Keep in mind your past is only a remembrance, and recreating it is a pointless journey. It is over. You are in today and that is all you have. And in the present is a good place to be because here is where your power lies.

Let's look at your life to discover your starring role and theme(s). Ask yourself some of the following questions:

- When I was growing up, what was I most praised for?
- What has been my greatest achievement?
- For what would I want to be remembered?
- What qualities would others use to describe me?
- What obstacles have I overcome?
- What have I had to endure?
- Who have been my adversaries? Why?
- What have been my biggest misfortunes?
- If I had to choose a character in a movie or book who most resembles me and my life theme, which would it/they be? (You may have more than one.)
- What is my greatest character strength?
- What trait would I not want to display?
- Who was wrong about me? In what way?

As you sincerely answer these questions, a recurring theme or pattern will probably emerge.

Your theme is a familiar one in which you feel comfortable, even though it is the source of despair and anguish at times. Your star personality is one you are proud of and that fulfills your image of whom you believe you should be.

But your ego identity also has fears of inadequacy it tries to mask, even from you.

Marsha was an administrator for a large hospital. She was extremely responsible and well thought of throughout her workplace. She was very attractive and always dressed in a professional and business-savvy manner. She had a vibrant personality and was on everyone's guest list. Men were always attracted to Marsha and she always had her choice of gentlemen to date. As one short-term relationship would end, another man would immediately appear from the wings. Her friends viewed her as confident, outgoing, and extremely successful both in work and her social life. Her single women friends envied her capacity to find available men in a world where they were complaining, "There aren't any single men."

Marsha had no trouble recognizing her role and theme as Scarlet O'Hara in *Gone with the Wind*. She saw herself as the center of men's attention, but also as a passionate woman who had a strong will. She was proud of this image and enjoyed the success in her career.

However, Marsha was suffering from loneliness and had a desire for a long-term committed relationship. In addition, unbeknownst to her company, she was nearing a burnout stage in her career. The constant pressure and responsibilities were taking a toll on her.

When she probed deeper, it became apparent to Marsha that her role as Scarlet was, indeed, an Academy Award Performance because Marsha's real fear was that she wasn't attractive enough, good enough, or worthy of being the one someone chose for a permanent partner.

Her countenance and posture of assuredness were attempts to deny her inner fears of inadequacy by demonstrating to the world she could take care of herself, be extremely successful, and attract a male partner if she wanted.

However, it was in her intimate relationships that feelings of inadequacy emerged. She unconsciously sabotaged the possibility of a love relationship by alternating between confidence and need. Not knowing her authentic power and the fact that she deserved to be loved, she was unable to be genuine or vulnerable in relationships, and ultimately either she or her partner left.

Her theme was originated in childhood when she felt lost in the crowd of a large family of girls, where she never felt the love and attention she needed. So she developed the ego and personality to get what she needed.

This role served her well in the workplace as an overachiever with an outgoing, tenacious personality. However, she was tired of the competitive environment in the workplace and wanted love in her personal life. She also found people at work didn't always trust her.

As Marsha gave up pretending and started finding her inner spirit, her life began to change. She dated fewer men, but the quality of the relationships changed as she gave up her starring role. Her career improved and she reported having more peace and time for other pleasures in her life.

Playing the high performance role had taken a lot of energy, which then became available for other activities. Her frenzied schedule and the demands of the ego had exhausted her. She now discovered new vitality and energy by aligning with her spirit.

I am sure her life will continue to improve as long as she stays committed to fulfilling her soul's purpose, which includes having love and compassion for herself.

Richard was a senior vice president with a large bank and seemed to have the world at his fingertips. He had a beautiful wife, a successful career, and two children—the American dream.

When being honest, Richard saw himself as the triumphant hero who always achieved victory and high acclaim. His theme of winning and being the brightest and best seemed to be working for him, based on his level of corporate status in the bank.

However, when I spoke with other members of the bank, it was revealed that Richard was a know-it-all who never allowed others to give their opinions or ideas. His arrogance was well-known throughout the branches. Also, it was rumored he'd had several affairs and was fortunate he hadn't had sexual harassments suits filed against him.

He was viewed not as the brilliant hero he believed himself to be, but instead seen by co-workers and staff as a pompous man, lacking integrity. He was not a good leader; his team performed well, in spite of him, and not because he helped them reach their potential.

And then, unexpectedly, Richard's docile and devoted wife served him with divorce papers. This action was not part of his plan and he was devastated.

As he considered his starring role and theme, he finally saw the denial his ego was holding in place to keep him from facing his immense fear.

When Richard was a boy, he had a very controlling mother who had high expectations of him. She was critical and demanding, and showed very little affection. Richard became the star of every team and had the best grades in every class. He was the valedictorian as well as a lettered athlete. It seemed there was nothing Richard couldn't do.

His belief he was not lovable was made worse with the companion torment of not wanting to be exposed as the bad little boy. His starring role was a mask for a small boy who was desperately afraid of making a mistake and losing his mother's conditional love.

Richard was not connected to his inner spirit or his authentic power. So all the accolades, and even the attention from women, would not fill the void in his psyche. Richard was finally ready to begin giving up his starring role and womanizer theme.

Richard's life began to change.

Unfortunately, it caused him great pain and anguish to look behind the face of his ego. But as he did, his leadership style improved, and people reported working in a better environment. His wife still filed for divorce, but with time, perhaps the relationship will improve if he remains committed to awakening from his false drama.

WAKING UP

As you start recognizing your leading role, you will see the workplace and your life differently. Initially, however, you will continue to play out your role. Little by little, you will begin to see the falsity of your play-acting and pretending. You will start waking up and seeing another way of responding to situations and people. The external world and workplace will become more caring and less threatening.

The desire to sleep and remain in your fictitious story is quite prevalent. The average person is living life on a day-to-day basis, unaware of being asleep. The individual assumes everyone else is living his or her life in the same manner with varying degrees of so-called success. Most people rarely question the source of their pain, usually blaming it on someone else. Attempting to be numb and distracted, they do not see the chance for freedom from the ego's self-destruction.

However, in everyone's life, periodically an opportunity for learning and for healing occurs. These chances for growth usually come disguised as obstacles or painful situations. Sometimes they are a loss of a job or a loved one, or other economic, emotional, or physical hardships. These challenging times can be the best learning opportunities—if the person so chooses. The world is experiencing such an influx of disasters, economic hardships, wars and conflicts, it is difficult to stay asleep and ignore the global tragedies.

Today, you have many chances to start confronting and disengaging from the painful web of so much suffering, and the constant interaction with others who push your buttons, goad your reactions, and create the high intensity of the overall world and work circumstances.

The important word here is *choice.*

Four constants that never change and are the framework in which we grow are:

- Time
- Choice
- Truth
- Death

We can't change time and we can't avoid death. But during the allotment of time between birth and death, we have many passages and stages in which we can choose to see things differently. We have opportunities to discover the truth within us instead of playing out the fiction we live in most of the time. And as we look at heroes, both past and present, we can see that sometimes disappointments and trials in our lives are blessings in disguise when they lead to expansion and evolution.

The interesting aspect of choice is that everyone has ample time to use their free will. Selecting the course that will advance the soul is the best action, but is usually not done because of the intense pressure from the ego to stay with the familiar illusion.

If you do not choose your inner spirit over ego, the lesson will continue to be presented. Your soul will direct you into further opportunities to rouse you from your sleeping.

Unfortunately, the resulting pain with each new experience is usually intensified. The early wake-up calls were ignored, and it now takes more to get you to take note.

So begin to identify, each day, how you follow a predetermined theme as you encounter people and events. Watch your reactions and ask yourself the following questions:

- Is this helping reinforce my ego identity as the star of my drama?
- Am I discovering the center of my being, or am I simply gaining strokes for my ego?
- Do I really need to be the star?
- Am I expecting others to play a role in my drama?
- Am I listening to what others say or paying attention to what they do? Do I have a script for them?
- Am I meeting my ego needs at the expense of others?
- Am I blaming others for my suffering?

To assist yourself in awakening from your imaginary tale, start to challenge some of the automatic ways you have been spending your day. Change some of the daily routines which have become so habitual. Let go of some of the structure, and allow more spontaneity in your life. Exerting a lot of control and over-structuring your life are attempts to be safe. At the same time, exerting so much control also limits your experiences and opportunities for joy.

The ego wants to keep you numb and unaware of your true essence. When you are insensitive you can operate on autopilot and live on the surface. You may feel safer but your life will be more mundane. It is like living in a black and white movie, instead of a full color world, or listening to an old radio instead of digital music with surround-sound speakers.

So opening up your senses and awakening to your environment can help you become more present and aware of your life. The following activities would be a good place to start:

- Take a different route to work.
- Buy clothes that are a different style or color than you usually select.
- Eat lunch at a new restaurant.

- Go to lunch with different people.
- Change meeting times and vary the agenda.
- Consciously look people in the eye.
- Walk instead of riding elevators, escalators, etc. whenever possible.
- Try a new food or recipe.
- Take a long bath and don't rush to get through it.
- Give yourself a treat—something frivolous. Examples: massage, ice cream cone, manicure, day off, extra round of golf, nap, anything new you didn't think you should buy.
- Walk in the rain without an umbrella.
- Take a walk in a park.
- Say hello and smile at strangers.
- Wade in a lake or pond.
- Go to a good movie or play without planning it ahead of time.
- Call someone you haven't talked to in a long time.
- Pay attention to colors, smells, textures, and sounds. Become more aware of your senses.
- Stop at least once every hour when you are working and come out of intense concentration.
- Skip television and listen to music or read a book.
- Continue meditating when you first wake up and right before you go to bed.

These methods will aid in "waking you up" just as smelling coffee and bacon can awaken you in the morning. These variations in your routines aid you in being in the present moment, which is all we have. Although routine is important for continuity, learn to recognize when it is an attempt to be secure and is a block to experiencing the fullness of your life.

When we walk around numb and not present to our lives, it is indeed a tragedy.

Living a facade and feeling vaguely satisfied is the way many people live today. Waking up for people who are somewhat satisfied is more difficult than for those who are hurting, ready to seek another way. The semi-alive people will not see the need as greatly, because they are in a state of resignation or artificial satisfaction.

"This is as good as it gets" or "It could be worse" is their belief system. Or, "Someday it will be better—when I get the new job, find the right mate, get the new house." For most people, the fear of the unknown is greater than the discomfort, so it is easier to just go on as they are. And with the current economy people are held in their positions with increased fear, grateful to simply have a job.

Many people will often describe themselves as happy the way they are when talking to others. The truth is, they do not want others to know how really discontented they are. You know many people like this. But when I ask my audiences how many of them sitting right there in front of me have had a major upset or difficult life situation in the last year, almost everyone raises their hand. It is sometimes easier to be honest in a group situation when we have some degree of comfort that others feel the same. But most of the time we feign confidence and nonchalance, rather than be vulnerable and a target for dominance by others.

When people feel oppressed in the workplace, they rarely confront those above them. But lashing out at peers is common. Reactions and counter-reactions increase the complexity and only escalate personal pain, lack of respect, low self-esteem and internal competition. So the lack of compassion coming from many leaders who are only concerned about the bottom line radiates out through the organization and ultimately, to the customer. The economic impact is rarely considered by those reading the spreadsheets. But the cost is immeasurable.

Employee satisfaction surveys do not represent the truth for several reasons. Denial is a strong factor because to admit anything is wrong would require the person to consider a change that is too frightening. To reply honestly about the issues in the workplace is far too risky because of the possibility of being discovered a betrayer, and finally, even if the employee is departing, the old adage "don't burn bridges" still applies.

Most people just continue working in this indecisive way, complaining at home each night and often resorting to addictive behavior to stop the pain and shut down the mind. But sooner or later, life usually brings about situations making it increasingly difficult to ignore their lack of true awareness and movement toward their genuine purpose.

Breaking through this wall of denial and automatic behavior is a process occurring only when the person is ready and willing. Getting to this turning point often comes when there is emotional distress, enough discomfort to finally get your attention. Sometimes it takes a broken heart to take down walls of fear and protection to find yourself.

If the ego keeps substitutes for genuine happiness in place (such as momentary pleasures, outside distractions, and external validation), the need to awaken is not felt so intensely. Even the misery in the workplace is denied as the ego uses all kinds of techniques to keep the truth below the surface to avoid acknowledging the anguish.

How long do you want to live your life in semi-happiness, or worse yet, extreme distress?

Many people are finally realizing life is too precious to waste in the sorrow and unhappiness perpetuated on the stage called the workplace. And the conclusion of many recent surveys indicates employee disengagement is a global epidemic. Organizations and people are not using their potential, because of low morale, uncertainty and fear. It is senseless and tragic in terms of the toll on individual happiness and business prosperity.

THE HIDDEN TRUTH

Behind the ego is powerlessness. The hold it has on us is from weakness, not strength. If we really knew this, we would let go of all the strategies and cover-ups faster than a hot potato. We would put our guns down and surrender to the greater self, our true essence, our innermost strength. Relying on the ego is a bit like a drowning person holding onto a rope to save them, only to discover it is not connected to anything and cannot rescue them.

Instead of fighting others, we need to confront our own ego. When you face up to your ego's fears, you will discover peace where you anticipated pain. You will start to see the ego is an actor with no authority, merely a substitute sent in by you to represent you in the world. Seeking your starring role and finding out how your theme is controlling your life will bring new freedom and peace.

When do we choose to learn the lessons presented in the workplace? When do we step off the stage and become the director of our life instead of an actor in a tragedy?

Why not now?

And as you do, it touches all those with whom you come in contact. You can be the light to help shine away the pain on the dimly lit stage at your workplace and the world.

PERSONAL RESTORATION PLAN
TO PRACTICE IN YOUR WORKPLACE

This week we will start becoming aware of some of the companion emotions to our starring role so it will become clear to us we have a theme that we keep replaying—expecting new results but receiving more of the same.

1. Ask yourself the following questions:

- What emotions did I feel this week at my workplace?
- What triggered them?
- How did I react in situations when I was feeling the emotion?
- What were the results of my actions?
- Did it produce the outcome I wanted?

2. Ask and record in your journal the answers to the questions from this chapter.

3. From this list of questions, can you determine a possible theme and starring role? What have been the costs for playing this role?

4. Watch how you interact with others in the workplace to determine how you substantiate your starring role. Try to listen more and assert less. Write down any insights you may have had.

5. In your next meeting, become aware of your participation. Are you bolstering your starring role or truly contributing needed information or ideas? Are you listening to others or trying to reinforce your own identity?

CHAPTER FIVE

Motives

*   *   *

As we individually choose to look within instead of blaming others, we will bring peaceful energy to the work environment. As managers and leaders begin to understand the true source of the fear and conflicts in the workplace, the consciousness of the organization will change.

PERSONAL RESPONSIBILITY

Many people assign responsibility for their lives and life situations outside of themselves. This perspective, of course, comes from the viewpoint of the ego who feels powerless. All occurrences and situations are drawn to you, based on your own unconscious motives. There are no accidents.

It is as though there is a joint agreement of unseen but compelling cosmic forces.

This vortex of energy, made of intersecting beliefs, produces a magnetic power drawing the necessary players onto the workplace stage. Your beliefs and thoughts create a force that brings about situations and people who will interconnect with you. Together, you play out your interaction of unconscious needs, desires, and motives. Depending on the nature of your beliefs and your unconscious desires, you attract various exchanges and events. As you become conscious and in alignment with your energy, you can compel the desired people and results into your life. This is usually experienced as synchronicity and coincidences.

However, if you have unconscious, competing assumptions, they will interfere with the energy and you may not get what you think you are looking for. But you will receive what your energy is attracting. So it is important to uncover conflicting streams of energy coming from you that dilute the power of your real desires.

In a sense, you employ others to meet the needs of your play. Your thoughts and words have a will that manifests into reality.

When you complain about your life, you are giving up your own autonomy. The point of view that sees effects as happening to you allows you to surrender responsibility for your life. This claim, accordingly, relinquishes your power to do anything about it. This perspective and consequent belief render you a helpless victim—usually a self-righteous victim.

Statements denying your power always create undesirable results, and cause confusion and pain. Disowning your influence is your ego's decision. However, your inner spirit is completely aware of your unlimited power and who you really are.

This way of viewing the world as a victim is hard to reconcile. If you say, "It is not my fault; I am not to blame for the things that have gone wrong in my life," your ego feels relieved. Your ego wants to be right and does not want to claim any accountability for anything that has not turned out the way you want. So you get to maintain your innocence.

But when circumstances do turn out the way you want, your ego wants to declare ownership and victory. You enjoy the attention when the outcome is positive and your image is bolstered by the success.

So when are you responsible for an outcome and when are you not? To clarify this, we need to better understand cause and effect.

Cause and effect are not opposites; they are really two parts of the same occurrence. There can be no effect without a cause; but conversely, there can be no cause without an effect. They are participating mutually in the same dynamic.

Most of us have this confused, so we immediately jump to finding fault in any incident and usually fully project the blame onto anyone, anyone but ourselves.

Being willing to see your participation in any cause-and-effect dynamic will free you from needing to deny or suppress motivations or fears. The very acknowledgment that you are neither a victim nor a villain is both releasing and empowering.

To illustrate this relationship between cause and effect, picture a batter at home plate. There could be no hit or home run, no matter how many times the batter swings without the ball being in the air precisely at the moment the bat is swung. The pitcher could have thrown the ball perfectly across the plate, but without a batter swinging the bat, there would be no hit. The impact would not have occurred without this mutual cooperation.

So ultimately, cause and effect are one dynamic occurring with synchronicity and mutual action. There are, therefore, really no accidents.

But the ego has selective interpretations.

It will claim to be the cause for the result if you deem it a favorable outcome. The ego believes a worthy conclusion elevates your status in the world. Conversely, the ego will deny being responsible for anything it feels is negative about you.

A good illustration of this is to be found in the story of Craig, a divorced man with two children. He harbors a great sense of guilt for having divorced his wife when his children were young. He also feels remorse for not participating as a father in the early years of their childhood, because of his business distractions and other involvements outside the family.

When the children were young, he was not always available for them. His son is now in college and doing well, but it's a different story for his daughter, the younger of the two. She has had all kinds of trouble, been involved in illegal drugs, and done poorly in school. She rebels against her mother and is unreliable.

Craig's ego takes credit for his son's success, which proves he was a good father. However, he blames all the problems the daughter is having on the former wife, citing her lack of discipline and poor parenting skills as the cause. His ego believes this exonerates him from the responsibility of any cause-and-effect dynamics with the younger child.

Here we can see clearly the dichotomy: Craig is claiming the good outcome and denying the bad outcome.

However, this denial causes Craig more pain and energy because it is difficult to keep the fears and doubts about himself from surfacing. It also requires him to keep blaming the ex-wife and daughter for their failures. This prevents him from having any kind of relationship with his former wife or his daughter.

He loves his daughter, but his constant criticism of her and casting her as a failure has caused the daughter to alienate herself. Now Craig further complicates this situation by blaming the daughter for not wanting to see him or have a relationship with him. Now he has cast himself as the victim—the good father who is rejected.

Failing to see and admit to himself that his daughter is acting out from pain in her psyche that occurred when she was very young prevents Craig from having any compassion for his daughter and her unfortunate dilemma of chemical addiction. His critical and unsupportive approach to her continues to add to the girl's lack of self-worth.

Craig's ego continually gives his daughter the message she is a disappointment in his eyes. Then Craig wonders why his daughter does not want to see him. He does not recognize his judgment is driving his daughter farther away and deeper into her addiction to alleviate the pain.

If this is hard to grasp, consider the powerlessness coming from denying responsibility for consequences. Understand all encounters in which you participate with another are mutual cause-and-effect dynamics.

Authentic power is willingness to be the cause in any matter, whether the outcome is perceived as good or bad.

Readiness to give up being a victim and recognizing your willing participation in the self-described victim role will empower you. In reality, you are not powerless—only your self- created ego is weak. And the ultimate goal of this book is to help you see that the ego is really powerless. As you do, you can begin to give up drama, blame, need for external-validation, and the helpless role of the victim.

Claiming your inner authority is the beginning of waking up and finding liberation.

What you so strongly want to refute, the secret you feel you must guard, is the very thing you need to look at. The very acknowledgment of and surrender to what you fear or to what you believe is bad will release you from your self-made prison.

Craig's acknowledgment of his contribution to his daughter's early environment would allow him to have compassion for her and her issues. Craig would then be in a position of non-judgment and caring, which would allow the daughter the freedom to return to her father.

Accepting his responsibility and having empathy for his daughter would give Craig the opportunity to truly help his daughter. However, as long as he is in denial of his responsibility, this will not occur.

So being accountable is really just claiming the power you already have, but have been denying. It is availing yourself of your true, inner spiritual essence and strength and then challenging the small role your ego wants you to play.

When you truly find your strength of character, you can consciously use your genuine power for the creation of love and tranquility in your life and the lives of others around you. You will stop designing the fictional stories that from believing you are weak and instead create a radical new path of courage.

When you heal and repair your own heart from the past, you can extend love and respect to people in the many relationships surrounding you. Until you give up those filters and layers of protection which are not allowing you to reach your own soul, you will see events and situations as outside of you.

DISCOVERING YOUR UNCONSCIOUS MOTIVES

Every movie or story has a plot. As the center of your performance, you are following a story line that will provide evidence to prove your motives, even if you are not aware of them.

The plot does not change, because you developed it from unconscious motives and continue to play it out with the same goals. Although the players may change, the drama will not vary, because you originated the plot to recreate and prove your long held belief system.

You may consciously think you are the guiltless one and the other person or people are to blame, but it really is not the case.

You may honestly believe you are seeking a new outcome, and you may genuinely feel you are trying to bring about a change in your life. But unless you change the unconscious motives and reassign the roles in your life, nothing will change. Since they are unconscious, your secret intentions must be brought to the surface where you can see and disengage from them.

Revealing to yourself your hidden motives requires an internal change that comes only with self-reflection. Until you willingly look back at yourself as the source of your feelings and circumstances, you will continue having similar relationships and situations, wherever you go. You may move or change jobs, but without your inner work, nothing will be different. There is often a honeymoon period, but when the shine wears off, the old dynamics reappear. The original insecurities come up again. You may even find yourself saying this person or another person reminds you exactly of someone else from a previous situation or former workplace.

You need people in your place of work with whom you can interact to corroborate your story. The other players, who take significant roles in your play, are chosen by you to reinforce and support your plot. And in the end, you get to be right, once again! Even if you are miserable, at least you are right. And you can once again view the world as unfair.

Your ego's goal is always to find support to sustain your story line and your belief that you are blameless. The other characters have the same goal, coming from different unconscious motives and plots. How do you feel when someone points the finger of blame at you?

As the emotional intensity increases in the workplace, you must play out your part and defend your position with mounting passion. As your emotional fervor builds, the other egos in the workplace react with rising vehemence. The plot thickens as the drama escalates.

The resulting scenes cause ever-increasing complexity and make it almost impossible to recognize the origin or even the point. The momentum of these racking emotions takes over, and the result becomes literally a scene from *As the Stomach Turns.*

The ego's plan is forever the same so it is amazing we fail to recognize how many times we have been down the same path. You always receive the consequences your plot demands, even if it is painful or disappointing on a conscious level. It is surprising we aren't bored. So, it is a good sign if you find even yourself getting tired of telling your story to your friends or family. It can be an awakening when you hear yourself say, "I am sick and tired of being sick and tired."

Your need to be innocent requires the substantiation of others so you don't start to doubt yourself. Creating allies who agree with you is part of the ego's plan to keep your belief system intact and prevent you from taking a deeper look at what is happening. Honestly, have you ever found yourself looking for evidence to make someone else the villain and then found allies who agree with you? Having a common enemy can make strange bedfellows. A common enemy is often the bond between allies—not only in the workplace between people and groups of people, but in the world, between countries. The extent of a "group ego" plot is literally staggering, resulting in wars killing millions of people. We send our children to battles for supremacy and power over others, in the name of national security. The attack and overcome theme has destroyed countless lives throughout history.

So why don't we change?

The answer is the ego wants the drama to persist. So while you are operating from the ego, you cannot see you created your life and now it is reflecting back at you. Instead, it feels out of your control and appears to be coming from outside of you.

It is as though you spent a long time preparing a beautiful dining table and then when you sat down, you said, "I don't like the way the table is set." You are not aware you are the one who set it.

A Course in Miracles says, "You see the world that you have made but you do not see yourself as the image maker."

What does it take to change your mind and to see the truth?

It begins with challenging yourself to discover the unaware motives directing your plot. The best place to start is to notice when your ego gets provoked and then gently ask yourself the following:

- What am I trying to hide?
- What do I think this says about me?
- What am I afraid of?
- What do I think will happen?
- When did I feel this way before?
- What really is the threat here?

Only by interacting with others and discovering your fears can you dislodge the hidden doubts and pains that are the source of your motives and ultimate drama. Even if you believe you are angry, justified, or wronged, the root of these emotions is still fear. Noticing even slight irritations or worries can be an opening to your inner self.

Learn to observe yourself and notice your language. What are you trying to keep inside and what are you projecting outside? Any statement from you has authority and command.

When the outcome from our account is desirable, we claim it. If something we consider negative or bad is occurring, we say it is happening to us. But even negative phraseology comes to fruition because you create your world with your thoughts and words.

Look behind your denials, your complaints, and pessimistic declarations. Observe what irritates you, upsets you, or causes you stress. Be aware those responses are coming from a deeper emotion such as guilt or lack of self-acceptance. Notice your protests: are they coming from a stand on a principle or a cover up to prevent disclosure of your inner guilt? "The lady doth protest too much, me thinks," is an often quoted Shakespearean line from *Hamlet,* describing one character's observation of another's defenses. What is the angst behind your words?

For example, the statement "I don't need anybody" is an attempt to cover the fear of vulnerability.

Positive intentions followed by commitment, perseverance, and action give you potent results and freedom to choose what you want. However, your unconscious intentions need to be revealed by looking behind the facade of the ego, to discover what you so valiantly defend. You need to expose your plot and motives to the light of day.

Your life experience will not truly be different, as long as the motives remain unconscious and hidden from you. Purposeful intention with right action can bring about a change in circumstances. This takes courage because the ego is so demanding and unforgiving, it will not let go of its tenacious grip on you without a great deal of resistance.

You will be tempted to deny that it is pain below the surface because if you allow it to emerge you will then have to deal with it. That is bad news for your ego, but good news for your soul. .

William was a senior vice president in a large hospital. He had been with the hospital for years and had always been a dedicated and committed individual. He was somewhat on the serious side and very analytical in his approach to management. Every person in his management group had very clear and specific performance objectives. He was relentless in assuring they were carried out—a good example of the micromanager. He exerted intense control over all those he managed and nothing slipped by him.

When the hospital hired a new CEO, William was somewhat nervous about the change in authority. The previous CEO had been in command for many years and this new change made William uneasy. He didn't know what to expect with the new leadership in place. William performed best when everything was in his control.

The new CEO seemed very dynamic and confident, but he made William suspicious.

It became fairly clear rather rapidly that the new CEO would be making some sweeping changes. As the weeks progressed, William felt insecure in his formerly well-grounded position with the hospital.

As this uneasiness within himself increased, he began exerting more pressure and control on his staff. The employees, who were already unhappy under William's style, began to feel even more anxiety and stress from the increased watchfulness and strict demands made by him. And as always, this led to infighting amongst his staff because they expelled their pain through lateral attacks on each other.

Within a few months, when the CEO had finished ascertaining the various roles and performances of different departments, William was offered an early retirement, which left him little choice. The control he had tried to enforce in an effort to make himself look good and keep himself safe backfired.

William was devastated and forced to step off the stage where he had spent most of his adult life. He spent almost a year blaming the new CEO and claiming his role as a righteous victim.

Because he was too young to want to retire from the workplace, William found another job. This time, because of the previous pain, he began to observe himself in a management position. William began to uncover the origin of his need for this over-diligent control of others and situations.

He had grown up an only child with very few playmates. His parents were overprotective and did little to encourage him to take risks or try new things. He was always a good student but very timid. He learned to operate in a small world with very little exploration because it felt safe and secure. The last thing he wanted was to call attention to himself in any way.

Because of his education, dedication, and faithfulness, he was finally promoted to a vice president position at the hospital. His management style was never questioned and only the people who worked in his department knew what an unhappy environment it was.

William's unconscious motive was to keep everything and everyone in place. His fearful ego led him to believe this would keep him protected.

It finally proved to be wrong.

As William began to open up with the new people and trust that they were capable of performing without a whip and checklist, he began feeling a new sense of freedom. He hadn't realized imposing all the rules in his former over-diligent manner was exhausting him.

He has continued to challenge his fears and give up the high control in his life, both at work and home. He is now happier in this new role on a new stage—only because he finally looked behind the strategy of his ego and at the unknowing motives—but it took a great disappointment and much pain to get his attention.

When we follow our unconscious motives, we are following the motivation of the hopeless ego instead of the positive intentions of our inner self. Our goal is to bring them to light, release them, and create conscious goals and intentions leading us to peace and understanding. Intentions are a powerful force we can utilize but if they are clouded by old, hidden mental constructs, we will be limited.

The work on your self is difficult because the ego is so shrewd and it stands at the door blocking the entrance to your higher self. The persistence it requires is the reason so many people take the path of least resistance by following the ego. But to discover your inner greatness, you have to flush out the impurities and remove the blocks you are defending and trying to keep in place. The work is rewarding as you claim your rightful heritage, your true source, and your unlimited power and abilities. You will be relaxed and you will no longer have to watch your back or play cover up roles.

EGO-DEFENSE MECHANISMS

The proof that the ego's thought system is strong is demonstrated by its intense desire to deny any uncertainties or doubts lying beneath the surface. The resistant posture is employed to prevent you from looking in the mirror that reflects the very issues you need to see to heal your soul. It is a mirror the ego would prefer not to look into.

You respond to a perceived threat with an instinctive fight-or-flight pattern. Wanting to leave a painful circumstance rather than looking at what is below, the ego will instruct you to bail out or put on the boxing gloves. The decision is usually made in a flash because your ego reacts immediately and automatically, rather than allow your panic to surface. The ego has a knee jerk way of reacting, so when you find yourself in a reactive state of mind, know this—it is time to turn the focus back on yourself. Have you ever noticed how uncomfortable and insecure you feel when you are being defensive? It is not a feeling of strength.

If you leave one situation you will, sooner or later, encounter an almost identical experience because the issue within you has not been resolved. The problem will keep showing up. Leaving may give temporary relief from anxiety, but it is only the short-term response of relief from the immediate stress and threats.

If you do not depart but choose to remain in the confrontation, your ego will direct a strategy to barricade and protect you. This ego-defense mechanism becomes an offense because the intention is to overcome or injure the source of the threat so you will remain unscathed. Your defense becomes a literal offense.

Denial is a tool your ego uses to prevent you from seeing clearly. Attacking another merely escalates the emotion and keeps your energy involved in the turmoil and off of yourself.

If you find yourself defending anything, you can be certain the very need to resist is an indication something deeper is going on within you. When an attack has no meaning or fear for you, your ego is not called forth to protect you. In other words, you only counterattack when you believe the assault on you or your character is true.

For example, if you are an excellent accountant and someone challenges your math, you would simply take a look at the financials and admit the error as a simple mistake. You would probably just correct it and reprint a new report. However, if you are concerned your accounting abilities are weak and your job is dependent on your skills, your ego would react quickly to defend your mistake, believing it would be costly to your security to be less than perfect.

I have heard people in the workplace say they are sometimes required to defend their position or prove their plan is a good one. I have also heard people say they have had to stand up and defend their honor.

Your honor or your position does not need defending. Your honor stands on its own. Defending anything takes a great deal of energy and attention. It requires covering yourself from having any weaknesses exposed. What a shame. What a tragedy to be unable to acknowledge and receive support in areas where you don't have all the answers. When we come from authenticity, we are our word, we are proactive, and we state our position with confidence, not defensiveness.

But the ego believes you must have all the answers and the solution, or it says something negative about you. But if you already have everything you need, why would you need anyone else? Why have teams? Why come together with others at all?

I have watched ego-driven leaders in organizations gather their team or senior management group for a meeting. The participants all agree with the leader and pat each other on the back. They use flattery and basic sucking up to assure their own position on the team. People chime in with comments intended to make themselves sound smart and they use buzz words and corporate jargon to sound informed and intelligent. Each member participates from a need to please and doesn't question the direction of the company. So no one is contributing in a meaningful way and the leader and organization are missing the creative force of group will. It is only when things start declining that the rats jump ship. As a breakdown occurs, few people will be accountable. Having not contributed from integrity and genuine support, they are the first to abandon the ego-driven leader.

An enlightened leader is not defensive or resistant and encourages different opinions for the betterment of the organization. This leader does not need a personal validation and is not looking for everyone to agree with him or her. An enlightened leader does not put up walls preventing group discussions and even debates. One of the common characteristics of a good leader is they are approachable.

Defense is the main strategy of the ego because if you were to look at what it is you are defending; it would be the decline of the ego.

Resistance is a barricade we construct that keeps others out and us safe. It is a contracting emotion much like a draw bridge across a moat protecting the castle. When we feel threatened we pull in our emotional draw bridge, closing us off from any perceived attack. What we don't realize is the contracting and resistance also makes us feel separate and alone.

But if we could take down our resistance and put down our swords, we would discover where we anticipated pain, we would, instead, find peace and joy. Our authentic power arises when we are willing to look within.

As you take down your guard, you learn your inner spirit is capable of unlimited strength and wisdom which can be counted on in all situations. You find a new kind of serenity, based not on being superior or overcoming others, but coming from your inner spirit, which is connected to the all powerful creative source—the universal power of love. Relying on God, Source, Creator, or love—whatever resonates with you—is the source of power and courage. So why would we count on the small, frenetic power of the ego?

The intensity of your defensive reaction can be the catalyst to discover the door to your higher self.

If you feel a great deal of emotion around a particular issue, it is because it is one of your bigger life lessons trying to present itself to you. The ego will naturally block this opportunity because your ego cowers in the face of your inner, true power.

The ego would rather have you rely on its tiny acting role as the center of your drama. No matter how stellar the performance, it pales in comparison to your mighty, eternal, unalterable inner source.

One of the most significant reasons we avoid looking at ourselves to discover our core issues is that we are hiding guilt and humiliation associated with hidden fears. There is a concealed core belief, deep inside, that is self-defacing and shameful. As I have said before, the true theme of the ego is, "I am not worthy." We believe there is something not lovable about us and if it is discovered we will be exposed and deserted.

The ego cannot accept any perception of weakness, knowing it to be its Achilles' heel. The fear is so great we must struggle boldly to uphold our image. Unbeknownst to you, shining a light on the origin of this belief is the key to freedom. The pain you expect melts like a chocolate left in the sun and in its place there is a beautiful gift. If you but knew the truth, you wouldn't put up the battle!

Getting past the ego's defenses is not easy. The ego stands as a lookout at the door of your psyche, allowing only beliefs that support its image to enter, even as it leads to a descent into hell, the depths of pain and suffering.

As the director of operations for a highly successful company, Sheila often felt put upon to carry the burden of the organization's structure and daily operations. Believing no one was as knowledgeable as she (and certainly not as dedicated), she worked long and tedious hours. Her family complained she was never home on time, and she herself begrudged the fact she had little freedom for family and leisure.

Sheila's children had been disappointed numerous times when she did not arrive to watch them perform in school functions. Her husband often had to take up the slack, even though his position with his company was just as important and critical to his company's success. Yet, he somehow managed to work regular hours and have time for the family.

As the years passed by, her promise to her family of things "getting better soon," just never materialized. Her endless commitment to work continued.

It was not until her children started having serious problems that she began to question her obligation to her company. She felt incredible guilt when the counselor described the children as having a lack of her parental support and love during their critical years.

Although her husband had done as much as he could, the children had often felt abandoned by their mother. Their sense of self-esteem had suffered. Sheila's husband was on the verge of filing for divorce because the stress and lack of communication had mounted to unbearable levels.

Through counseling, Sheila began to look at what was driving her to such levels of workaholism. In actuality, the hours she was keeping at her company were not really required if she worked more efficiently and delegated some of the work to her staff.

The unconscious motives originated in Sheila from her early childhood anxiety of being abandoned by her parents.

Sheila was the oldest in a family of five children. Her parents were often gone and did little to attend to the children. She was unconsciously angry at her father's lack of discipline and depressed by her mother's frequent absence. She began taking over many of the responsibilities of the mother: ironing, cleaning, cooking, and watching the younger children. It was an effort to please her parents and hold everything together. She thought if she could fix the problems she would be loved and could cover her fear that they were somehow her fault.

Her efforts were not rewarded, so she felt herself the victim of an unfair world.

When her friends were having fun going to parties and school dances, she often bore the responsibility of her siblings and the household. She hated her life, but Sheila felt she had no choice. She believed she was the only one responsible and accountable.

When she married her husband and had children, she always believed she would be a wonderful parent, having been for all intents and purposes, the "mother" for her sisters and brothers. However, her husband seemed to do such a good job with them and her job was so demanding, the years just slipped by.

Sheila finally recognized her over-extended hours to her business were motivated by an unconscious desire to be the unappreciated, righteous martyr.

She saw she somehow got a strange reinforcement when no one thanked her or gave her the praise she deserved. She finally saw that the lack of gratitude offered by the company gave her the evidence she sought to prove to herself that the world was still unfair. The situation fed her desire to be needed and allowed her to continue being the noble, sacrificing heroine of her drama.

The sad part of Sheila's story was the discovery she had abandoned her own children, much as she had been deserted as a child. But because she was able to acknowledge this unconscious action, she was able to stop defending her position.

Through this realization her ego's need to play out the old theme of being victimized began to diminish, and she started talking to her children from her authentic self.

She was able to establish a new relationship, based on honest communication, listening, and demonstrating real interest and compassion for them. She asked them to forgive her for her continual focus on her job at their expense. Her relationship with her husband also changed as she gave up her martyr role.

When you uncover your unconscious motives, you can begin to start making conscious decisions and purposeful intentions.

Since all our motives (conscious and unconscious) have power to create, reclaiming your responsibility and your ability to set your intentions from your powerful source will change the direction of your life.

CREATING CONSCIOUS MOTIVES/INTENTIONS

How do you recognize your hidden motives before you hit the wall, have a crisis, and have no choice but to seek a better way?

One way is to look at your life right now. Are you living the life you want? Are you at peace? Do you have the elements in your life story that fulfill your conscious wants and desires? Are you happy, with good relationships? Is your life purposeful and enjoyable? Are you healthy?

The life you are living, the family, the job, the home, the friends, and the lifestyle—all are results of your motives, whether they have been conscious or not.

There are no idle thoughts. We create our reality, based on our belief system, motives, and choices, whether realized or not. If your life is not in harmony, you can know you have contradictory goals. Your discordance is a result of conflicting desires and choices. Incongruence in you creates an incongruent life.

Look at the areas in your life causing the discontentment. As you identify these undesirable areas, start to discern the possible rewards or reinforcement you are receiving, in spite of your complaints about them. This is difficult to do because we believe we would not have chosen these problems. But as you see you are responsible for all the consequences you are experiencing in your life, you are also giving yourself the freedom to make new choices and new intentions.

Your true destiny is one of peace and contentment, joy and creativity, love and compassion. If you are not experiencing these feelings, then you are playing out a drama, based on contrary goals. Your energy is being split into different directions and your incongruence is showing up in your life.

For example, Joan was a manager with much responsibility over several departments. She complained to me that the women in her workplace didn't like her and never included her in their conversations. However, it wasn't just her employees in her management groups, but other managers as well, who were cool to her.

I asked her if this had ever been a problem before. She conceded there had been other situations when women didn't seem to care for her. She admitted she thought they were probably jealous of her. She didn't understand why, though, because she tried to be friendly.

"Why do you think they are jealous of you?" I asked.

She thought it was because she always dressed so professionally, was very efficient in her work, and was very accomplished.

The interesting dilemma, I told her, was that I knew many women who dressed beautifully, did an excellent job, etc., but were well liked by their fellow female associates.

I asked her to gently try to look at herself as the possible source of the problem, instead of projecting it fully on the other female associates.

Joan had grown up in a family of very pretty sisters who were still very close. Joan had always felt she was the least attractive. In fact, she called herself the "ugly duckling." She had grown into a very attractive woman, but as a child, she had felt homely.

When she felt depressed as a child, she would go off to be by herself. The retreat from others gave her some relief and temporary peace.

Even as an adult, she was still striving to get her sisters' approval and continued to feel she was not worthy of their attention. She still felt unequal to them in beauty and talent. This was a childhood belief system that was not true, but she lived her life as if it were factual.

She now began to realize she had maintained this theme of unworthiness into adulthood. She then found the proof to support her hidden belief that she was unlovable. Her countermeasure was to appear worthy by acting confident, superior, and invulnerable. With this attitude emanating from her, people—especially women—were repelled, and though they were civil, they didn't want to include her. Her desire to maintain her image would not allow her to see she attracted this behavior, and her need to be right and blameless exceeded her desire to be happy.

But now she was ready to look at other possibilities. She realized she was the common denominator, so to speak, so she must be the important part of the equation. She started looking at ways she isolated herself at work that caused other women to distance themselves from her. She began noticing the things she did that may have caused someone else to feel uncomfortable around her. She became aware that she often attempted to act superior among women in an effort to deny her actual feelings of being inferior.

Joan is now learning to recognize her motives from the past and the thought stream that causes the actions and reactions with others. She is recognizing her thoughts at their source and stopping them before they become full blown beliefs and behaviors. It is an automatic way of viewing the world so it takes time to extinguish the old thought patterns. But with consistent attention she will be able to do it. She is also making conscious steps to extend herself to females at work, to work better with others, and even to have some fun at work. Humor in the workplace helps people feel happier and more trusting of others.

If we looked at Joan's life, we see that the ego is very deceptive and shrewd. Joan had felt helpless to change the situation and was really very miserable and lonely in the workplace. Her ego, however, got the satisfaction of being right—her belief that the world can be cruel, made up of cold-hearted and jealous women.

The key to revealing the ego's unconscious motive is it will always have a negative side, even as it seems to prove you are right in your viewpoint. And there will always be a loss or cost when your ego claims you are the victim and you are correct in your opinion. Looking at this side of ourselves requires courage because we don't want to see our unsavory qualities. Until we do, they hold us fast in a tightly shut world.

For Joan, the cost was isolation and having few friends.

Do you want to discover your ego's unconscious motives? Do you want to begin releasing these hidden agendas that lead to your unvarying plot of unhappiness? If you do, it takes willingness to be responsible for your life, to stop being the injured party, and to courageously face your inner fears. It is time, essentially, "to go where no man has gone before"—to inner space, the place where your soul and deepest desire reside.

The following questions will help you take the steps to do this:

- What situations make you most unhappy in your life?
- Who are you blaming for these consequences?

- Do you notice any defenses or denials? Ask yourself, "What am I defending?"
- Although a situation makes you unhappy, are there also some benefits? (being right, getting sympathy, admiration, etc.)
- Can you say to yourself, "Perhaps I am wrong; perhaps there is another way to see this"? Can you find another way?
- When in the past did you feel a similar way in a comparable situation?
- What is the cost or loss in your life when you maintain your ego's position of being right?
- Are you willing to admit how you can be a fake, holding a pretentious image to fool others? (This is a tough one.)
- What would be a new positive intention to replace the ego's unconscious motive?

Let me warn you this may take a lot of practice. The ego does not give up being right very easily.

Your ego will want to resist looking at you as the source of your own pain. You look most easily at others for blame and then find corroboration. Changing the reactions you have is not easy but it is most difficult to stop the automatic blaming and defending when you are in the middle of a heated situation. The opportunity to learn about yourself occurs in a flash if you are willing in the heat of the moment to stop your old pattern.

Here's an example that demonstrates how hard it is to identify what is happening in a conflict. This is what happened in the middle of an argument with my friend John. He is someone I care very much about, but one day while we were talking on the telephone we had a disagreement about something.

Somehow, our usual friendly conversation turned into an argument. I was amazed because I was sure I was right and he was so wrong. It surprised me he could be so adamant and belligerent. I felt a strong need to defend myself and make him understand my point of view. The emotions were very high as we came to a toe-to-toe confrontation of two egos, each of us wanting to be right. We were at the point of hanging up on each other, each sure we were right when I suddenly realized what was happening and said, "This is a perfect example of two egos battling—coming face to face and each wanting to be right. One of us needs to stop and look behind the face of our ego and to stop trying to win."

"I don't know how," he told me.

I didn't know if I could do it either, so strong were the emotions going back and forth between us. I was thinking to myself that I was really disappointed in him, and quite frankly it would have been much easier to just hang up.

But I also knew it really takes only one person to begin unraveling the chain reactions and escalating emotions. I was hoping it would be him!

I finally decided to try. I took a deep breath, and although I was feeling very angry, I stopped myself in the moment and said, "I'm sorry I'm being so insistent that I'm right. It really isn't my intention to hurt you or make you miserable"—which was exactly what he was feeling, as was I.

I was attempting to look at what this lesson was telling me about myself while also trying to see his point of view.

"I want to hear what you're saying. I am sorry I have been so resistant. It's my desire to understand you and stop this stalemate."

As I said these words, I began to feel myself calm down. As I continued, soon I started to feel sincere in my words. I was able to tell him I cared about him and I realized this standoff was only hurting us both.

The pain and anger I was feeling only a few moments ago began to dissipate as I gave up my unconscious motive to be right and to win. I realized we were each feeling like a victim, even though neither of us really was.

I was figuratively putting away my gun.

I changed my motive to a conscious intention of finding peace and resolution between us. I gave up my ego pride and the need to prevail. And we both benefited. And as I put my gun down, what was he able to do? I made it safe for him to put his gun down as well.

The wonderful thing about giving up needing to be right and choosing to learn the lesson presented, is it releases the other person from needing to maintain his position. The other person usually learns the lesson almost simultaneously because he can then stop feeling the need to blame you.

In my case, my friend immediately said he also wanted to understand his lesson and he also cared about my feelings. We were able to move forward in our relationship. We had learned it was possible to give up the battle, even in a heated moment. We were both then truly the winners. And years later, we are still wonderful friends. I could have killed off the relationship in an effort to be right and maintain my superiority.

Practicing these opportunities to become free of the ego and your unconscious motives takes perseverance. It also requires the belief that you are worth it. I have found it helps to go to a quiet place to unplug from the noise and chatter. As you allow the external focus and consequent tension to melt and fade for a moment, you can feel your deep inner connection to the tranquil, inner source to which we are all connected.

There, you can invoke your inner spirit to help you get past the formidable gates of your ego. You can relax and feel your inner strength dissolve the grip of the ego. Your ego takes it as a personal affront when you point the finger at yourself, and this quietness can help you move past its constraints. Every time you are able to surrender to the quietness in your inner world, you are moving toward freedom and release.

If you are having a really difficult time looking at yourself as the source, you can ask your inner spirit for the courage and guidance to do this. Just before you go to bed at night is often a good time for to ask for clarity and recognition of your blind spots.

You may then have a dream or you might, upon awakening, suddenly have a clear picture of your role in your own suffering. Understanding that you have a powerful will, whether it is coming from the ego or the higher self, is important here.

I once had a dream that was so clear about my unreasonable desire to be a perfect mother. Even though I intellectually knew no one is perfect, I was unknowingly harboring guilt and the trepidation that I had fallen short in my role as a mother. The dream was filled with past experiences and emotions but ultimately showed me parts of myself I hadn't forgiven. The dream was so clearly a message of how I was stuck in some areas of my present life because of unacknowledged guilt. The dream ended with the words "My Life" rolling down like credits on a movie screen. It couldn't have been more explicit and it allowed me to see the aspects of myself I hadn't accepted. It was amazing because I was able to relax and relinquish some of the expectations I put on myself. I discovered my desire to be perfect (a totally unrealistic goal) was only preventing me from accepting myself as I am. These negative feelings had been blocking me from moving forward in other areas of my life.

I highly recommend sleeping with pen and paper nearby your bed to record your dreams the minute you awaken. Dreams are very instrumental in understanding yourself if you commit to paying attention to them. Some will reveal your fears and others will show you your aspirations. Most dreams help us express and expel some of the stress and emotion from the day to day events. But some are messages from your soul and are worth paying attention to.

If you are honest, what qualities in yourself do you find unacceptable? The intent of this chapter is to help you uncover hidden motives directing your life forward or holding you back. By doing this process, you will move toward integration and alignment with your authentic self.

Restoring yourself to your whole and complete self, without the need of external props and drama, is the destiny of every soul. Having conflicting beliefs and opposing motives is the source of confusion and misery, in the workplace or any place else in our lives.

You willingly participate in all experiences and interactions. This means you "will" yourself into the circumstances and relationships in your life. They didn't just happen while you were looking the other way. It is hardest to comprehend when you are in a terrible upset or upheaval. "Why would anyone wish this upon themselves?" you ask. But even the most difficult circumstances hold the seed for something greater in your life. The death of a loved one is usually one of the most painful life experiences, but even the loss of someone you love can provide deep learning and understanding for those left behind.

But the truth is, the past is over, and replaying the old scenes is tiresome and painful. When you discover your belief system and motives you concocted from your past, you are free to set and achieve the magnificent, conscious intentions that you are capable of attaining. You will be a clean and clear lens for your energy to shine through, illuminating your life and everyone with whom you come into contact.

Choose a new, bright, happier future by reclaiming your heritage and birthright to live in peace and tranquility. The strain the ego places on you is so arduous. Aren't you willing to let it go, even a little? Start by looking at the way your ego is addicted to the workplace drama. Be a true hero and have the courage to look at yourself as the source of pain. This process will lead to the greatest opportunities for the evolution of your soul. Making new conscious intentions from your deepest self will dramatically and permanently alter your life both at work and at home. Reruns can be a thing of the past, where they belong.

Conscience intentions create the life you want. Paul J. Meyer, founder of Success Motivation Institute, and a forerunner of the human potential movement said, "Whatever you vividly imagine, ardently desire, sincerely believe, and enthusiastically act up, must inevitably come to pass."

To powerfully attract the results you desire, begin by relinquishing fears and protective layers of the ego, and then clarify and envision exactly what you really do want. Invoke your emotions while thinking about your goals because strong desires and feelings create deeper impressions in your mind, according to scientific research. It explains why frightening and emotional experiences from the past are so etched in our mind and have such an impact on our life.

Recognize that setbacks from the past are only lessons that better prepared you for your new intentions. A very successful movie producer who recently spoke at a convention I attended pointed out an important life principle. He humbly stood up after all his amazing accomplishments were cited on a huge screen and told the audience that for every success he has had, there were also dismal failures. The secret, he said, was to just keep going and to never give up on his dreams, in spite of perceived failures. The next success is just around the corner.

Life is full of challenges, but we don't have to suffer through them. We can greet them with enthusiasm and see them as opportunities to create and serve the world, as we learn to clear the negative layers clouding our vision. We can choose gratitude and appreciation for being here and having so much abundance on a beautiful planet. As Louis Armstrong's heart stirring recording expresses, "I think to myself, what a wonderful world."

When we give up and give into doubt and uncertainty, it is merely our ego telling us we are too small. Stop the stream of thinking at its source—the ego. Lift your eyes above the old patterns and see the vast horizon ahead. Don't look down, so to speak.

Set a target date or intermittent steps with target dates. Nothing is quite as motivating as a deadline. Write down your intentions and timeframe and tell them to someone who matters to you. This action will help solidify your commitment and assist you in manifesting your dreams. It is so easy to procrastinate when your intention is hazy and you have no timeline or date for attainment.

Take action. When you truly believe a goal is worthwhile and achievable, and you have a target date, the only way to achieve it is to take the necessary action. When you are excited about what you are doing, you feel engaged and the desire propels you forward. The work becomes satisfying, invigorating, and joyful. Your inspiration may come from a higher source, another dimension, but you are the one who has to take the action. *Spirit can write the music, but you have to play the piano.*

Whether your intention is to get a degree, start a project, lead a team, get a promotion, start a new business, create a masterpiece, or find a new job, it starts with removing the hidden agendas that have stopped you in the past and clarifying your new intention. Your focused energy will draw to you the people you need, the situations you require, and the outcomes you desire. I call it miracle thinking because it attracts magical experiences, coincidences, and synchronicity.

Become unstoppable. Avail yourself of your inner, spiritual greatness and step into the life you want. Set free your imagination, hopes, and dreams. Nothing is holding you back but yourself.

PERSONAL RESTORATION PLAN
TO PRACTICE IN YOUR WORKPLACE

1. Begin this practice by choosing an intention in your workplace or your life. Describe it clearly and visualize what you would like to happen and describe it clearly in your journal. Envision yourself experiencing the joy from achieving it. The more specific you can be, the better. Identify the ego thoughts that have limited you in the past and refuse to be held back by them. Set a target date for completion and write down the action steps. Some people even like to make a vision board with pictures illustrating what you want, which helps increase your commitment and motivation. Include the following:

- Intention
- Identify past barriers
- Target date
- Action steps

2. During your work week, pay attention to your motives for various activities. Ask yourself the following questions:

- What is my biggest complaint at work?
- Describe a situation where this comes up and write it down.
- What do I get out of this complaint?
- What would be a better intention that would help me to be proactive rather than reactive?
- Do I share my complaint with others? Do I look for evidence proving I am right and "they" are wrong?

3. This week begin practicing, at least once an hour (more often if you can remember), to stop and bring yourself to the present. Take a quiet moment to remind yourself of your sacred, inner being. Take a deep breath and allow yourself to unwind from your focused attention on the

activity in which you are involved. In addition, if you have any other moments in the day where you feel stress and tension, repeat this action:

- Deep breath.
- Withdraw attention from activity.
- Connect with inner self.
- Maintain this moment until you feel calm and clear.

Brief moments throughout the day connecting to your higher self will give you a sense of grace and an inner calm. This little practice will assist you in waking up and unhooking from the trance of activity at work. It will also help clear your mind and let you work more effectively and efficiently.

CHAPTER SIX

The Director and Script

*　　*　　*

THE DIRECTOR

By now you are probably getting some new ways to view your business environment and the people you see every day. Continuing with the metaphor of a theatrical performance, it might be helpful to see how you make decisions and communicate with others from a script and a directing voice that arises from experiences earlier in your life.

The director can be recognized as a voice that is calling forth the course, the action, and the outcome of the scenes. The direction is based on the ego's need for confirmation of its leading role of passion and, usually, suffering.

The voice of your ego is on non-stop auto-play and is so incessant you are never without it. Even as you try to stop it, it will continue directing you. You listen to it and sometimes you will even argue with it, but it is never silent. The fact that it is not really you, but the voice of the ego, is demonstrated by the fact that you can observe it and distinguish it from yourself when you focus and become present.

The voice of the director takes on many different tones. Sometimes it is the sound of your mother, warning of impending danger. Sometimes it sounds panicky and other times, persuasive. Often it can sound like a critical voice, limiting your faith in yourself with statements such as "You are not capable," or "You will fail and make a fool of yourself."

The inner saboteur's director voice is coming from your ego, which does not believe you can achieve your desires without many external validations, such as money, other people's approval, status, or some tangible support. This is because the director, coming from the voice of the ego, is attempting to hide its shameful secret of not being worthy on its own.

The director believes you need other people to validate you, but the ego is also afraid and intimidated by others. This causes a peculiar kind of dilemma because you need other people but you also lack trust in them. It is like being drawn to a fire while being afraid you will be burned.

The director will guide you through episode after episode and scene after scene to authenticate the ego's performance and protect you from harm or shame. Fearing others' criticism and still needing others' support for the drama are the motivations behind the director's supervision.

Hearing the tone and origin of the director's voice can be very helpful in discovering that the director is just another aspect of the ego, coming from your past conditioning. Learning to become aware of the voice and identifying it, from the long-ago cast of characters in your life, can assist in finding liberation.

Sandra was a co-owner of a very successful service business. Her clients were other businesses, and Sandra had developed a skillful presentation and had faith in her employees' abilities to carry out and deliver the service. Her partner was a man whom she had known for many years and they had formed the joint partnership about five years previously.

There were several other similar businesses in her area, and although her company was doing well, two larger competitors had a bigger market share and contracts with some of the key prestigious businesses in the region. Frequently, Sandra was up against these competitors in a proposal process, and for some reason, even though her firm had demonstrated great success with some of their existing clients, she did not win very many engagements when she was up against one of the bigger firms.

Sandra was also having some problems with her partner. Even though they were equal partners and he was always polite to her, she felt he treated her in a subservient manner. When she tried to discuss this with him, he denied it. He basically dismissed it, and the conversation always ended with her feelings not heard.

When the company had their staff meetings, Sandra again felt inferior in power, even though she was the co-owner. Her partner often took the lead in the meetings and then appeared to support other people, rather than Sandra, on some major decisions.

In addition, Sandra had some problems with a couple of employees. Not by coincidence, these two were the same ones her partner always seemed to agree with. This only compounded the problem. Although she had equal economic power, she acquiesced to him in running the business, even against her better judgment.

When I talked with Sandra, we began exploring why she was afraid to be more assertive with her partner. She said she knew there was something deeper going on because, as miserable as she felt sometimes, she couldn't seem to stop herself from backing down and giving in to his wishes.

She also noted that when they were giving a presentation to a prospective company, she felt less confident if he was with her. When she took other employees for the group presentations, she always performed much better and the employees often complimented her on her great skills.

So what was going on? Why was she feeling intimidated by her partner?

One thing that she recognized and her partner failed to comprehend was that this dissension between them, as well as between her and the employees with whom he sided, was draining the positive energy force and potential from their business success in many ways. Their combined leadership was muddled at best, and resulted in the employees resorting to gossip and alliances.

From Sandra's viewpoint, it was her partner's fault entirely. The two employees were very opinionated and disloyal to her. She was angry inside but felt powerless to change it. So she just went home at night and complained to her husband. Nothing changed, except her stress level, which was increasing.

The turning point arrived when one day after she learned she didn't get an account she had worked very hard to land. The incident was the straw that broke the proverbial camel's back and her doubts and insecurities loomed up. Sandra was reaching her limit of pain and discouragement. I asked her what she was thinking about herself that made her feel so inadequate. Losing the proposal was disappointing, but it was only one account. There would be others.

She couldn't explain it, but she felt like she was never good enough. As she talked, her comments about herself were very negative and self-effacing. At this point, she seemed totally lacking in confidence and inner spirit. Finally, she agreed to spend some quiet time by herself, and listen to herself to discover where those negative messages were coming from.

The next time we talked, Sandra had finally realized the voice she was hearing in her head was her dad's voice. And he had been dead for twenty years!

The director of her drama was still the voice of her father, who had been extremely demanding and always told both her and her sister they just "didn't do anything quite well enough." He was punitive and insensitive and no matter how hard she tried, she could never please him.

Even when she did her very best, getting good grades, making the team, or accomplishing any goal in her school days, he always told her she could have done better. She now continued to carry out this scenario of disappointment in herself, based on her father's voice. Her motive was to find evidence that she would never be quite good enough and would always be second best.

It was a long held belief of which she was unaware and she replayed it over and over. The amazing (or not so amazing) part was her partner had a commanding personality like her father, and her ego now responded to him just as she had reacted to her dad. She had unconsciously replaced her dad with a business partner to validate her belief that she was not good enough. So her partner hooked her into old beliefs, and by being a mirror to her deeply imbedded fears, he made it possible for her to recognize them.

It brought incredible freedom to Sandra when she realized that her feelings and emotions were coming from the past and she could change how she saw her partner. He was just playing out his drama the way he learned it, but she no longer had to play out her role or be in his drama.

Her genuine power emerged. She was able to talk to him directly with honesty, conviction, and courage. She learned to challenge her ego and her father's voice every time she heard it. With practice, she became more and more confident and influential in her business and her presentations.

The effect on the company was also dramatic. The staff meetings went better and communication improved because they became aligned toward the success of the company, instead of goading and challenging each other.

Beginning to self-direct from your own higher self and becoming proactive rather than reactive are goals for your soul's evolution. The influence from a past authority is not really directing a new performance at all; it is simply a previous experience being recreated again and again. Choosing to consciously make decisions in the present moment with inner serenity and clear focus is not only empowering to you, it allows others respond from their genuine selves.

Actions and scripts directed from the inner authority of your own voice are not dependent on approval from others or on the ego-driven opinions of others. This internal guidance has genuine inner confidence, and therefore, trusts in the process and power of universal energy. The inner spirit directs with a certainty that can move mountains.

The ego's false guide is relying on its own charade to lead you through your scenes. The ego's power is artificial and is therefore being fueled by external and unconscious thoughts and judgments of others. The ego's director listens to voices from the past—causing fear, doubt, and worry.

When you are listening to a voice that causes you to feel anything other than peace, love, and respect for others, you can be sure you are listening to the ego. Do not be beguiled or misled.

THE SCRIPT

The script includes dialogue, with words and lines the actor uses as the scenes unfold. In many places and business environments, the script contains a certain language people understand.

As part of my consulting experience, I learn the language of a particular industry. For example, the people being served could be clients, patients, citizens, consumers, patrons, customers, members, residents, employees, users, or investors. The product could be a professional service, financial services, devices, toys, food, consumables, produce, manufactured items, technology, art, entertainment, education, property, health care, or any of thousands of categories.

The language becomes part of the culture and is used to help one fit in and be in the know. Each industry and business has its own cultural vernacular and nuances, in addition to the general business language. The world of the computer and the Internet has added an ever-changing and growing language. The language and vocabulary change as fast as the technology. In addition, the buzz words and trends change and being up to date with the language is considered necessary to demonstrate you are current and knowledgeable about cutting edge concepts and trends. If you around long enough, you begin to see the same principles reoccur with new vocabulary to describe them.

Group speak is what happens when a certain language becomes imbedded in the culture. Certain terms, even slang, start showing up in conversations. The need to be included combined with the imitator skills of the ego all sustain the verbiage. You soon hear many people sounding like parrots. It is fear of being excluded that elicits this response, even by even senior management team members. I could list many of these jargon words, but by the time you read them they will have changed again.

Being part of a group's culture can also cause one to abdicate personal responsibility. When it is the company—or the company policy—that is speaking, individuals can pass the buck. This group speak can also result in people compromising their values because everyone else is doing it. Implosions in corporations and government are always preceded and accompanied by people looking the other way or even actively participating because of personal fears regarding their own needs and security.

I find it interesting how many workplace scripts and lines include words that are military combat terms, such as:

- Launch an attack
- Defeat the competition
- Go in for the kill
- Guerilla marketing

- Strategic mission and tactical plan
- Work in the trenches
- Call out the troops
- Corporate warfare
- Damage control
- Gather the arsenal
- Join the ranks

I believe this is just a reflection of the competitive atmosphere of businesses today. Competition has increased between businesses, but more significantly, this has created increased internal competition among people within a company.

Competition instead of cooperation leads to dissension and lack of unity. People end up comparing themselves with others, which usually only creates more envy, antagonism, insecurities, and victimization. Then add to it the individual scripts coming from each person within an organization.

The dialogue includes lines we have used before to communicate and get our needs met. We are usually unaware the words we speak are memorized from having said them before in previous melodramas. You can sometimes recognize an unconscious script in yourself and others when you hear the lines and words repeated verbatim in different conversations.

Dave, a marketing executive in a large company, has had the same complaint about several previous companies in which he worked. "Those guys [the other managers] have no drive. Why don't they work as hard as I do? What's the matter with them? I outperform everybody . . . and I never get a thanks."

He has failed to see his script is always about him pitted against everybody else. He is the righteous one. His disdain for the other co-workers is felt. Although he is respected for his marketing abilities, he is not liked very much by anyone. Nor is he trusted.

His script is the same with different companies and people, directed by his ego. I mentioned this to him and for the first time he noticed it for himself. Not without some denial and defenses, I might add. Admitting he seemed to have a script led him to look behind his ego's direction and discover why his lines are always the same. He is working on discovering his hidden, unconscious motives, and also challenging himself when he starts to go down the same path with the similar never-changing script.

Noticing the script and then following the thread or pattern linked to an earlier period is helpful. If you are honest with yourself and courageous enough to look for your deeper motives, you can find insight into how created experiences are the source of your director's voice. Through giving up resistance to looking inside yourself, you can allow your authentic voice to emerge.

GIVING UP THE DIRECTOR AND SCRIPT

Perhaps it is time to try another way of operating and begin to align yourself with your spiritual essence, instead of the insistent and persuasive voice of the ego.

Although the ego tries gallantly to make you look good and protect you from its imagined fears with the correct dialogue and dramatic lines, it is also a traitor willing to sacrifice your best interests in order to remain in control. *Your ego says things you wouldn't allow anyone else to say to you.*

Coming from lack of any genuine self-worth, your ego will whisper in your ear and secretly remind you of your weaknesses. The ego is a harsh critic. It is condemning, shaming, and accusative. It limits you and keeps you from following your inner purpose by pointing out obstacles and reasons to have doubt and fear. Your ego is shrewd and can sound realistic, thoughtful, and convincing. It can persuade you to believe it is the voice of reason. The voice is often very analytical and intelligent, making statements that sound prudent and rational. Your ego can be so undeniable that you don't even question its validity. Powerful intentions can be derailed when you listen to the hesitations, misgivings, and negative consequences projected by your ego.

Your ego will then counter this perceived attack on you with support, justification, and explanation for your fledgling self-esteem. It truly believes in the drama, even though it is a fearful recreation from past times.

The director will do everything to warn you of the impending danger. And finally, the ego offers to protect and defend you from harm. If you trust in this false claim of security, you will go around in circles, riding an endless roller coaster and wondering when you can get off.

Scripts allow a person to stay asleep and not be present to the moment. They require little attention to the interaction occurring. Your ego is listening to a prompter so you will know when to spew forth the lines from long ago. Scripts do not oblige you to listen to another and they cause you to sleepwalk through your life until something happens that is startling enough to finally get your attention.

One way to wake up is to practice listening deeply to others when they are speaking. This involves focusing on another's actual words rather than listening to your own internal dialogue. We rarely do this. It takes commitment and constant attention. It also demands you to wake up and operate in the present. You cannot connect with others in any meaningful way without focused, deep listening and attention on the other person.

Giving undivided attention requires stopping your inner conversation and concentrating completely on the other person. Look into their eyes and patiently allow them to express their thoughts, ideas, or concerns. You don't have to have an immediate answer but you do need to truly listen. With the connection on this level, you will find you can respond with acceptance and honesty rather than just words that come pouring forth. The calmness and interest you are presenting is a gift to the other person. The free exchange of energy between you will be felt by both of you. It cannot be done when you are anticipating their words and working on your own script.

FINDING YOUR AUTHENTIC VOICE

Listening to the voice of the director that comes from the ego is so automatic it takes deep attention and great effort to stop yourself. But bringing into your awareness the voice that commands the action will allow you to cut the cord and bring forth your true essence. Your words will become meaningful and helpful to others, and you will speak truth instead of platitudes and old clichés.

How do we find our true voice and authentic words?

As you start questioning your automatic response in many interactions, you will clear a space for your authentic voice from your higher power to speak out. When you discover the pattern of action and unsuspecting, unthinking words you have been using, it will seem so glaringly obvious you will wonder how you didn't notice you were only starring in reruns.

It is not a sin to follow the direction of the ego, but it is a delay in peace and happiness for yourself. The delay keeps you from experiencing the pleasure and contentment coming from within. If you really comprehended and believed this, you would stop taking your dialogue from the ego, and choose the exquisite joy and freedom your higher self offers.

The funny thing is that it is easier to see others' scripts than your own words. In fact, others' patterns and scripts may seem quite transparent to you. Recognizing your own takes sincerity and the readiness to stop pretending. But the inner force and energy that can then emerge will make the effort well worth the time and commitment to yourself. You may even reach the point where your script is laughable. When we can laugh at ourselves, we are truly living in freedom.

The ceaseless conversation of the ego is ever present. The chatter and commands of the director drown out the "still, small voice" of spirit. The authentic voice will take you to new episodes of creativity and joy if you allow it to surface.

Finding your inner authority takes waking up to the present and allowing stillness to enter your mind. It demands reclaiming your inner serenity, even in the midst of a dramatic scene. It involves a commitment to maintain alertness instead of the tired path of the ego.

Your ego would rather sleep through life and miss the aliveness and adventure of living truthfully. And you will do anything to prevent an assault on your belief system.

Picture a very drowsy little child sitting up in his high chair or stroller. His little eyelids keep dropping shut, but he jerks awake at a sudden sound or nearby movement. He wants to fall asleep.

The ego is a child wanting to sleep rather than to challenge the artificial world it created. It takes great effort to wake up—but it is time. It is time, not only to awaken yourself, but also your brothers and sisters with whom you live and work. All the heavens rejoice as you begin to wake up! All the angels celebrate your awakening!

Standing up and stepping out of the muck of all the competing noise and chatter requires giving up some behaviors you have been using for years. Coming out of the hypnotic trance of the delusion in your workplace and the world takes committed effort.

The joy you will experience when you take direction from your inner spirit cannot be compared to the shallow artificial happiness in the ego's drama. You will find your genuine voice.

Joe was the CEO of a large company employing several thousand people. He had reached high levels of success and was now reaping the financial rewards he so duly earned. He had always been a driven man, graduating the highest of his class and going on to receive a Harvard MBA. He climbed the proverbial corporate ladder, but his intensity, courage, and competitive nature finally brought him to the top of his company.

Unfortunately, he was not as happy as he would like others to believe or as all the extravagant homes, cars, and travel would indicate. He finally recognized, with the willingness to look inside, that he had been listening to the voice of his father all his life. He strove to gain attention and recognition from his father, and it was a continuing torment. He jokingly shared with the group in the workshop that he was fortunate he made a lot of money so he could now afford the psychiatrist to help him heal and resolve the damage from listening to a controlling, demanding father. He had reached great success because of the constant pressure he felt from his dad, but he wasn't particularly happy and had a lot of issues with relationships.

As you understand and practice listening for the authorities from your past that command your current life you will bring forth new responses from both yourself and the others still in the drama. As you disengage from the web of interacting scripts and dramatic episodes you will find a new kind of freedom. This is how you begin to bring light to the stage. This is how to rise above the chatter of the crowd and become a true leader.

PERSONAL RESTORATION PLAN TO PRACTICE IN YOUR WORKPLACE

1. Pay attention to your inner conversations. Begin to discern whether it is your authentic voice, or a voice from the past still directing you. Ask and write the answers in your journal:

- Who is speaking here?
- Where have I heard this voice before?
- What will happen if I don't follow this direction?
- What is the fear behind this direction?
- Have I said these lines before?
- Is this a rerun of a past scene?
- Am I really listening to what another is saying?
- Has this script ever worked before?

2. If certain words or directions repeatedly stand out in your mind, try to distinguish whose voice it is (mother, spouse, etc.) and then ask yourself if the words are really true. Question the validity of the instructions. Do you believe these ideas anymore? Or are they from a default program from the past? Write down any conclusions or realizations.

3. Pay attention to other people's conversations and notice how they often say the same things. Begin to realize when someone else is speaking from a script; they are not aware of it. And then recognize that neither are you. It takes focused attention and the desire to rise above the noise of confusion!

4. In all meeting and interactions at work start to notice your authentic voice guiding you to give up the following:

- needing to prevail or triumph over another
- needing to be superior
- needing approval of others

- treading the familiar path
- being the victim
- accepting the roles and definitions of self and others
- trying to fix or change others
- blaming others
- occupying center stage

Write your insights, the responses of others, and your feelings of authentic power in your journal. Continue your practice of being grateful and record any new experiences for which you are happy. Enjoy the new lightness that comes from giving up the burdens of the ego.

CHAPTER SEVEN

Judgment

*   *   *

Judgment is the lens and filter through which we view our world, including the people with whom we work and the circumstances in which we find ourselves. It is simply an opinion, coming from our ego, but it seems real to us. Its validity is rarely questioned even though it is only our interpretation.

Our judgment arises from our own narrow perception, based on our own experiences with different people, diverse situations, and various conditions over the years of our lives. Many of our opinions were instilled in us by significant authority figures and we now simply accept them as true, and are not even curious to discover whether or not they are even factual.

OPEN MIND

Viewing the world through the filtered eyes of judgment is the pervasive way we see everything. We cannot stop judging but we can become aware our interpretations are not necessarily the truth. When we can discover we are suffering, not because of what is happening but because of our explanation of what is happening, we will find freedom. We will find liberation from the belief systems that keep us locked in a small world of misperceptions.

Wisdom is usually attributed to living a long life. Over the span of a lifetime we are presented with different opportunities to explore relationships and conditions from different vantage points. Walking through various experiences is a process in which we grow and develop understanding. However, not everyone gains knowledge or insight. When we follow the guidance of the ego, we just keep taking the same voyage, arriving at the same destination. It only appears different—for a while.

It is as though we are walking down a winding road and although we can't see further down the path or what lies around the bend, we create an image in our mind of what we think we will encounter. Our future is based on the road we have already traveled. We will continue to have the same outcomes until we expand our scope and see life from a higher perspective. Imagine lifting up and seeing from a bird's-eye view, observing the landscape from horizon to horizon. We wouldn't have to make up the scenery or the journey, and we would see in all directions. Giving up the rash conclusions and snap judgments of the ego is comparable to rising up from the path and seeing the vast beauty of the entire landscape.

We can increase our understanding and discover new adventures only when we have an open mind, not a fixed point of view. With an open mind we will grow in our own wisdom from our higher self. But if we insist on maintaining our tiny conclusions and resist seeing another perspective, we can be sure we are operating from our ego. We can also count on the future being just more of the same, only increasing in intensity. The unwillingness to listen or to see another's point of view comes from the ego's enormous need to be right.

A good example of how a closed mind operates is to observe teenagers. Watching their behavior gives us a glimpse of how firmly the ego attaches to its opinion. If you have ever interacted with a teenager, you have seen that the teen knows everything. The teenager will fight to be right and is totally closed to the advice of the parent or another adult. The teen will not give up their viewpoint without a battle and they want to win at all costs. They do not have the perspective of experience and time but they are convinced they are right even from a very limited life. Teenagers are often not willing to listen and when we, as adults, are so opinionated that we can't hear another's position, we are much like the know-it-all teen.

Unfortunately, many adults have strongly held beliefs and ideas and stubbornly stick to their story. A conflicting idea or outlook from another is too threatening to the ego. The ego cannot stand the perceived assault on its thoughts and beliefs because we believe we are our thoughts and beliefs—we think these opinions represent who we are. The unwillingness to hear another point of view comes from the deep insecurity of the ego and fear that we will be diminished if we are discovered.

THE EGO'S CAMERA

The drama taking place in your workplace is viewed through your ego's camera, which ultimately censors and filters all the action. Identifying the significance of the camera is essential because judgment is so all-encompassing, we don't even know we are doing it. The filters coloring your vision of your life and workplace are based on your history and experiences with significant people. Most often this includes parents and other influential people in your early childhood. Unresolved issues, pains, and insecurities, even though masked with attempts at artificial roles of superiority, eventually collapse when the pressure mounts.

The past is a memory. Viewing the stage through your camera makes the past come alive again on this new stage.

A judgment of another person is simply assigning a person a role in your drama that benefits your ego. The roles you have assigned people are not, of course, the roles in which they see themselves. When you judge other people, you are basing it on your narrow perspective from your small corner of the world.

Other people have their own version of their identity and the plot of their story. Because you have assigned them their roles based on your needs, regardless of what they say or do, you will often see and hear what you expect from previous scenes with other people.

Even if others don't deliver the lines you assigned them, your lens will be blurred by your ego, and you will often see and hear what you anticipated. Only when you can suspend judgment and practice deep listening can you hear what another is telling you.

Notice how you listen when someone you don't like or with whom you don't get along is speaking. It could be someone at work or even a politician from the opposing party. Our filters allow us to hear only what we want, the views confirming what we already believe. This closed mind is rarely noticed by the one who has it. It is felt to be the truth—but it's not.

VIEWPOINT OF THE INNOCENT CHILD

Children's view of the world begins with their parents and other influential people around them. When parents don't provide the love and support children need, their automatic assumption is to believe they have done something wrong and they have caused a parent(s) to act the way they do. Children attempt to get the recognition and love they need and when their needs are not met they blame themselves. The feeling of not being loved and accepted is compounded by their belief that they are guilty.

Children often make up stories to explain disappointments or rejections in an effort to make sense of their world. Blaming themselves is so sad, but for a child, even a fictitious interpretation is better than the unknown. Children grow up and unconsciously carry these original beliefs and accompanying guilt, which held themselves as the cause of the problems in their family or early childhood.

Although it is a parent's responsibility to provide the love, guidance, and structure a child needs to grow up and become independent, parents vary in their emotional maturity and ability to provide these primary necessities. Their own dysfunction gets passed down to their children just like it happened to them—a chain of reactions that has been occurring for generations. Transformation in our world will occur as we, one by one, each restore ourselves to our powerful, inner spiritual being. Our personal restoration will be transmitted to future generations.

The effect of our childhood dysfunction shows up in our current landscape, but we go unaware. We walk around with protective, invisible shields. We deny the impact of our childhood and sometimes block out our early memories completely. If we are asked as an adult about the role of our childhood in our current life, the mind will have all kinds of rationalizations and explanations for our childhood experiences, usually dismissing them as "not that bad" or denying any problems existed.

I can't tell you how many people have told me their life was like *Leave It to Beaver*. If we do acknowledge painful circumstances, we usually have logical or analytical descriptions of how we have already dealt with the issues. But the rationalizations are coming from an adult's point of view, and we remain unaware and disconnected from how the innocent child felt who had no such understanding.

Catherine was a powerful and influential businesswoman with a mind like a steel trap. She was extremely confident and sat on boards as an advisor for other large corporations. She was a strong supporter, and often the leader, for political campaigns because she had intense convictions and a good understanding of legislative and government structures.

Catherine had grown up in a family with one sister, a father who was very powerful in the region—"everybody knew him"—and a mother who tried to keep everything together, usually with manipulation. Catherine recalled always getting her father's approval by being the best at everything she did. As long as she was successful at meeting his expectations everything was fine. When she didn't perform, which was rare, his smoldering temper and negative reactions were unbearable. Even when she was doing well he was not a warm or demonstrative man, but when she failed to measure up it was agonizing. Her mother was small in stature and seemed to have no real influence in the family. As she got older she came to understand her dad was an alcoholic and his addiction resulted in erratic and cruel behavior. Being very analytic she studied the syndrome and over the years recognized the patterns of behavior were all symptoms of an alcoholic personality. She dismissed the rejection and carried on with her life.

Catherine had a great deal of success in her business life and a seemingly happy marriage with three sons. She was a much more involved parent than her own mother had been and she loved her sons dearly. Her husband was a very kind man but definitely let her take the reins in all family and other important decisions.

Catherine's only issue seemed to be that she had no real friendships or relationships with people other than colleagues from business or government. For the most part, it didn't really matter, she claimed. But occasionally she wondered if people were kind to her only when they needed something. Also, at the same time she was pondering these things, all three of her sons had moved out of state, either for college or jobs. Her life started to feel empty and her business relationships were becoming less than fulfilling. The turning point occurred when her father died.

In spite of the negative childhood memories, her father's death elicited an unexpected emotion and a profound sense of loss. The pain she experienced brought into focus her unrealized desire to receive love from her father as she now knew she would never get it. She was surprised at her feelings because she thought she had already dealt with his lack of caring. She understood the alcoholic syndrome. But in her grief, she finally realized the truth: the little girl she was then didn't have those logical explanations for the rejection she felt. Little Catherine thought it was her fault. She had spent a lifetime wearing invisible armor to keep herself safe. She had achieved great feats and accomplishments to quell her sadness and inner doubts. This new awareness and understanding helped her to finally know it wasn't her fault.

She suddenly felt a new sense of lightness where she formally felt a burden. She found herself forgiving her father for not being able to meet her needs. And as she forgave her father, she also forgave herself; she hadn't done anything wrong. She was not the flawed person she had secretly believed she was. This knowledge caused a softening in her heart and allowed her to see her world through new eyes. It opened a door she didn't know was closed and led to a deeper, more meaningful appreciation of herself and all those in her life. Her perception of her world dramatically altered.

RECOGNIZING JUDGMENT

Acknowledging you are judging others, circumstances, and most of all, yourself is the first step in bringing about changes in your life.

As you become aware how much you do censor the world, you can also start to realize it is just your opinion. Discovering it is simply an opinion opens you to the possibility you could be wrong. Perhaps you are wrong. Just considering the prospect you might be mistaken is an opening for change and a new perception. Being able to be wrong is a big step!

Secondly, you need to recognize how you have interpreted the actions of others in a way that confirms your expectations, which is also a judgment. This step is also very difficult.

The ego finds not knowing all the answers hard to accept because your ego has been using its expectation of others to verify its belief system for a very long time. Interpreting another's actions to meet your ego's requirements is such an unconscious, automatic process it takes persistent and deliberate focus to recognize it and then to challenge it.

Thirdly, you have to admit to yourself that by keeping the judgment in place, you get the satisfaction of being right, which to the ego, is one of the strongest motivations and reinforcements for its existence. Being victorious, you believe, causes you to feel powerful. In reality, however, the ego is still powerless.

And finally, when you come to the realization that the source of your anxiety and fear is your own judgment of the world, yourself, and others, you are on the path to freedom. When you see you create the limiting beliefs about yourself, the frightened thoughts about the world, and the negative opinions of others around you, it will release you. While holding judgment, we cannot see our interconnections and similarities. Our judgments hold us as separate. Our perceived differences are the basis of prejudice, inequity, discrimination, and denigration of others—our fellow human beings. This spiritual isolation leads to greater fear.

In the workplace, you may feel disconnected even as your own judgment drives others away. The need to be right and to win is so strong you won't even see you are the cause of your own isolation. You will see yourself as the victim of this sad situation and not the cause.

The ego's judgment and the companion need of wanting to be correct have huge consequences—the loss of love, peace, and joy in your life and the lives of others. Wars are fought in the name of whose god is the true god, whose religion is the right religion, and whose culture is the superior culture. When are we going to see we are one global family with one source?

Giving up judgment of others is one of the most difficult lessons in human dynamics because judgment is the habitual and unconscious viewpoint, permeating the workplace and all our relationships.

Judgment in the workplace keeps people from trusting one another and unknowingly operating from fear. The truth is, when you judge others, you are seeing in them what you cannot face in yourself. Your inner critic seeks to project judgment outwardly. Those harshest with themselves are the most disapproving of others.

Judgment flows from a perception of what your ego believes is the way the world operates. But your ego does not have enough information to know how the world really functions. Have you ever had a critical boss who always finds things wrong with your work? Chances are this person is highly critical of themselves. And you probably believe you are the cause and take it personally.

Our opinion of others occurs with haste. We fill in all the blanks. It is as though we see someone's toe through a doorway and think we know what the whole person looks like. It is like having a Cocker Spaniel and believing we know what all Cocker Spaniels are like. Most of our decisions stem from other people's opinions that we have adopted as our own, not suspecting that they aren't true.

Judgment is taking a small piece of information and making an assumption that you know everything else. It is ludicrous, but your ego convinces you it is the truth. You live your life as though your beliefs and interpretations are real. They are not. But you frequently cling to them with tightly gripped fists and refuse to let them go. If you really comprehended how your suffering is a result of your mental perception and what you tell yourself is happening, you would understand the cause of your torment.

The lens and filters in your camera prevent you from seeing anything clearly. You do not have a wide-angled lens. Nor do you have a high enough vantage point, because you are down on the stage amidst the drama. It is so difficult to shoot your scenes with any accuracy concerning the reality occurring on your stage. You create an explanation and then accept this blurred and undeveloped image of the world as real. What we don't understand is that nothing is outside ourselves and the world we see is a reflection of our beliefs.

Another reason our viewpoint is so out of focus and foggy is we don't have enough light to see clearly. This book is intended to help illuminate the stage. Every time you rely on your cloudy interpretation or someone else's opinion, you short circuit your spiritual connection. Your ego cannot reach your spiritual source anymore than plastic can connect with electricity.

Your inner self adjoins with the universal source of energy, providing a conduit to authentic spiritual power. The result is love and creativity surpassing anything you can know or achieve on your own. This light within will brighten your life as you simultaneously give up the ego's unquenchable needs and ceaseless judgments. When you surrender your ego and its false pretentions, you allow your authentic self to emerge. Relinquishment of the ego leads to liberation and enlightenment.

Judgment by the analytical mind causes so many problems at work, as well as all the other arenas of your life, it is amazing you continue to side with it. It limits your life by creating problems where none exist. Judgment obscures communication and alienates others because your ego will not allow for any point of view besides its own. When you can recognize and acknowledge this process of denying your participation in the drama, you are taking a gigantic step forward in the advancement of your soul.

WHY DO WE JUDGE?

Why do we make judgments so rapidly and with such limited information?

The answer is we are afraid of others, and we dread asking questions in which we might not receive the answer we want. We just jump to our own conclusions rather than delve further. We are fearful the answers will reveal we are mistaken or inadequate. So we make assumptions and then carry out the unconscious plot and motives that satisfy our mind. In the workplace, people are often afraid to ask a question for clarification because they don't want to appear stupid. Even when the leader says, "There are no stupid questions." Because we judge ourselves so harshly, we believe others do too.

Another misperception occurs when someone does respond to us. We often hear only what we expect to hear, based on our own story of the relationship. Our interpretation of what they are saying can be completely off base—not what they are communicating at all. We believe our own script, and we do not let others interfere with our depiction—even at the expense of our own happiness.

What are we afraid of?

The sad truth is we are afraid of being judged by others as not valuable. We are afraid to speak up and to be our true selves because our ego tells us we will be rejected. When we are having a conversation with anyone, rather than ask questions and clarify what others are saying to us, we make up our own lines for them.

Because we are judgmental we project the same qualities on others and see them as judging us—and not always the way we would like them to view us.

We don't communicate our feelings and thoughts to others, but we often expect them to read our minds, understand our reactions, and applaud our dramatic performance. We even sometimes believe we are a victim of an attack from lines they never even delivered. We wonder why others don't respond to our pain and anguish when we forgot to give them the script! We are living in our own little world, so confined by our mind. We judge everyone from the position of our ego and our starring role even though it causes us pain and loneliness. This myopic point of view is so prevalent and normal it goes by completely unnoticed.

To demonstrate this, think about what happens when you enter a large room with lots of people. It goes something like this. First, you judge them on whether you think they like you, respect you, admire you, want to talk to you, already know you, remember you, wish they knew you, hate you, condemn you, value you, trust you, or any number of other attitudes you think they might have about you.

Secondly, you then judge them for their initial and observable characteristics and how they compare to you. Are they better looking, smarter, more talented, more confident, inferior, fatter, thinner, better dressed, sexier, more articulate, poorer, older, younger, better, worse, funnier, taller, shorter, or wittier than you?

Then you begin sizing them up, based on your past experiences. Your ego starts casting them in your drama. They don't even know they are auditioning!

Do you know why they don't know they are auditioning for your drama? Because they are all doing the same thing you are doing: auditioning you and others for their own drama!

Did you know you were trying out for a role in their play?

Your ego sets about creating the image of itself it wants to project to others. It evaluates and interprets all the other characters and what their roles are going to be. For your drama, your ego does not need any further information because it believes it has enough experience from the past to recognize all the characters on the present stage.

Your ego will even suppose it knows how others think and feel. What arrogance the ego has!

Harry was a high-level manager in a large company showing some big losses in the past quarter. There were rumors of downsizing. One day, as he was walking on the administrative floor, he saw some directors from the company emerge from an executive session that had been going on for several hours. Three of them stopped and were quietly talking in the hall.

As Harry walked by, they seemed to stop talking and nodded grimly at him when he passed by. Harry felt a sinking feeling and went home that night to tell his wife he was probably going to be laid off and should start getting his resume together.

His wife was very upset because she didn't work, they had a wonderful lifestyle, and she didn't want to see it change. The next few weeks or so were going to be a very depressing time for them.

The same morning, shortly after Harry had left the floor, Bob, the vice president of the sales department, came down the same hall. He was feeling good because he had lined up some major accounts that he knew would really help the company recover from the reported losses. As he passed the same three directors, they looked at him and nodded when he passed.

Bob felt a sense of pride, knowing they were probably discussing what a great job he was doing for the company and how he was saving them from more financial shortfalls. Bob felt certain he would be getting a promotion and probably a big bonus for his significant contributions in generating revenues for the company.

Interestingly enough, the three directors were discussing an upcoming golf round they would be playing in the afternoon. The last quarter had been tough, but things were looking up for the company, and they all were feeling good about themselves and their powerful roles in the leadership of the company. Neither Harry nor Bob's name had come up at all during the morning meeting!

Harry and Bob had not only reached their own conclusions about the conversations they believed occurred in the meeting, they proceeded to live the next few weeks as though their beliefs were reality.

This is a demonstration of the power of the belief system and our ability to create our own reality. We live our lives as though our limited perspective is the whole picture. Our world is made up of our interpretation, not what really happens.

The real question is: whose direction are you going to follow, your ego's or your spirit's?

Living through the judgmental world of the ego is like living in a tiny little house with the blinds pulled tightly shut. You do not let the light of day shine into your small and enclosed environment. The ego is fearful you will discover you don't need this identity, so it must keep you in the dark and prevent you from waking up from this drama.

The reinforcement for holding judgment over others is the false sense of superiority.

Through your camera and lens, you can view yourself and others in any light you choose to validate the story line you are following. The ego doesn't even need the supposed enemy to agree with its opinion. If you want to see yourself as a victim, for example, you will believe it is true even if others don't substantiate it.

The ego will always see others as the cause of your pain. If you don't get agreement, your ego will lead you to people who will corroborate your story. In fact, these alliances, based on reinforcing the identity and motives of the ego, are the most common kind of "friendships."

The bond that ties many relationships is the mutual support of each other's drama. They are not authentic friendships and can be cast aside with changing stories.

True friendships are much rarer. In an honest friendship, each person feels safe to be vulnerable and to not feel judged as good or bad. Trust is the result of non-judgment. The combination of judgment and fear of others prevents most people from being truthful in their communication. The authentic relationship is based on a deeper bond that transcends ego needs. Each person supports and honors the other's choices and ideas. One does not attempt to control the other but offers gentle support when asked. The exchange of energy is free and balanced.

Since most people are operating from the ego and looking for validation of their stories instead of the truth, relationships that are based on spiritual honesty are extraordinary.

Spiritual relationships open doors to new ways of communication. Each person benefits from the relationship and expands as a result of mutual sharing. The friendships, whether between friends, family members, lovers, spouses, or other people, contain within them the opportunity for rising above the traps and disillusionments of the ego world.

When people can find good friends in the workplace it adds to job satisfaction and feeling part of the organization. In fact, the Gallop Organization found that those who have a best friend at work are seven times more likely to be engaged. Those who don't have a best friend have slim 1-in-12 odds of being among the engaged. Building authentic relationships in the workplace is good for individuals and for the company.

However, relinquishing the ego's usual reactions from its well-worn path requires courage. It may require you to no longer validate someone else's strongly held story. For example, although you still lovingly listen to their account, instead of agreeing, you help them look outside their own judgment at other possible options. By honoring the inner spirit, especially when the other is steeped in an emotional drama of blame or suffering, you help them find their inner strength and potential. Not siding with their opinion, which is coming from their wounded ego, is not easy, but it is the highest honor you can bestow on them.

You might even say to them, "I honor you too much to see you as the small self you think you are right now. I see much more in you than you are feeling at this moment." Words like these can be said caringly and given with the promise you will be there for them. Your refusal to confirm their story of victimization may cause their ego to react to you with temporary disappointment. But your inner support and love for them, coming from authentic power, will genuinely elevate them on a level you may not even be able to see.

In other words, you do not read the lines in the script they wrote. Playing out the role for them and telling them what they want to hear would strengthen their ego, while causing much greater harm to their spirit. Unfortunately, this false support for others occurs more often than sincere honor for others, both in the workplace and the world. The false support is not loving or honest; it is simply self-preservation (also known as sucking up).

Ron, a warm and loving guy, was carrying out an insane drama with his girlfriend of six months. She was having doubts and fears about the relationship, coming from her early childhood wounds, so she kept giving him mixed messages. She would offer him lots of love and attention for two days, and then withdraw and tell him she needed "alone time" for several days. He was not supposed to call or "suffocate" her during these periods apart.

Ron would be very hurt and disappointed when she would withdraw after they just had a wonderful weekend or couple days together. He would suffer and wait for her to call, and then when she did, he would try even harder to win her love. He bought her jewelry, took her on trips, and did anything he could to please her.

The push-pull pattern continued with Ron playing the puppet role, just waiting for her to pull the strings. This was especially hard to watch because he alternated between exhilaration and, conversely, severe pain. He was on hold, just waiting to be called back into the dance with her.

In the workplace, Ron was the CFO, in charge of the accounting department for a large construction company. As a CPA, he was not only bright, but also very experienced in the industry. People admired and respected him as a businessman and saw him as an extremely reliable and confident person.

Why would he be giving up his power and personal happiness to this woman who it appeared didn't seem to have much compassion for his feelings? Most of his friends refused to say too much because of his obvious emotional involvement in this relationship. They would agree with him when he said she wasn't fair, it was all her fault, she was an insensitive woman, etc. But then he would go running back to her. So they watched silently and started getting tired of the scenario.

One day, he asked advice from our mutual friend Karen while the three of us were talking. I was very proud of Karen when she would not agree with his claim of being the victim of the girlfriend's unfair treatment. She said in her southern accent, "Honey, y'all must like it. You chose it! If you didn't like it, y'all wouldn't keep goin' back for more." Even Ron had to laugh.

Then we discussed how he had given up being the director of his own life and had handed the whole stage and script to his girlfriend. It was time to start being the authentic director of his own life. Karen's refusal to validate his story line, which was based on his judgment from the past, helped him gain a new perspective.

Ron's ego had been playing out scenes from the past of a mother who also had given mixed messages. Of course, it took Ron more than one momentary glance at the part he was playing in the drama to bring about a change. He started looking at the interaction and saw how he was responsible for his own part in the dynamics of the relationship.

In addition to taking charge of his own story, he also gave his girlfriend freedom to love him without his projection of neediness on her. As he asked for less, he gave her the opportunity to love him more.

My wise daughter, Stephanie, who is a very old soul disguised as a young woman, has dropped many pearls of wisdom for me over the years. When she and her brother, Kyle, were teens, I was so preoccupied with their lives, I sometimes made myself miserable. I thought I could control things and keep a handle on their behavior if I was protective enough. My life, during those times, was filled with anxiety, and it was Stephanie's words that helped me let go: "Mom, why don't you get a life of your own? Then you wouldn't be worried about Kyle and me all the time."

She was right! My attempt to manage situations that were out of my control anyway was making me a prisoner. I stopped my overanxious worrying, and we all survived their teen years.

What I can now say to Ron and others who focus their lives on someone else in an attempt to get happiness and security from the person is: "Get a life of your own and be happy." Then you will be the kind of person others can love freely.

We often agree with another's judgment or opinion because our ego wants to be liked and validated. It is easier to agree and lie to people than to answer them honestly if they ask you questions. I have had to honor myself and not validate someone's actions and perceptions when I was feeling hurt. It is not always easy to take a stand for yourself or for someone else when an ego is attacking you. But when you rely on your inner power from your spiritual source, you can withstand the assault from anyone's ego.

Challenging your opinions, which are based on the past and your preconceived ideas about how the world and its people operate, is the way to freedom. When you refuse to limit your world with unfounded judgments, you make way for love and freedom to flow into your life.

Your ego makes the assumption that everyone views life and, in particular, the workplace stage in the same way. This is absolutely not true. Each person is making judgments all the time and rarely do the interpretations match. Understanding there are two different dramas and scripts in play when you have a conversation or especially a confrontation with another will help you untangle the confusion.

Peggy was the new marketing director for a company that had multiple locations. She was very enthusiastic and had lots of plans to implement to help achieve the strategic goals of the company. Part of her job was to work closely with the director of operations, Lance, who managed each of the sites. At first he seemed very welcoming and supportive of her marketing program. They were intended to work very closely, and she was eager to hear his ideas and what he thought of her marketing plans. Although he managed each of the sites and the employees reported to him, there would be areas where there would be overlap and some of his employees would have some responsibilities in assisting with events, projects, etc. The employees seemed eager to participate and even had ideas of their own.

Somewhere along the way, Lance started acting a little strange. He resisted some of the ideas they had previously agreed on and now had different thoughts that seemed to conflict with the steps they had already implemented. She would ask questions, but he would say things that seemed unrelated. It was subtle, but she felt an invisible wall between them.

To make matters worse, the Chief of Operations, to whom they both reported, made some suggestions to her that she and Lance work out their differences. The COO implied that they weren't on the same page and that he was saying some things that were quite different from what she said. She felt a mounting sense of suspicion, but for what, she didn't know. It was extremely important that she and this colleague work well together.

Her growing apprehension caused her to start avoiding him and have only absolutely necessary conversations while she debated what to do. Although they were at equal levels in the organization, he had been there much longer and seemed to get a lot of respect from everyone. But so great was her dread of him and his possible criticism, she just evaded the situation.

Finally, she decided to pose some questions to herself. What was she so afraid of that she couldn't address this situation and get some resolution? What was that fight or flight feeling she had that felt like she was back in junior high and one of the boys wouldn't play fair? She became aware of an old sense that the boys in school were right and got their way, and girls shouldn't argue; they should be nice. For a liberated and evolved woman, these old unconscious beliefs surprised her when she was honest enough with herself to look deeply. She became determined to push through this wall of fear and address the problem with him—without blame.

The next day she asked him to go to lunch with her. When they had ordered their meal and had time to talk she told him that it was extremely important to her for them to be a united team. She said sometimes she felt some resistance from him and that she wanted him to trust her. She added that her respect for him was great and his ideas, thoughts, and support were necessary for her to do the job that would help the company grow. And after all, they were on the same team.

He seemed surprised at her candor and finally admitted that he hadn't trusted her, partly because the COO was making comments to him that caused him to wonder about Peggy's motives. Lance felt Peggy was trying to undermine him in some way and he wasn't sure why. So it seemed the COO was sending mixed messages to both of them. Their process of learning to work together, which in most situations can take some time, was impeded by the confusing comments.

They continued talking and made some decisions to really trust each other and agreed that when there was any confusion they would stop and each express their thoughts. They also decided that when the COO said anything to either of them that implied they didn't get along or were not saying the same thing, they would adamantly support one another and reassure the COO they were on the same page. If necessary, they would get all three of them on the phone to confirm their alignment.

Over the next few years their relationship strengthened. With time she knew she could always count on him, and he trusted her completely. When anything came up, as it always does in a workplace environment, they could directly face it and come to a solution. She even told him that when she first arrived she felt like a school girl sometimes, trying to talk to him, and felt like he wasn't interested in her ideas. He confessed he grew up with an older sister who was bossy and made him feel like he didn't have power. They both agreed that knowing each other expanded their understanding of themselves, helped in their ability to communicate overall, and benefitted the company as well.

In truth, his need for recognition, a sense of power, and admiration had initially caused him to push her away. His judgment of her was validated by a boss who was often incongruent and had a habit of stirring up trouble without having all the facts. Her fear and judgment of him was immobilizing her and preventing her from doing her job or talking directly to Lance. When Peggy broke the pattern by sincerely communicating, the whole scene changed to one of respect and cooperation.

JUDGMENT CREATES YOUR WORLD

It is characteristic of the ego to make up rules for itself, based on false assumptions of the world, and then to try to live by them. Most of these rules are made by your ego's judgment about how you should live your life to prove to yourself and others you are a worthwhile person.

"Following my rules will make you acceptable and worthy to yourself and to others," says the ego.

These arbitrary rules are the guidelines and structure for performing your role on the various stages of your life. They are the standards by which your ego then evaluates and critiques your performance.

The problem with most of these guidelines is that since they are made by the ego they are really just attempts to alleviate self-doubt and fear of inadequacy. They don't work, because you judge yourself so harshly you will never be acceptable in your ego's eyes. When you don't follow your own made-up rules, you then beat yourself up. It would be funny if it wasn't so painful.

This lack of acceptance of yourself leads to projection and lack of acceptance of others.

Finding fault with others becomes a constant way of viewing others through your shadowy filter and lens. It gives you some temporary relief by focusing the camera on others.

Ed is a very educated and well-read man. He is a lawyer and has learned a lot about critically evaluating all decisions and strategies in all arenas of life.

His keen mind is an asset in the courtroom, and he is a much-sought-after, high-cost attorney. His quick ability to ascertain a situation and determine contributing factors has made him an excellent litigator.

Socially, Ed is not so highly esteemed. He has an arrogant nature that seems to come from a very elevated opinion of himself. He is quick to point out others' faults or frailties. He always knows more about any subject than anyone else, and his conversations are more like lectures than interactive, friendly communication.

His criticism of others is not always blatant, but it is always felt nonetheless. It usually comes as sarcasm or laughter at another's expense. He often subtly puts others down by ridiculing a movie or book they might have enjoyed or characterizing as trivial anything he deems beneath his stature or interests.

He is also critical of others not present. He rarely has anything nice to say about anyone. He is quick to point out others' weaknesses and failings.

He seems to have a toxic statement about everyone, and he smiles as he dissects others. Finding fault with others gives him an illusory kind of pleasure.

Ed also spends great attention on his own appearance. His clothes are the finest, his shoes are spotlessly polished, and he drives only the most luxurious cars. His jewelry, watches, and accessories are designer label only, and even his casual look is straight out of a men's fashion magazine. He is perfectly attired, all the time.

In fact, he is pretty much perfect in every way except . . . no one likes him, not even his wife, who left him after years of high control and criticism.

What Ed doesn't realize is his intense criticism and unappeasable attempt to be perfect are belying his incredible disdain and criticism of himself. His attempts at flawlessness in himself and criticism of others are to mask to his own suffering and self-hatred.

He couldn't bear to look within himself at the shame and disgust he is carrying; instead, he projects all of it outward. His ego has been so terrified, even the incredible pain that he has gone through in his personal life has not penetrated it.

You know people like this. Huge fears build thick walls. I don't know what it will take for him to look behind the face of his ego. It takes what it takes!

The goal of this book is to help you put the spotlight on yourself to gently bring clarity to the confusion. The ability to see clearly is worth the effort because it will bring authentic relief to your pain. Self-acceptance leads to acceptance of others, and acceptance of others leads to self-acceptance. As you learn one lesson, you simultaneously bring about the other. Self-acceptance is followed by patience with yourself and others. You are also able to find compassion for yourself and show the same caring attitude to others.

The Golden Rule applies here, not as a rule to try to follow but as a natural law of cause and effect. You can't help but follow it. As you "do unto others" is exactly what you do unto yourself. And "as you do unto yourself" is exactly what you do unto others.

There is no other alternative. You cannot give love and compassion to others, for example, if you cannot give it to yourself. And you cannot give it to yourself if you do not give it to others.

And if what you offer others is unforgiving judgment, it is because it is also what you offer yourself, and vice versa. Herein lies the closest opportunity to comprehend that we are not separate. We have the same mind and we all are constantly projecting and reflecting.

If you can see this, you will understand Einstein's statement that it is an "optical illusion of consciousness" that we are separate. This discovery alone can change your entire life!

THE FINAL STAGE: JUDGMENT DAY

By now, I hope you are beginning to see the path of the ego has been one of fear and denial, pain and projection. We might begin to wonder why one wouldn't recognize this as a journey into hell.

Indeed, it is!

Because the tiny, fearful ego is so judgmental of itself and others, it must also project the same judgment onto the all-loving Creator. The ego throughout its life gradually attempts to build up defenses in preparation for its unavoidable destination—its ultimate fear—Judgment Day.

The ego instinctively knows it will never survive after physical death, even though it longs to believe it will go to the everlasting place, the hereafter it wants to enter. And indeed, it dreams of the Promised Land for the rest it needs because, quite frankly, the ego is exhausted from all the energy it expends in the big chess game of life. The ego has spent a lifetime in the ever-vigilant roles it has created for itself.

But the ego doesn't believe it deserves heaven. The ego is only an actor and knows it is not worthy of a final resting place of any kind, not even in the ground. So the ego sees the point of death, the Day of Judgment, as its greatest fear coming to fruition. As it comes before the Creator, it will finally be found out. The jig is up. It will finally be exposed.

The ego is a fraud.

And from this terrible position, met by the Maker Himself, the only choice, the only justice would be everlasting hell: to have to remain eternally in the pain it has been in all its life, only amplified a thousand times.

The ego will now be with the pain and suffering it has tried to deny all its life, but which is now its never-ending future. This is the justice the guilty ego believes is its only reward, its just deserts for a job well done of fearing and preying on others for its sustenance.

So the ego says, "Confess your sins. Admit your guilt, so God will allow you to enter the Gates of Heaven."

This is the final conflict: how can the ego give up its defenses in the face of the Creator, the One who knows how much of a fraud the ego is? Here, the ego comes face to face with its greatest fear. The fear is so great and so terrifying, all other perceived threats pale in comparison.

Hence all the stories of dying if you see the face of God, the fire and brimstone of hell, the whole concept of Judgment Day, and the endless admonitions from the leaders of the churches throughout centuries of fear.

The fear is unconscious, but it is so great that the ego has found ways to attempt to lessen the fear: Confess your sins, do good work, give your money to churches and other worthy causes, and finally, project your guilt onto others. Disconnect from it, go to counselors, take seminars, read the Bible and self-help books. Seek answers to find peace and relief from the pain and stress of living a lie.

But every attempt, even the admirable paths, all lead to fear at some point because the ego knows it will be confronted in the end, and then its powerlessness will be exposed.

So once again, the ego plays one more game: it bargains with God.

The ego promises to be good and righteous "if you'll only let me go to Heaven" when its time on the planet is up. But *good* is a relative term. How good is good enough? How many sins can you commit?

Therein lies the ego's challenge: trying to appear good enough for God, but really never measuring up. The ego knows, ultimately, it is not worthy.

So the fear that unconsciously resides within every soul is a pain deeply embedded in the psyche. There is no escape. Hell becomes a reality because it isn't someday—it is now!

Life is a living hell for the ego.

Moments of clarity and joy occur, but the massive consciousness of the ego's world is so great it is difficult to not be swallowed by it almost every step of the way.

So where is the door out of this painful maze of self-deception and fear?

The only possibility is in opening the door to that which has never seen the light of day, the door the ego has locked shut and for which it has thrown away the key. But the key is right here. You must have the courage to challenge your ego, your false self-created identity, which has never given you anything but pain and exhaustion.

You have the key. Great teachers like Jesus, Gandhi, and the Buddha cannot give it to you. They can only point the way.

The way home points back to yourself: the judge, the jury, and the warden of your self-imposed prison.

Only you can set yourself free. You must challenge the seemingly powerful ego to finally give up the battle and surrender to the incredible inner spiritual greatness residing beneath its shabby imitation of your true self.

It takes great attention, it requires fearless dedication, and it demands focus and awareness in the present moment of every passing day. You are waking up from a deep, deep sleep, and the desire to go back to sleep is almost overwhelming.

You must fight the urge to sleep by challenging the ego's attempts to hook you, to make you believe it is real, to lead you back down the familiar path of perpetual pain and misery. The process of facing your ego would be extremely difficult if it wasn't so powerfully reinforced by your soul.

Your soul wants you to awaken.

Many of you are now trying to wake up because the terror and demons of the nightmare are becoming too painful and unbearable. The fracturing of the old system is becoming intolerable. And just as a nightmare wakes you out of a sound sleep, so can a crisis or painful experience wake you up from the ego's dream. You can decide right now to wake up, to be restored to your true identity—the beautiful soul you are.

WAKING UP NOW

Isn't it time to let up? Isn't it time to let the light of peace, love, and acceptance shine into your life and workplace?

People everywhere are tired of this wearisome dance. As we, one by one, shine light on the stage of the ego, the radiance will begin to penetrate the misery and web of pain with the gift of acceptance and appreciation of each other, as well as for ourselves.

We can create an environment of trust and compassion by giving up judgment of others and ourselves. Because judgment is held by so many, it is difficult to see it is not the true picture. Mass agreements will only change as we individually give up our own false proclamations.

How do we do it?

Begin by asking yourself the following questions:

- Do I compare myself with others?
- Am I striving for personal glory?
- What are my grievances at work?
- What are my criticisms of the government?
- What are my complaints about society in general?
- What wouldn't I want others to know about me?
- What do I find most unacceptable about myself?
- What about my appearance am I most critical of?
- What do I most mistrust in people I work with?
- Do I know what someone is going to say before they say it? How could I?
- Can I learn to ask questions for clarity instead of making assumptions?
- If I were to meet my Maker today, what would I fear would be my worst sin?

Looking at the answers to these questions will tell you about the source of your judgment and help you recognize how you evaluate yourself and others. You will see how you project your own insecurities out into the world.

It is time to start challenging your ego's threatened opinions.

If you look at the base of judgment, you will see it is not power. When you judge, you are operating from the ego. Judging is an attempt to weaken or disempower another, even if only in your private thoughts.

Your ego believes if you can discount others, you can hamper or minimize their power to hurt you. Interestingly enough, it is much easier to see judgment in others than in yourself. But the damage inflicted on yourself is far greater than any threat you perceive from others. Allowing them the freedom to just be, accepting them for exactly who they are, is the most loving and enlightened thing you can do.

It is not a sin to follow your ego's direction, but it always delays your path to freedom and enlightenment. It takes watchfulness and concentration to notice the slightest thoughts and irritations that are the seeds of judgment. Not allowing them to grow into full-blown judgments is the best thing you can do. Snapping them off at the roots and weeding the garden frequently will keep it free from the overgrowth of weeds that would take the sun and sustenance that belongs to the healthy plants. Stop the stream of thinking that fuels your ego world.

As your awareness grows, you will be amazed at how many times during the day you make judgments or form immediate perceptions of others. By letting go of these opinions as quickly as they occur, you will cause them to dissipate, and in their place, you will feel and see the radiance, beauty, and joy that are your natural inheritance. It is your heritage, your birthright as a human being living in these times. It is your destiny to awaken to your inner greatness.

You will replace your negative emotions through giving up judgment with a new, softer feeling of respect, love, and honor. The feelings of the heart will rush in to fill the void that was formerly filled with judgment, prejudice, pain, and walls of fear. You will see a new, brighter, freer world as you continue to relinquish judgment, day by day.

Your continued success in releasing your judgments will reinforce this new way of being. You will become strong and detached from the outcomes of daily events because you will no longer have a personal agenda attached to them. You will experience an independence you have never known and you will feel physically lighter and more energetic, joyful, and peaceful. Most of all, you will feel released from the weight of trying to control others and situations, both at home and at work.

Controlling your world by trying to influence the actions and choices of others will become a thing of the past. You will realize it was an illusion anyway. To give up judgment calls forth your trust in the universe and your innate spiritual integrity. It requires becoming present and giving up the past, which has been dictating the workplace and the world.

Giving up your interpretations requires the companion ability of trusting that you are not needed to direct the daily drama. It allows you freedom because you are no longer holding yourself responsible for everyone else.

The drama in the workplace, as well as the world, is comprised of complicated scenes in which you are both judging and participating every day. Therefore, unraveling this multifaceted drama can be complex. So keep noticing your judgments and then ask your inner spirit for help in giving them up.

Dispel them. Unleash your freedom, peace, and joy, which have been enshrouded in clouds of judgment. Just let go.

Understanding how judgment creates your world is the missing link to your freedom from pain and misery.

The ego wants to make others smaller when our work is to empower others, to release them to their true greatness, to help restore them to their real identity. But we cannot do this by diminishing them from the viewpoint of the ego who wants us to be superior to others. Judgment and criticism from the ego-driven leader douse the sparks of creativity. An enlightened leader fans the spark of brilliance into flames of passion and imagination. As a leader, understanding how and when you criticize others is a most crucial lesson. You can't help those you lead through your ego's eyes. You help them when you transcend the ego.

UNIVERSAL LOVE

Universal love is the source of all energy and light. Universal love is the power that sustains you and all of life.

Love lights the world. It shines on everyone and opens hearts and minds to the beauty of creation. Love radiates like the sun, a joyous expression of the magnificence of our spiritual essence. It recognizes all is well and bathes the world in its loveliness.

But if love is the sun, judgment is the cloud that obscures it. Clearing away the clouds of judgment is the way to freedom of expression and the ability to receive love, joy, and inner contentment in your life. So powerful is love, it disarms and melts away the ego's falseness. Love, in its purest form, unhampered by judgment, cuts through all of the ego's negativity.

In addition, love is practical and masterful. It operates from dedication, persistence, and resolve. It doesn't cower in the face of obstacles but stands strong. It builds hope and faith, fortifies your strength, and increases your intensity. Love flourishes in spite of uncertainty, dissolves all fear, and moves mountains. Love is the very reason you exist. Who would not rely on this power if we truly understood?

Seeing others as enemies is a result of judging; you see their actions as causing your feelings. Holding others responsible for your feelings is a gigantic misperception. When you begin to see how judgment permeates and colors your entire world, you will begin to see it also destroys your peace and harmony.

Judgment is so persistent it takes focus and constant attention to give it up. But the results will reward you a thousand-fold.

You will see the world differently when you release judgment. You will enjoy the beauty of the human experience and receive the rewards for helping to elevate understanding and compassion. As you practice your new insights by demonstrating to others and yourself that you accept them as they are, you will become an enlightened and powerful leader.

One of the greatest results of giving up judgments of others is you simultaneously give up judging yourself. This love and acceptance of yourself is freedom at the ultimate level. It is your ego's self-loathing and fear that created the whole drama to begin with. It is the ego's lack of self-worth that directs the drama to deny its fear.

Here is your freedom!

Can you see it is through the practice of giving up judgment that you will become authentically strong, whole, and complete? Giving up judgment will remove the barriers preventing you from being all your soul desires. If you really trusted this information, why would you not start right now?

PERSONAL RESTORATION PLAN
TO PRACTICE IN YOUR WORKPLACE

1. As you go through your day at your workplace, focus on the moments when you are quick to make a snap judgment of either another person or a situation. Before taking any action, look within yourself and acknowledge that you are judging and your point of view is limited. Ask yourself:

- Could I be wrong?
- Am I attempting to minimize or disempower someone?
- What other interpretation could I make about this person or situation?
- Am I trying to elevate or protect myself?
- What other ways could I respond to this person or situation?

Continue doing this at every opportunity. Write down your insights at night and continue to seek clarity as you confront your ego's judgment.

2. By looking at your judgments of yourself, you can find more personal acceptance and compassion for others. As honestly as you can, answer some of the questions posed in this chapter, such as:

- What wouldn't I want others to know about me?
- What do I find most unacceptable about myself?
- What about my appearance am I most critical of?
- What do I most mistrust in people I work with?
- If I were to meet my Maker today, what would I fear would be my worst sin?

As you answer these questions, write down your answer so you can discover your own fears and inadequacies. Watch your mind and see how it tries to deny, even to yourself, what you believe are your weaknesses.

After compiling your list, try to bring acceptance and forgiveness to yourself for not being perfect. As you release judgment of yourself you will see the workplace, the world, and others in a better light. The world will become a happier and safer place.

CHAPTER EIGHT

Understanding Rivalry

* * *

In a world of ever increasing uncertainty, many people are recognizing the need for more compassion for one another. I live in Seattle, and when the Dalai Lama visited he nearly filled Qwest Stadium, home of the Seahawks. The attendance of thousands of people was a testament to the growing desire for a better world. However, the workplace is still an arena where kindness is often in short supply and many people are too harried to take the time to recognize the need for compassion.

Unfortunately, the temperature in businesses is heating up, so to speak, and people are in dire need of healing. As business leaders increase their pressures and demands, the internal competition swells. Rivalry, mistrust and antagonism permeate the business culture creating low morale and lack of faith in business leaders. If you are dealing with a competitive work situation, what can you do? First we must understand the underlying source of the dissension.

Rivalry in the workplace feeds on fear and insecurity and is accelerated by the desire to be recognized or appreciated. Few can withstand the discomfort and pain of being criticized, attacked, and blamed. The desire to feel significant and valued cannot be stifled and when people are treated with disdain or lack of respect, it feels literally like being stabbed and deeply wounded.

Fear in the workplace, when it comes up, wastes the energy of every man and woman. Fear *becomes* you. If allowed, it can overtake our perception of the world. Fear flows through us like a mighty river. When blocked, it builds up and gets stuck within the body, hardening like frozen ice or concrete, finally stopping all the healthy, normal emotions and actions from flowing.

The pain is then absorbed into negative emotions creating physical illness, addiction, or morose feelings. Attempts are made to expel the pain by blaming, attacking, or lashing out at another, which only leads to greater rivalry, competition, and jealousy in the environment.

Fear, blaming, and attacking someone else gives the one doing it a false sense of superiority, a feeling they are above the source of the threat of destruction. The perpetrator is not aware of the deep pain they inflict on others because it is not felt when they are in the attack mode. But this sense of triumph over the enemy is short-lived because another rival will soon show up.

Emotional assaults are occurring every day at every level in the workplace and the world. The prognosis for this ongoing dysfunction is not good. It is an unending process leading to the continuing deep lack of self-esteem. Self-worth will never be found in perpetuating drama.

WHO IS THE ENEMY?

The enemy is the root of all your troubles, so believes the ego. The enemy causes unbearable pain and brings up incredible apprehension. The opponent, therefore, must be dealt with to diminish or to completely remove the suffering. This is done by destroying the cause—the enemy.

There may be more than one enemy. But even with several enemies at once, the dynamics are always the same.

In literature, movies, and television shows the hero is seen as the one who becomes the victor when pitted against formidable opponents or incredible obstacles. We face many challenges in our workplace and our ego wants to claim victory as well. The alternative, we believe, is to surrender, which is disgraceful and humiliating to the ego.

If the opponent appears to the ego to be mightier or more powerful than you, it will engender even greater fear.

The enemy in the workplace is such a central character in your life, you can become obsessed with and often even immobilized by the intensity of the danger you believe is coming from him or her. Your ego may direct you to hours of suffering and anguish over how to deal with the situation.

The enemy is always the one or the situation that is seen as a threat to your security and well-being.

Many times the enemy is the source of pain because of envy of what the other person has or has attained. It could be status, a position you wanted, material wealth, beauty, or any number of external things your ego covets. Jealousy, the green eyed monster, has been the root of battles between individuals, families, communities, and even nations throughout history.

The source of major dramas, even sometimes leading to death, is the fear of losing the beloved to the rival. The eternal triangle has been the motive and story line of unbearable pain and resentment for centuries. The fury of "a woman scorn'd" represents this passion played out. Men have dueled and fought wars over the person they loved.

Intense passion and misery over the beloved arises because the attachment formed in the love relationship offers such significant and powerful opportunities for joy as well as pain. Unrequited love, or "love lost," has been one of the most excruciating experiences for humans throughout history. However, even these dramatic, heartrending situations can offer healing and new understanding if those involved choose to learn the lessons.

To understand this more fully, let's look at how human beings have responded to the enemy in all its forms—the other who is perceived as a threat to the welfare of individuals and societies.

Cave men found weapons to defend themselves and provided security for themselves with the threat of force. In the Middle Ages, people built castles with high walls, moats around them, and drawbridges for protection from the enemy. Early settlers in America, traveling in wagon trains, circled the wagons for protection, and then they built forts with high walls and lookouts to keep the enemy at bay and keep those inside safe and secure.

In modern times, nations battle in the name of national security and have departments of defense to orchestrate military combat to ensure their country's safety.

But when does the defense become the offense?

Humans, on an individual basis, both in the workplace and other environments, continue to build walls and defenses to protect themselves. But these protective walls are also barriers to communication and relationships with others. The many layers of fortification add to the impenetrable space between yourself and other people.

The strong need to keep your belief system in place leads to a variety of behaviors. In addition to its defense mechanisms, the ego also develops its team of allies to help combat the enemy, just as nations do in wars. The alliances, formed with individuals who agree with your viewpoint, are usually based on the bond against a common enemy. The enemy could be a situation, a person, or a group of people.

In the workplace, I have seen people who do not even like each other come together when it supports their contempt for the adversary. They feel the power in numbers and believe they are fortified by having others in their camp. Having allies helps reinforce the artificial power of the group, which is battling a common opposition. But this group is operating from fear disguised as teamwork. Cronyism in government and the workplace is an example of egotistical alliances based on meeting the needs of those in the group.

Conflicts and battles resulting from the chain of actions and reactions to the perceived threat from one another can grow to horrendous proportions. With large groups it becomes unwieldy and the intensity can be overwhelming to those participating in the clash. When nations see each other as enemies, war is often the deplorable result.

So who is your enemy in your workplace?

The irony of the drama around the enemy is different people view different "others" as the enemy. The ego creates the rival, based on its point of view. Who you deem worthy to be your opponent is the one who holds the greatest threat to you and your personal security. If the person whom you view as a danger is in a higher position than you in the workplace, the intimidation will seem more intense because of his or her perceived power. But even then, you can learn to deal with the fear and have an authentic conversation if you understand the dynamics. In my work with various companies, it is always so clearly evident how each individual is the star in his or her personal drama and the enemy is cast by the individual.

For example, several people may tell me a particular person is the source of the problem in one department or at a certain level. But several more have an opposite perspective or at least do not share the same enemy. Then I talk to someone in the accounting department, for example, and he is oblivious to the names mentioned by the others, but is certain the real enemy is another accountant by whom he feels most threatened.

If people weren't so terribly miserable, these dramas would be almost laughable because the enemy is so clearly an illusionary creation, all based on viewpoint and perception. Human beings feel separated from their spiritual source and they see themselves as separate from each other as well.

The creation of enemies is the result of personal fears being projected outwardly, assigning the part of antagonist to the one who could do the most damage in your own personal drama. We see ourselves in a battle between "them" and "us." It is a delusion but it seems real to us.

The ludicrousness of this belief of separateness from our fellow human beings and the resulting creation of the enemy is most clearly illustrated in examples from our recent world history. Russia was considered an enemy of the United States, and then was suddenly recast and was no longer the enemy after decades of the Cold War.

When I was twenty years old, I traveled through Europe and we stayed a few days in Germany with a relative of one of my traveling companions.

He had been a German Panzer officer. As I mentioned earlier, my father was a World War II B-17 fighter pilot and was shot down on a mission over Berlin. After parachuting out, he was captured and placed in the prison camp Stalag Luft 1. He was held captive as a POW for nine months.

He was six feet tall and weighed 185 lbs. when he was captured. He was twenty-seven years old and a 2nd Lieutenant in the United States Army Air Force, proudly serving his country. During his imprisonment he lost 70 pounds. His feet were frozen, and he lived with lice and horrible, unsanitary conditions, and dealt with near starvation.

Now here I was staying at the home of the enemy. This man was a wonderful person with a lovely family. As we talked one evening we both saw the tragedy and unbelievable insanity of war, as we realized that during the war he and my father would have killed each other if they'd had the chance and did kill each other's countrymen. And now, I was his house guest. What changed?

When are we going to see our oneness with our fellow brothers and sisters on this planet and stop the wars and fighting? This is a key question:

"How can we have compassion for people across the globe and bring about world peace if we do not have compassion and honor for the people we see every day—our families, friends, and co-workers?"

FIGHT OR FLIGHT

When a human being feels threatened, the instinctive response of "fight or flight" is often triggered. Since the ego cannot bear to have an assault on its thought system, it must react swiftly and without delay.

In battle, the troops retreat when the enemy is too strong; they wave the flag of surrender. Animals will fight unless they see the opponent is too fierce to overcome and then they retreat. This fight-or-flight syndrome is universal.

However, in the drama of the ego, the retreat has become a way to avoid facing the fears of the ego. Retreat can come in the form of refusing to have further conversations, an impasse. It can include shutting oneself off in a closed office. Sometimes one even leaves the current workplace for a better opportunity. However, if the lesson or occasion presented is not used for learning, the drama will follow. So you may just leave a situation, not even consciously knowing it is fear that's driving you away.

The ego's plan is to protect our image, save face, and keep anxiety below the surface, where it does not have to be acknowledged. Denial and repression are such automatic and powerful tools, we are not even aware we are using them.

Lyle was a fairly new manager in a company that was aggressively growing and expanding its customer base. There was often a lot of competition among the managers and departments, and each leader's compensation was based on their incoming revenues. This competitive environment did not help build collaboration or bring management together to work as a team.

Lyle was feeling pressure to build his department, so he became passively combative with the other managers. He tried to assert his weight in decisions he felt helped his position in the firm. He was very skilled in making articulate arguments, and he usually was able to put others down with a disguised sarcastic remark carrying a zinger for the recipient.

What other managers and employees didn't know was Lyle was operating from fear. His passive attacks were followed by retreats. One way he retreated was that when he was in a confrontation in which he started to feel threatened, he would say to his opponent, "Well, I'm not going to argue with you."

This left the other person feeling shut down because saying anything in response would be confirming that this was an argument. Lyle would then leave the conversation, close his office door, and be relieved he didn't have to receive any more attacks. His door was closed most of the time and his shut-out mode kept people away unless he chose to come back into the group. This passive attack, followed by a retreat, was unknowingly causing Lyle more harm than safety.

Other forms of retreat, such as silent treatments or pouting, occur in various environments. These scenes sometimes remind me of children in the sand box, throwing sand, hitting each other with shovels and pails, and then finally retreating into the corner. "I'll take my toys and leave," says the ego.

Wendie was an articulate, optimistic woman who had a relationship with a man she cared very much for. Because of the intensity of the relationship, they would unknowingly bring up each other's issues, becoming much like a mirror for each other. It was disappointing to her that they could not seem to break through to direct communication. Whenever the conversation brought up his hidden fears, his response was, "Oh, ple-e-ease. Don't go there." He would then shut down and refuse further conversations.

He described to her how he and his former wife had similar conversations that resulted in arguments, and he wasn't going to ever do it again. "You sound like Mary Ann!" he told her. This was his passive attack on her—casting her in the role of the ex-wife, also known as the enemy. He wouldn't play if the dialogue didn't fit his script. Her need to be loved and appreciated caused her to try to fix the relationship for a while, so it would continue. Although they had many wonderful times together, he wouldn't allow the block that kept coming up to be penetrated and, she couldn't deal with the rejection. She finally realized she was unwilling to continue in a relationship in which she was cast as the enemy. She couldn't walk on egg shells to fit into his ego's script and avoid opening up his old wounds. He didn't want any conversation outside his rules and the relationship ended.

When you are isolating, fleeing, not speaking to someone, shutting down, or using any form of flight, the question to ask is: "From what am I fleeing?"

It is not that you're fleeing other people whom you perceive as the enemy. You're running from the dread within you—a panic that other people merely trigger with their words or actions. This is where the ego does not want to look, so it places the cause with other people.

When flight or isolation is not chosen as a response to a threat from a perceived enemy, the other reaction is to defend with a fight. The need to defend is the key here.

If you would gently look behind your ego's need to defend, you would begin to discover what is holding you hostage and keeping you in bondage. The moment you feel defensive is the exact second you should look within for the cause. But your ego will not let you.

Defense is the ruling force in the ego's world because to look at what lies beneath the facade would put an end to the ego. It would be liberation.

Defensive reactions occur in varying degrees of intensity, depending on the size of the issue the ego is denying. The facts are: the more heated the response, the deeper the pain and the bigger the defense, the greater the fear. A strong wall is needed to protect a false belief system. For example, rage is covering an enormous fear even though it may appear powerful.

Whether you are choosing fight or flight in a confrontation with an enemy, you are still being driven by the ego. Within you is something you have concealed from yourself, and you believe attacking or fleeing will keep you from having to look at it.

The key to unlocking the door to this self-imprisonment is knowing that the fear is already inside of you. It is lying within, like a serpent, waiting to attack at the slightest provocation. A smart little boy I know said, "Mommy, ghosts can't scare you if you're not afraid."

What can you do to help heal yourself and the workplace of this reactionary internal competition? The only remedy is to stop reacting, attacking, defending, blaming, and fearing to look at your own wound. Who is the source of pain? Why do you allow the attack, and most of all, why do you believe them?

Pain and suffering are not the results of the actual problems, they are symptoms of resistance. The remedy is to face it squarely, revealing what needs to be healed and resolved.

Staying with the pain, not running away, and allowing it to arise so it can be released is the only way you will discover deliverance. As you allow the pain to be felt, you will gradually have memories of other painful experiences. This is your opportunity to witness to yourself how you received these ideas and descriptions of yourself and how these fears have become you!

Discovering your true self, your beautiful self, is difficult to do when you have incorrect beliefs about yourself blocking your experience of joy. Clearing out the fictitious thoughts requires the willingness to stay with your emotional pain long enough to release it. This courageous act will strengthen your inner core of authentic power, for you will be facing your greatest fear. It only takes going to the source of pain, briefly. You do not have to replay this scene of emotional suffering in your physical world again. Allow the pain that has been hurting you for years to now be the door to your release. It can only be done by you, on your own journey to the source of the lies about yourself.

The truth is we are glorious beyond our own belief—all these little beliefs we have created are nothing but shadowy veils. These veils of protection keep us from being fully alive and joyous by filtering the light and shrouding us from seeing our true selves.

GUILT AND SHAME

Understanding what we are trying to hide leads to acceptance. There is a hidden core belief beneath the surface that is self-defacing and disgraceful. Your ego believes there is something so reprehensible about you that it is unacceptable and unbearable to look upon.

Why do people give up their energy and power when an organizational environment is dysfunctional? The truth is our fear of punitive action from those in authority causes most of us to deny our own emotions and follow the direction of those with the perceived power. This stems from unconscious and often buried childhood emotional experiences of being scolded by a teacher or another older authority, such as a parent. These memories have created in us conditioned responses to those who seem to be in charge, whether it is a boss, the corporate office, or leaders in government.

This fear of authority can be released if you understand the source. If you know what it is by facing the troubling emotion, you bring illumination and clarity. You discover its very origin and looking upon it sets you free. The new-found freedom ends your need for the defenses, plots, and battles your ego thrives on. You release the stranglehold grip of the ego from your soul.

But your ego does not want you to be free.

The peace you would experience from ending this intense battle would be so profound you would be changed forever. A new, light energy would flow in, replacing the frenetic and frantic action stirred up by the ego.

You would be filled with a soft and exquisite serenity. The thrashing and turbulent waves of emotion would give way to the gentle lapping of calm waters. The cloudy storm would subside, and the sun would come shining forth upon still waters. Literally, the difference would be that amazing.

Who would not choose this beauty and tranquility of spirit over the chaos and uncertainty of the ego?

The ego has you so baffled and disconnected from your true source. You believe its incessant direction, so you rarely question if there is another way to see things.

ADDICTIONS

When the ego fails to keep this dissatisfaction and shame buried deeply enough, you become very anxious. It feels to you like a general sense of undefined apprehension and disguised nervousness. Some people may experience anxiety attacks.

When this internal discontent is at its worst, the ego may attempt other methods besides fight or flight.

The goal of the ego is to keep you numb and distracted. The mental jockeying and play acting is so draining, we must seek ways to stop the mental chatter and get away from the restless mind. If the methods already employed—such as defense, flight, alliances, gossip, sabotaging, grandiosity, intimidation, blaming, being the martyr, and manipulation—are not keeping you anesthetized, the ego will seek other options.

For example, you may try to render yourself numb with self-medication in the form of alcohol, drugs, food, and other addictions. Even anti-depressants prescribed by physicians keep the ego from fully experiencing your pain by reducing the uneasiness and self-recrimination. These methods, therefore, help the ego avoid its suffering by changing or altering the mood or state of mind. Sometimes it is necessary for short periods, but when it continues the drugs often become addictive.

There are a variety of other temporary fixes or mood-elevating methods that are also capable of becoming addictions. These include gambling, eating, sex, shopping, working, or any frenzied activity that gives you a high or mind-elevating, temporary pleasure. It helps one escape. Many people report that they can literally feel themselves go unconscious when they engage in emotional eating—barely aware of what or how much they are eating.

However, the ego becomes insensitive to the effect and begins to need more and more of the drug of choice to keep dissatisfaction in check so the high can continue. The frequency, intensity, and amount of the drug needed to attain the satisfaction increases, thus escalating the compulsion for the drug or producing the need to replace it with a stronger drug. It is the nature of addictions.

Then at some point, the addiction itself becomes the problem, e.g., alcoholism, drug addiction, eating disorder. The pain becomes unbearable for the self and others. As the compulsion for the drug grows stronger, the lack of self-worth intensifies, leading to feelings of desperation, self-loathing, and fear.

However, this self-inflicted trap can lead to an opportunity of great advancement through a breakthrough in consciousness, if the individual decides to surrender. The obsession for the drug is running the whole show, and the denial is intense.

But when the painful recognition of the addiction in one's self occurs and the individual finally surrenders, healing is then possible. This is the turning point that you see when someone hits rock bottom and chooses spiritual growth through counseling or a support group, such as AA or others.

Liz is one of the most accomplished women I know. She has a successful career and still maintains time to do hundreds of other things. She is a fabulous gourmet cook, putting on great parties at the drop of a hat. She sits on a number of boards and seems to be the head of nearly everything she gets involved in.

Her house is spotless, her gardens are always beautiful, and she seems tireless. Her children are grown, but she spends lots of time with her beautiful grandchildren. She belongs to so many groups and has so many activities that she is rarely home.

It has been only recently Liz has started to notice something is missing in her life. She is so busy being busy she has little time to be introspective or wonder about the actual quality of her life. Liz told me she finally realized she is terribly lonely. She is truly afraid to stop this frenzied activity for fear she will have to face solitude and aloneness.

The attainment of inner peace through being content to be alone is a necessary part of the evolution of the soul. Seeking this busy lifestyle to avoid being in touch with herself and her doubts is exhausting Liz. What she doesn't realize is that being alone frightens her.

Avoiding facing the unknown is causing her deep anxiety and pain. Letting go and confronting the uncertainty will bring her a new calm and acceptance. Until she connects with her inner spirit, her many activities and worthwhile accomplishments will not satisfy her soul. They are external efforts to keep her numb and to substitute for being needed and loved.

Unfortunately, this is not just Liz's story. I know many women like Liz. I also know many men who can't bear to be alone and quiet with themselves. Over-busyness or needing to be with someone at all times is a strategy to distract you from your real opportunity for growth.

The ego will block your journey back to yourself with all kinds of external activities and diversions, but the only way to peace and joy comes from self-reflection.

Liz is already a step ahead of many people by being aware of her addiction to activity to avoid facing herself. She is practicing spending more time alone and is feeling some relief. She is discovering that the resistance to being quiet and alone with herself is more painful than doing it. As she allows herself some silence in her life she is finding a gentle presence of peace, a tranquility and relaxation in place of the former anxiousness.

The ego finds it so difficult to relinquish all these constraints. However, the spirit within can use any pain or circumstance to help you restore yourself to your true identity if you sincerely desire to transcend the prison you are in.

Recognizing and recovering from addiction is a powerful way to spiritual growth and freedom because you have to overcome intense denial surrounding the fear of being exposed. It takes great courage and trust, but the rewards are freedom, peace, and love. And the relief is immeasurable when you discover you are not guilty and you needn't feel shame.

VICTIM OR ENEMY

How do you deal with the enemy in your workplace?

First, it takes courage and a willingness to face the unalterable fact that the enemy is your opponent only based on your casting the person in that role. The ego will fight this vehemently because the ego truly believes the other person is really a threat. Your ego has projected all the blame on the other person and has cast you as the victim.

The situation with which you are struggling is really not the issue. Its only validity is in your ego's purpose: to strengthen or defend itself. Either position stems from fear. Those people whom you believe are causing so much turmoil may not even know they have been cast in the role. Or they may consider you the enemy and think they are the victims!

So the question is: Who is attacking whom?

What appears to be an attack from another is their ego defending them from being in their own role as the victim. You think you are the victim, but so do they. You each assign the other the role of the perpetrator and yourself the role of the victim. How can this be? But this is what is happening with individuals, groups, companies, communities, and nations.

When are you the perpetrator and when are you the perpetrated upon?

Claiming to be the virtuous one is so easy to do. But realizing you are doing it is much more difficult. I was in a large city for one night and one of my former clients lived there. We decided to meet for dinner and catch up. Half way through dinner I started noticing how righteous he was. He was the good guy in all his stories and everyone else was the villain. Whew! When I got back to my hotel and thought, what a self-righteous victim he is!

While relaxing and thinking about this, I suddenly said to myself, "Have I ever been self-righteous?"

"Of, course not," I retorted. Then I thought about it some more.

As I contemplated this, I suddenly had a vivid memory of a client who had canceled a long term consulting contract with me. I had been disappointed and hurt and felt it was unfair. I had done such a good job for them, I told myself. But as I looked at the situation in retrospect and with more honesty, I realized I had been getting tired of working with them and hadn't truly had the motivation I had in the beginning of the engagement. And they really deserved the opportunity to work with someone new and fresh. As I realized that I wasn't a victim at all but had harbored this feeling of being wronged for several years, I sat up in my bed and laughed out loud! What an immense relief to give up this story and see the truth.

Have you ever felt you were unfairly treated? Perhaps you were but, it is also possible you played a part in it—hard to admit, but possible. On a larger scale, I have even seen business leaders turn their clients or customers into the enemy and see themselves as justified for providing service without integrity.

A large insurance company was falsifying reports and turning down claims from the very people who were paying the premiums to keep them in business. They had people within the company forging doctor's names and writing reports that disallowed certain procedures and surgeries so they would not have to pay out the expenses incurred for medical charges.

The company was fearful of a negative cash flow position. This fraudulent denial of claims was a demonstration of frightened egos, accelerating their need to prevail into an offense. The very people they were supposed to protect became the enemy and suffered the consequences.

When it was exposed, the company justified their actions and even at the end the CEO would not acknowledge his responsibility. He saw himself as the victim. He acted amazed that this could have happened to him and didn't believe his company deserved the consequences.

I had a friend who volunteered to help me on an out-of-town project. It was an hour-and-a-half drive and, by the time we would get back, it would be an all-day commitment. I had not requested his help, but he offered and seemed excited to go with me. I was very appreciative and relieved to have his help. Fewer than twenty-four hours before we were supposed to go, when it would be difficult to find someone else, he decided to try to withdraw his offer.

He asked if I really needed his help because he had some other things he would "kinda like to do." I said I really did need him now because it would be too late to get someone new. He sounded irritated but said, rather curtly, he would be there.

In the morning he called again and tried to make a couple more excuses and said he would be late. One part of me felt like a victim and I was tempted to say, "Just forget it." However, on a deeper level, I knew his ego had turned me into the villain and was causing him to do something against his will. I was just holding him to his word.

I told him he was trying to make me the enemy now. I recognized he was hoping to make me feel guilty but it wasn't working. I joked with him and made him laugh, but I did not let him off the hook he had put himself on. The happy ending is he later thanked me for expecting the best from him.

He recognized he had a pattern of making promises in the moment because it made him feel good to offer to help people. Then he would try to back out if something better came along. The way he unconsciously got out of it was to make the other person wrong. His ego believed it would justify his not keeping his word. I refused to play the role, and it forced him to see his own pattern.

THE CLIMAX: FACING THE ENEMY WITHIN

The point arrives in the drama when the main character must face the enemy. The alternative is to continue suffering or to depart. This moment comes when the hero is prepared to take a stand and face what he or she dreads.

Now this can result in the ego attacking or confronting the enemy who is perceived to be the threat. This ultimately leads to another continuing drama which escalates with the same enemy, finding a new rival, or moving to a different stage. Nothing is resolved or learned. The blaming of others for your pain or situations is abdicating responsibility for your own feelings. The problem with doing this is it gives you no out, no road of escape from the pain. It is a terrible place to be because it appears so hopeless to you, which it is not.

Reclaiming your power over yourself, your feelings, and your circumstances allows you to change your mind, to see things differently, and to stop being held hostage by yourself.

If you look behind the image of yourself, you will see your powerful higher self and realize others do not have the authority to harm you, unless you give them the role. As Eleanor Roosevelt said, "No one can make me feel inferior without my consent."

It is important to understand your reaction is not occurring because of what is happening with this person. The enemy in the present circumstance is hooking your ego from a past scene because you have assigned this person a role from your long-ago cast of enemies. It is here the chance occurs to see other people differently—not as figures meant to serve you in a role you gave them, whether friend or foe.

You or the other person have to stop for a moment and see that it is the judgment and subsequent expectation of the other, coming from the ego, that is the cause of the conflict.

But this would require you to step out from behind the face of the ego and to be willing to see you are equally responsible for the basis of the painful battle with the enemy. The automatic and usual tendency of the ego is to simply project it fully onto the other person, rather than looking at the self, making the other person wrong.

What is the way out of this dance of pain and suffering?

Choosing to learn the lessons presented is tantamount to the opportunity for freedom. If we knew this to be true, we would welcome challenges and see they are the portals to joy and freedom.

The only answer is to face your suffering. You will find the way out when you stop resisting the pain and let it fully arise. You can finally see what it is you are afraid of. The ego's path has led to nothing but misery and suffering, blame, and shame. Why not try this new courageous way to deal with the situation?

You start by turning the focus inward to discover what your own doubts are, so you can stop projecting and blaming the other person. The conflicts between you are the very gateways to moving to a higher level in the evolution of your soul and your ability to relate to others without fear.

This effort to recognize your ego's judgments and expectations takes deep concentration. After all, your ego wants you to go back to sleep.

Focus on this task of recognizing the ego's efforts to control things by casting you as the victim. Commit to your own spiritual growth. Your pledge to your inner growth will lead you out of the anguish and suffering and bring about the peace you so desire.

If you would really like to start having different results and find joy in your life, take some quiet time to contemplate and truly comprehend the dynamics in which you are participating. If you can let down the self-protection and look at how you have been reacting, you can then learn a new way to respond coming from your deep self.

Recall a time recently when you felt resistant, irritated, worried, or threatened by someone or some event. Recall it as vividly as you are able to do. And then ask yourself:

- How am I really feeling?
- Am I hurt, mad, indignant, annoyed, outraged, sad, or some other emotion?
- Whatever the feelings are, it is important to allow them to arise and be felt.
- What is my perceived threat with this person?
- What am I afraid this says about me?
- What is my resistance telling me?
- Am I frightened of losing face?
- What am I afraid is going to happen to me?

Secondly, recognize this person is giving you an opportunity to heal yourself from some inner pain lodged in your psyche. This person's presence at work and in your life can lead you to a new freedom and strength if you use it to let go of old fears and the death grip of the ego.

Ask yourself the following:

- When have I felt this way before?
- When have I faced this enemy before?
- What would happen if I expressed my real feelings?
- Which automatic strategy do I follow—fight or flight?

- What is the benefit to me? What is the loss?
- What is my goal—to win or to be at peace?
- Can I see perhaps I am wrong?

The next step is to plan how you can find freedom from this automatic way of reacting, and instead create a new experience. Imagine a similar experience occurring in the future with the same person and the same feelings arising in you. It is important to remember the exact moment of feeling the fight or flight response. But this time do the following:

- Pause and take a deep breath.
- Say to yourself something calming (e.g., I am strong, I am calm, I am authentic).
- Consider these possibilities:
- Perhaps I am wrong here.
- This person is playing out their drama.
- I can choose whether I am cast in this role or not.
- This says nothing about me unless I believe it's true and I react and then it validates it for both of us.
- I am free to express myself honestly but without blame.
- This person is not my enemy (but is telling me something I need to heal in myself or I wouldn't have had this reaction).

Can you see how this would change the interaction and free you up to be true to your inner self and not be a puppet in someone else's drama? How would this response change the outcome? How would you feel? As you see that you have choices in how you respond when you are calm and generating your true energy, your life will change profoundly.

The true victory and finally peace are realized when the ego discovers the only battle is with the self. It is here that an opportunity to bring about a true armistice occurs. For it is at this point that you can choose to recognize you have fully projected the blame and cause of the conflict and your suffering onto someone else. This realization can bring about a true reconciliation of you with your authentic self.

So the challenge is to give up being the victim, give up blaming, give up the envy and fear, and instead place your trust in your inner spirit—your higher self. It is not easy when your ego is in control. But when you begin, the possibilities for freedom for yourself and others are endless.

TRUE ARMISTICE

As you answer these questions, you will gradually take ownership for the feelings you are experiencing. You will make the slow, but powerful, distinction that you alone are responsible for your position.

This is the beginning of independence.

If you have the power to cause the emotions in yourself, then you are also capable of releasing these discomforting thoughts and feelings. The dawning of this profound idea is your means to freedom. Peace resides within you. Only you can allow the negative and usually fearful emotions to enter.

You are bound to have relationships that cause you stress or discomfort in the workplace. The greater the sense of anxiety created when dealing with the individual, the more powerful the opportunity to heal and rebuild the relationship.

The workplace provides time and frequent interactions in which to learn and practice this new way of owning your authentic power and changing the relationship to a higher level. As you progress in this process, you will learn to notice even the slightest moments of uneasiness and learn how to release them before they take hold of you.

It will not be as easy to let go of painful responses and reactions in the intense conflicting relationships. But with time, you will come to know it works in all situations—from the most emotionally turbulent relationships to the slightly stressful ones.

You will learn to uncover the causes for conflict in relationships even if there is no communication or if the person is deceased. The emotion you are holding is not really caused by the other, only by you.

As you can feel the pain underlying the negative emotion and finally identify the origin which is some situation from childhood, you will come to fully realize the current individual is not the root of your anguish. The person is simply a mirror helping you remember the beginning of the thought system you formed as a child to protect yourself.

As you have experiences in the workplace that activate old reactions and cause you to relive emotions of the past, they become opportunities to let the feelings and reactions be disclosed and released. You will also see other people's behavior is not about you, but is a result of their own thought system. The tendency to take it personally is profound, but the truth is: it is not personal. It is part of their drama, as is yours, but most of all, it is not real. As you acknowledge your misery and its self-creation, you will see the other people you previously blamed are not guilty. You can now forgive them and give up the grievances coming from blame. As you give yourself mercy, you give it to others.

Peace comes the moment we stop putting up barriers to it. In the past, there has been little peace. But we can move into the future to a place where love prevails and compassion is the order of the day. We can be part of the evolution and the new presence sweeping our world with lightness and renewal.

We can share this new gentle way of relating with our children, and they can share it with theirs. Children who are given choices in a loving, disciplined way as they make the passage into adulthood will usher in a more peaceful future for all the coming generations.

The ego seeks substitutes for joy outside itself. The attempts are temporary distractions that lead only to needing more from outside the self, rather than to the source of joy, which is within. It is like drinking sweet beverages to satisfy your thirst, only to become thirstier.

Joy is our natural inheritance, our birthright. It is not learned. It cannot be sought after. It cannot be imitated. It emerges when you lift the veil of illusion. The veil of delusion was created by the ego who knows it is not worthy.

Connect with the universal source from which you came. Be a part of all that is, and exist as a witness to the strength and glory of love shining in all its beauty, bathing the world in tenderness, with equality and respect for each and every individual soul. It is your destiny.

PERSONAL RESTORATION PLAN
TO PRACTICE IN YOUR WORKPLACE

1. Begin the practice of facing the enemy by writing down the answers to the questions in this chapter. Then apply the steps including:

- Recognize the moment you felt fight or flight.
- Identify the actual emotions and some of the strategies you used.
- Recall when you first had these feelings.
- Imagine the same encounter only this time doing these steps in your mind:
- Take a deep breath.
- Make a calming statement to yourself.
- Realize these possibilities:
- Perhaps I am wrong.
- It is their drama. I don't have to validate it for either of us.
- I have choices.
- I can express freely without blame
- I am responsible for my own feelings.
- Now visualize the new outcome and how it feels to take your energy back. Feel your inner strength when you respond from your authentic self.
- Write down your discoveries.

2. Use the previous experience to help yourself respond from strength when you encounter a similar disruption in your workplace. Notice your improvement in handling touchy or difficult situations. Write down your experience.

CHAPTER NINE

Leading with Spirit and Compassion

✳   ✳   ✳

STRENGTH OF CHARACTER—GENTLENESS OF HEART

The power to lead is possessed by those who are willing to look within their own hearts. Enlightened leaders operate from strength of character and gentleness of heart. I cannot think of a single great leader, now or in the past, who did not face enormous challenges before they emerged as a significant leader. A life without struggle rarely prepares one to lead or to have the wisdom of a broad vision. The foundation of leadership is respect and honor for those one leads, coming from humility and equality.

Nelson Mandela was the first president of South Africa elected in a democratic election. He was elected after he served a twenty-seven-year imprisonment for his role as a civil rights leader. He stood for freedom and helped end apartheid. Bill Clinton said it was Nelson Mandela who taught him about forgiveness.

Clinton said he asked Mandela if he hated the guards who had held him captive for so long. Mandela told Clinton that he was briefly angry. But as he walked out of the prison for the last time he said to himself, "They had me for twenty-seven years. If I still hated them when I went through the door, they still had me." He said, "I wanted to be free." What an incredible illustration of the power of letting go of a grievance—even one that would seem so strongly justified. Nelson Mandela endured his extended captivity but came back to lead his country, to win a Nobel Peace Prize and to inspire other world leaders.

Looking at other great leaders who have made sweeping changes in the course of history, it is clear they all courageously dealt with difficult obstacles and circumstances to become great leaders. The courage of a great leader comes from giving up the fearful voice of the ego and relying on their inner core of strength. Without the recognition of the voice of the ego, you will continue to star in your melodrama and tragedy. You will be unable to make a significant difference in the lives of others because you will not be a conduit for the powerful energy force on which great leaders rely.

False pride has a need to keep reinforcing its image and blocks the source of true wisdom. When you are pretending, it is impossible to express the kind of qualities enlightened leaders possess. Moment to moment, you must choose whether to align yourself with the pride of the ego or the authenticity of the spirit.

Many leadership development courses teach business people how to behave and act like a leader. Most of these programs are unknowingly methods to train the ego to become an even better actor. Leadership is not changing your behavior by finding new ways to act. Enlightened leadership is an internal transformation that allows vision, character, and clarity to arise.

Students of these courses are not expressing the spirit within—their true inner greatness. The facade of artificial leaders is recognized by those they lead even though they have no authority to do anything about it. Pretending to be a good leader does not create synergism, respect, or collaboration needed to accomplish the goals of the organization.

I recently heard a former government leader being interviewed on a national TV show. He claimed it was the job of government to "convince the American people" of his beliefs and ideas. He didn't seem to understand that in a democracy the leadership represents the desires of the people, not the other way around. Lincoln's words from the Gettysburg Address flashed through my mind: "That this nation, under God, shall have a new birth of freedom—and that government of the people, by the people, for the people, shall not perish from the earth."

Enlightened leaders lead with trust and compassion. They pronounce truth, point the way, inspire wounded souls, and lift others from pain and suffering, whether it is in a workplace or a country. These great leaders inspire passion and incite energy to move forward. The tumbling of false leaders in today's business and government is testimony to the lack of authentic power of greedy, ego-driven leadership. It is leaving in its wake a field of new opportunity for resurrection and new potential in our world.

The current inflexible business structure, which has been in control for two hundred years, needs to change dramatically. As we confront this obsolete model of business we can begin to disconnect the lines of support. As the underpinnings of the old system weaken, the current leadership will lose its stranglehold on business and government and there will be a redistribution of power. Leaders and businesses from the old models have started and will continue to collapse. New, enlightened leaders will emerge from the ashes.

Enlightened leaders are not concerned with their own image and do not need to appear superior. They do not require props to hold them up, palaces to live in and empires to rule. Their humility is a hallmark of their authenticity. Enlightened leaders know they are not the identity the role requires; the position is simply a vehicle to allow them to serve. They see everyone as equal, regardless of their role.

Jim is a general in the Air National Guard as well as a partner with a large law firm. He is a leader in both the military and the private sector. His experiences and understanding from working with hundreds of people have led to his enlightened leadership.

He intuitively knows that regardless of their rank in the military or their status in private industry, people are all the same. He does not place himself above or below others and in fact recognizes everyone at all levels for their inner spirit.

Being a general comes with many external acknowledgments because of the deference to rank. For example, if he walks into a large room with hundreds of military men and women, they all stand. When he flies into a military base, he is greeted with salutes from everyone, and a staff car awaits his arrival.

Jim says there are a few officers who believe these accolades and military courtesies elevate them above the masses. These few believe their role as an officer is their true identity—an identity they consider superior to others. "They are overcome by their own fumes" is how he describes the facade these individuals want to claim.

In the private sector, Jim honors all others in his law firm on an equal basis. He does not allow office size, position, or gender to be reasons to see people as separate or inferior. He walks his talk and expects others in his firm to treat each other as equals.

Jim does not require personal fame or attention because he is connected to his inner authentic self. Anyone who knows Jim recognizes this wonderful quality in him. He is the kind of person people like to be around, and because of his sincere approach to life and others he is held in high esteem. He does not seek this recognition. He is a man who operates from integrity and always expresses himself with honesty.

Yet even Jim, with all his inner confidence and experience, has had those subtle thoughts from the ego slip into his dialogue.

"I wonder if I have one too many stars or stripes," he has asked himself. "I wonder if I'm not operating several levels above my competency."

If someone operating at the level Jim is can momentarily feel self-doubt, it is easy to understand how the ego-driven leader who has no inner power must be operating from massive fear.

I asked Jim how it is he doesn't get caught up in the two powerful roles he plays on different stages. Jim thanks his wife for keeping grounded and not taking it all too seriously. For example, on one occasion she picked him up from the airport when he returned from playing one of his dignitary roles and reminded him he'd forgotten to take out the garbage.

I cannot stress too much the intense dilemma that occurs as you continue to challenge your ego. Looking behind the ego's mask is a huge step that demands surrender of the ego's need for the external. Few pass this test easily, and it is given to you over and over again, in many different scenes and episodes. The answer is to always put yourself in the hot seat—not someone else.

Invoke your inner spirit to help you see what the lesson is for you in any situation that brings up the slightest anxiety, irritation, or emotion. The ego almost always finds this difficult because it automatically wants to blame an outside source. Only as your belief and trust in your inner authentic self grows stronger can you allow yourself to know you are responsible for all your emotions. Every time you refuse to be ruled by your ego, a new, lighter energy will infuse you with happiness, relief, and true inner confidence born of the spirit.

DEMONSTRATION IN THE WORKPLACE

Practicing the new insights as situations occur in the workplace is essential. Your new understanding will not last if you don't demonstrate it to yourself through right action. Much like a dream, which upon waking up is so clear but then slips into the unconscious mind and is lost, your new learning will evaporate if you don't practice it with others.

Demonstrating to oneself and others takes persistence and commitment. You are like a baby beginning to take his first steps. Picture the child, standing and tottering, falling and getting up again. He continues getting up, tottering, and falling. But the steps begin to get steadier, and the child grows in confidence. The child never gives up but delights in his progress as he steadily becomes proficient.

Insights not practiced or demonstrated are useless. Reading and studying for the sake of accumulating wisdom will result only in a person who talks a good story but doesn't walk his talk.

Continue recognizing the opportunities when your ego is engaged. Take a moment to remind yourself to breathe, to be calm, to allow feelings to arise and know you can respond honestly when you are calm and non-resistant. These are the occasions that give you the chance to practice your insights.

Many times it is still difficult to resist the ego's immediate desire to react.

Bring yourself to the present situation and remember you do not need to replay the past. Feel the quietness you are able to bring to yourself. You are waking up from the unconscious belief that this is reality.

If the ego is still unrelenting, remind yourself this is not about the other person—this is about you. Repressing, denying, or rejecting the feelings keeps them under the surface and holds you hostage to your ego. Identifying the source and then releasing it will lead to freedom.

When you do this you begin to embody the principles in this book. You will live your life fully and be filled with grace. It is your destiny to awaken to your inner greatness. As your awareness increases and you become in alignment with your spirit, you are a paragon of truth for others.

Here are the stark contrasts of living through your ego versus choosing the path of the inner spirit:

Ego (Fear)	Spirit (Love)
Defends	Is non-resistant and relaxed
Attempts to be superior	Accepts everyone as they are
Controls outcomes and other people	Trusts
Gossips	Expresses freely
Blames and attacks	Is responsible
Needs to be right	Can say I am wrong
Creates enemies	Extends love to everyone
Judges others	Sees everyone as equal
Holds grievances	Practices forgiveness

Ego (Fear)	Spirit (Love)
Is a victim or martyr	Is responsible for own feelings
Is cocky and arrogant	Possesses humility
Is self-righteous	Has compassion for others
Wants admiration	Draws respect and honor
Wants the first and last word.	Is a deep listener
Is anxious and nervous	Is tranquil and relaxed
Uses addictions to stay numb or get high	Feels inner joy and contentment
Is incongruent and conflicted	Is focused and clear
Complains	Is satisfied
Lacks self-worth	Has inner security
Needs external validation	Relies on internal, eternal, unchanging spirit

I would also like to reemphasize that the ego is not bad. We simply give it too much power. We need our ego to live in this world, but we must challenge it when it is running the show. I compare the ego to a passenger in our car. We do not let it drive, but it is helpful on the journey. Sometimes it can sit right up in the front seat with us and at times it must ride in the back seat. I have even had times where it was necessary to lock my ego in the trunk.

My friend Pat, who is working very diligently on her path of evolution, said there are times she would like to "kick her ego to the curb." But then, she realized she would have no personality at all.

It is a fine line as you travel on your spiritual assignment. Be gentle with your ego as you would be to a little child. It is, after all, operating from the past when you were a little child.

But you do need to repeatedly challenge it and its belief system with the right questions. The questions that help you choose spirit over ego always direct you back to yourself.

LEADERSHIP IS NOT FOR PERSONAL GAIN

Many employees report that those in upper management are seeking financial gain and personal glory. They treat employees as the method to bring that about. Elaborate schemes to protect the wealth of the dominant few have made the business system so complex, with many layers of protection.

True leaders do not see others as stepping-stones to their own personal empire or platform. An enlightened leader honors the freedoms and rights of others and leads with spirit and compassion. Great leaders understand the intrinsic rewards of operating from integrity. Greedy leaders who are tumbling from their positions in the current market exemplify the attitudes of ego-driven leaders.

Tower Perrin's 2005 survey of 5,424 employees in the U.S. health care found that, most disturbingly for health care institutions, health care workers do not have confidence in senior management. Only 43 percent say senior management is sincerely interested in employee well-being, the number one driver of health care employee engagement. What's more, 37 percent say senior management sees them as just another part of the organization to be managed, and 15 percent say senior management treats them as if they don't matter. Further, only 40 percent believe senior management communicates honestly and openly.

The lack of trust and confidence is occurring in business, organizations, and the government at an epidemic level. Restoring faith by leaders operating from integrity and deep convictions is the only solution and it starts with each one of us.

T. J. Meenach was my grandfather. He was one of the finest men I ever knew and he was a wonderful example of an enlightened leader. He served as president of the local park board and was a leader in the development of the park systems in the city where I grew up. He worked tirelessly, and many beautiful projects were created for the enjoyment of generations to come because of his efforts. He was a civic leader but also served briefly in the state legislature. He was disturbed, even during those times, at the compromises being made as businesses lobbied to influence state law.

He chose to work on city issues where he felt he could make a difference. He was also a very successful realtor but never had need for personal recognition. He worked quietly behind the scenes in the humanitarian actions he performed. Because he didn't seek after fame or material acquisitions, he was very financially stable. When the depression hit, he was one of the few not threatened by it.

What he did do was to confidentially help many families who were struggling during that time. He loaned money and gave many people the lifeline they needed to survive. Even today, prominent people whom I meet tell me their family business would not be here today were it not for my grandfather.

He worked toward the betterment of the community and taught strong values to his own children. My mother, the youngest of four, recalls the Christmas she begged for a new red bicycle. All her friends were asking for new bikes and their families were less prosperous.

Christmas morning arrived and there next to the tree stood her older brother's used bike, hand-painted red. We laugh at the story because he could have easily afforded the bike, and many of my mother's friends did, indeed, get shiny new bicycles that year. And it was not that he was not generous because he was. He came forth on many occasions to help his children, but he also taught them values and honest virtues. My mother learned at a very young age that keeping up with neighbors was not important. Her bike worked just fine.

He died when I was fifteen years old, but he left a memorable legacy for all of us. Although he never sought personal fame, after his death a prominent bridge and street were named after him. Before moving to another city, I had the gratification of working on some volunteer civic projects and often felt his presence when I worked with others carrying on what he started many years earlier.

GROUP WILL—TEAMWORK

Group will is the powerful and dynamic force that results from the alignment of individuals within a group toward a common purpose. Group will is available when the leader is the conduit for energy and creativity flowing from the group.

Group will is the force cutting through fear and obstacles to reach a common vision with the energy and creativity to accomplish it. It is so powerful it attracts the right people, circumstances, and events needed to achieve the goal.

It is through group will that those extraordinary accomplishments occur. When people are drawn together for a significant purpose, they become realigned and united. Group will is a powerful force elevating all the participants and their vision to previously unattainable levels. The synergism and synchronicity resulting from a united group seem almost magical, as if unseen forces are at work. A sense of camaraderie, collaboration, and respect are the basis of the relationships and together they reach heights no one could achieve separately.

In a compassionate culture, projects are assumed with enthusiasm, based on the natural desire to create, innovate, and improve. People working in groups of shared respect and responsibility have a greater sense of belonging and a stronger desire to reach common, beneficial goals. Positive relationships and friendships ensure the involvement and reinforcement for innovative group processes.

Cooperation is the result of respect and honor for one another and elevates performance. Conversely, internal competition within organizations depletes the energy and exhausts the individuals. Fearful environments do not promote friendships and instead cause suspicion, paranoia, rivalry, and insecurity. Working in a fear-based culture not only impacts work performance but also blocks teamwork and cooperation.

Many leaders employ individuals to meet the goals of the company; unfortunately the goal is accomplished through coercion and suppression. People are not productive under this structure and few can withstand the criticism coming from fear-based management. Applying pressure to those who are working well restrains their enthusiasm, eventually crushes their desire to do well, and distracts them from the actual goals of the company.

In these uncertain times, enlightened leaders are needed more than ever before. Leaders who can inspire others to work to their full potential, within teams of honor and respect, will reach levels of success and innovation otherwise unattainable. As a leader or manager, you can make the most significant difference in your organization by creating an environment of trust and compassion, rather than fear and insecurity. Leaders who understand the concepts of mutual engagement and group will can motivate others to the highest levels of performance.

Throughout history leaders have inspired group will among thousands and even millions of people. The desire for change is the most powerful reason for people to come together. Having a goal that benefits and rewards everyone causes unified action and commitment. This kind of teamwork is what companies are trying to build but they are missing the core elements. Too often, they offer only platitudes and empty slogans that do not inspire people.

An obvious characteristic of a group, who is truly practicing teamwork and availing themselves of the power of group will, is the lack of scrambling for personal gain and recognition. Individuals acknowledge each other for their contributions and accomplishments. People are happy to see each other succeed and they are appreciative of each other's efforts.

Using a simple metaphor, working in alignment feels something like this. I was new to an aerobic class where all the other participants were familiar with the dance steps. It was very uncomfortable as I struggled and kept taking steps that were not in alignment with the group. With some practice, I learned the steps and was able to be in rhythm with the others. I felt my energy rise and my enjoyment increase as our steps as a group were synchronized to the beat of the music. Instead of feeling drained, I was invigorated!

Open and trusting communication is essential in the group process and the leader must provide this coherent atmosphere. Learning to recognize when others are in their ego, especially if they are being defensive, is a crucial capability when guiding a group. Not allowing their ego to hook you or others is an ability that comes only from challenging your own ego.

One thing I have noticed in real teamwork is that the word *we* is used in most situations. The frequent use of words such as *I* and *my* is usually a red flag that egos reign instead of the spirit of the team—the esprit de corps.

I have heard CEOs who claim to be benevolent and team-oriented use language like "my company," "my outlying property," "my" this or that. They are unaware their language betrays their ego's need to build a personal empire. They don't understand how setting a goal that rewards more than the leaders and their personal agendas is what drives a real team effort. The deep inner satisfaction of true teamwork that elevates everyone is absent.

I had an occasion to visit Chad Little and his race car team in Charlotte, North Carolina. I didn't know much about NASCAR racing, but I always thought it was a one-person sport—the driver. I learned on this trip that was not the case at all.

Every person who was part of the team used the word *we* when referring to the actual race. "We won third place last week." "We are racing in Darlington next week." Whether you worked on the engine, changed the tires, or drove the race car, you were all a part of the team. Only the driver was given the public recognition, but nobody cared. They were all part of the team.

FOCUSED LISTENING

Most of the focus of this book has been understanding yourself. It is also important to know how we can help others who may be operating from the ego, especially in the workplace. Assisting others in taking down their barriers can help open the free flow of communication. Your effort to help others in your workplace, your family, and other arenas contributes to the consciousness of everyone.

How do you deal with someone individually or in the group who is having difficulties, who is operating from the ego or using defense mechanisms?

Asking the right questions is the best thing you can do. Making assumptions is what we do most often. Talk to someone who is stuck in the ego in a voice of gentleness, as though they are little children, because at that moment they are.

Your gentleness can bring down walls and help them stop feeling that they must defend or resist something. The emotion that they are experiencing is inside them and not really caused by others. Seeing the spirit in others also requires not validating their ego when it shows up. They are in fear but do not know it.

Recognizing the spiritual essence in other people is done by recognizing that their egos are not who they are. With focused or deep listening, you can begin to hear what the other is really saying, looking past the flares of self-protection and warnings not to come too close.

This can be especially affective at times when the other person is acting out an intense emotional reaction. It is important here to give feedback recognizing their inner essence, not the ego's identity. Although it is difficult to not get hooked, focused listening even in the face of someone who is angry can help the other person wind down and become calmer. Your focus on their sanity rather than their insanity can reduce their rage.

With practice, you will become better at deep or focused listening. It is more complicated when the other person who is steeped in a drama or defensive posture is in a higher position in the company. I have seen powerful adults throw temper tantrums, slam doors, growl at people, or look like they are going to explode. None of these behaviors are coming from authenticity but they can be intimidating. It takes even more concentration so your own ego is not provoked. But the most obvious conclusion, when you are present, calm and aware, is that they are acting out from the fearful child within them.

When we give power to another's ego belief system, it can control us, but only until we recognize its insanity. That is really all there is to it. It takes only a moment to suddenly see clearly and then it is not long before that is the only way you see. This is true restoration, the true integration of yourself with your authentic, spiritual self. And someday, everyone will see the ridiculousness and insanity of the massive game of the ego. That is why A Course in Miracles says the world will end in laughter.

Practicing inner serenity during intimidating or fearful situations created by egos in the work force will help you hear the fear in the other's drama. This may sound impossible, but if someone is really acting out, it can help if you gently ask questions, as one would when speaking to a tiny little child. It will help the other feel understood and accepted and at that moment you are talking to the child within. When the other feels acceptance, the barricade of fear can come down more easily and disarmament is possible.

The ego has been in charge for a long time. It goes unchallenged because we believe it is who we are. We have been responding to our own and others' egos for so long, it has become automatic. We are conditioned so deeply, both individually and collectively that we are almost constantly living in ego drama. So committing to inner tranquility, especially when those around us are not, is crucial. It takes discernment and patience as you learn this new practice of remaining authentic and listening with deep presence. Developing the quality of focused listening will help you free others to express themselves, but it will also free yourself as well. This is a basic and vital step in becoming an enlightened leader.

Disengaging from the ego conversations and dramas is the only way you will be liberated. It requires the following:

- Feeling the quiet centeredness and inner serenity of being present. This quietness allows you to feel your inner spirit and keeps you from being aggravated by the ego's drama.
- Noticing conflicting thoughts and running judgments and letting them go. They aren't true.
- Recognizing the inner spiritual essence of the other. This allows you to see past the words and actions of the ego.
- Deep listening and acceptance, so the barriers can start to come down.
- Gently asking questions that will reveal the true needs of the other.
- Asking how you can be helpful.
- Acknowledging and giving feedback to their real self, not the ego.

Wounded people cannot be productive and creative, or reach their full potential. The workplace needs healing. Like a giant machine, it cannot run with faulty parts. The machine will work with integrity only when the parts are whole and complete. Creating an environment for restoring individuals in the workplace to their true identities expands the potential of individuals and the company as a whole.

The tidal wave of escalating events occurring in the business community and the world today needs to be challenged. Countermeasures need to be taken. Toxic environments need a solution and poisonous ideas need an antidote. You can be the remedy. The process of unhooking from the intertwined, complex web of chain reactions will help unwind and detangle the confusion. It is most successful when the leaders become aware of their own misunderstandings and initiate the steps, but anyone can begin to find their own inner peace, whether they are the official leader or not.

It starts with the seeds of recognition that you are more than your ego. A growing sense within you will build, causing your ego to diminish. Every time you give up assigning the role of the enemy to anyone else, your own inner personal power grows. The more you stop your frenzied schedule to just be aware of the present moment and your inner sense of who you are, the more your authentic power expands.

As your authentic power grows and you are restored to your true identity, you will be able to help restore others to theirs as well. We each add to the collective consciousness of our workplace, and gradually this will restore the atmosphere to one of trust, respect, honor, and compassion. In this environment, people will thrive and companies will exceed their goals for success. Prejudices and past discriminations can be put aside. And like the sunshine, the light and energy of love can shine equally on everyone.

Janice is the owner of a very successful restaurant in the downtown business district of a city in the Pacific Northwest. She is in her mid-forties and has owned her popular Italian restaurant for ten years. She had no formal education and spent much of her early adult years as a waitress.

The mother of five children and a very energetic and loving person, she knew she wanted to do more than work as a waitress. She studied and became a licensed stockbroker, but that didn't fulfill her passion. She found herself feeling intense pressure to succeed, and didn't feel the joy of her own creativity.

Janice always had a connection to her inner spirit. She calls it "the light." Ten years ago she heard about a restaurant that was not doing very well and was for sale. She offered the owners half of what they wanted and they took the offer. She somehow managed to gather the money, mostly on a wing and a prayer.

Today her wonderful little Italian restaurant and bar are always busy with people from the nearby businesses as well as from all over town. It isn't just because the food is good, although it is. And isn't just because the atmosphere is very cozy, with overstuffed chairs, wicker furniture, and a variety of antique pieces.

Going to Janice's restaurant just feels good. It seems to have its own personality. Whenever I mention going there to my associates, they always agree they simply love it. It exudes warmth and old-world charm. People like to go there year round.

What is the secret to her success?

Janice said it has to do with light. She believes the restaurant is an entity—it is a whole energy consciousness made up of the people who work there. And if anyone isn't feeling a part of the light—if they are in darkness—she gives them more light.

As the leader, she is responsible for sharing her light and helping them all be a part of it. They return it to her and each other, working as a team.

She compares it to all the employees being in the same boat. Why would you not want to do everything to make sure everyone in your boat is happy and it is on course? She believes each individual is integral to the success of the business. For example, the dishwasher is extremely important because without clean dishes the restaurant couldn't operate. Each person is part of a symphony—each with a different instrument but playing the same tune. If on occasion, someone is so unhappy that the light from the group doesn't seem to help, then they might leave, which is okay too. She doesn't want darkness in her restaurant.

Janice's two sons work for her and do an excellent job. One time she had an employee who was complaining about her sons. This employee was about the same age as her sons. Rather than becoming defensive, she looked at this young man and said to herself, "I think he needs some mothering light. He wants to be a son."

She began shining extra light and attention on him; the complaints stopped. In addition, he started working harder because he felt more of a part of the "family" and had a greater commitment to the team. He became a shining example of what kindness and compassion can do for a person whose ego is feeling insecure or threatened.

Janice intuitively understands the energetic power of synergism and group will. Her restaurant continues to prosper and draws people not only for the delicious aroma of garlic and Italian cuisine, but also for the sense of friendliness and warmth filling the restaurant. This comes from enlightened leadership and her genuine light.

ENERGY AND LIGHT

An enlightened leader has a consciousness that is light and energetic.

Science tells us that we are each an energy system and that everything is energy. How we use our energy is our choice. We are circulating our energy all the time. Where we direct our energy is our own choice. Balanced energy between people is best, whether in a marriage, family, or business. I have watched people sacrifice their own energy, exhaust themselves, give it away, suppress it, or let it explode in anger. Our emotions are waves of energy traveling through us but when blocked they have severe consequences.

Energy can be felt, and our inner guidance is always responding to it. When we are around someone with genuine enthusiasm it lights us up, too. And conversely, have you ever felt the energy drop or change during an interaction with someone? Have you ever had a disappointment that feels like the wind was knocked out of you and you feel your energy drain?

Working in a stressful, controlling, and unhealthy environment is so energy depleting. The energy of the ego leadership radiates down and the dysfunction at the top results in the breakdown of the teams. The agonizing episodes of high drama are very tiring and they cause you to feel heavy and burdened

Humor in the workplace has not only been found to reduce stress but also to increase performance. Laughter releases endorphins that help us feel better, experience less pain, and even reduce blood pressure. This lighter energy spreads throughout the environment, lifting spirits. It is hard to be light, however, if the leadership is not creating an environment of safety, trust, and respect.

Meditation and deep relaxation can help us balance our energy and allow it to flow freely through our bodies. In our relationships with others, the more we have an equal exchange of energy, the better we can work together and accomplish mutual goals. The qualities of trust and compassion in the workplace are the conduits for unleashing the exchange of energy, ideas, and imagination.

The most powerful way to elevate your energy and authentic power is to invoke the divine energy from your source, the power beyond yourself. It doesn't matter whether you are calling forth God, the universe, or nature. Allow yourself to feel the subtle spiritual vibrations flow into you. You can practice most effectively in meditation but you can also receive it at any moment throughout your day. And then you will radiate your positive energy to everyone—much like adding pristine water into a lake. A new, strong infusion of energy coming to this planet is available to everyone who is aware. And as you wake up to the vibrations and light, you can awaken your fellow brothers and sisters.

As we grow in our own spiritual path, our vibrational level becomes lighter. We are a means of expression for an energy emanating joy and acceptance to others. In addition, we feel brighter and more vital. Synchronicity and spontaneity occur frequently and naturally for enlightened leaders because their positive energy attracts others. Their transparency draws people to them, to a vision that represents and honors everyone. The authenticity of true leaders is recognized and experienced, and these leaders are sought after.

JoAnn never planned to be a leader, but it seemed to be her destiny. Her life just unfolded in the direction naturally. She worked in a large bank and through her intelligence, integrity, and ability to make clear decisions she rose through the ranks to the vice- president level. She was later persuaded to go to work for one of the largest companies in her city, where she also rose to the vice-presidential level.

JoAnn, at 5'3", has an angelic face, soft voice, and very kind demeanor. She is not the picture of the power woman one might expect. JoAnn never needed the pseudo-aggressive approach adopted by many women in an attempt to climb the corporate ladder. But then, JoAnn never attempted to rise up through the corporate structure. Her authentic power and ability to contribute to the success of an organization were recognized, however.

One of her former bosses, a respected CEO of another bank, told me JoAnn was one of the finest people he had ever known. He also said to make no mistake about her power, despite her petite stature and gentle acumen. He described her as having an ability to have great insights into things he hadn't even considered and for which he was very grateful.

They had a great team at this company and they interacted freely in the workplace. She walked into his office any time she wanted to talk to him. However, he knew something serious was on her mind when she made an actual appointment with him. A scheduled appointment was a signal for him he better be prepared because she always spoke with very clear intention.

Even if he resisted at first, her ideas or suggestions always ended up being absolutely right, causing him to see something he had not thought of. He was very indebted for her recognition of possible obstacles that hadn't occurred to him.

He recalls she was also more than able to deal with some of the egos in the workplace. One particular person was causing a big drama and trying to exert his pressure and influence on others in a way to fit his personal agenda. He had issued a memo earlier in the day to all the employees that not so subtly put JoAnn in a negative light and made it sound as though she was unfair. Most people were intimidated by this person, but not JoAnn.

The bank president watched her unobtrusively walk over to the man's office door, go in, and close the door behind her. He heard a loud exchange of voices—not yelling, but a very vehement conversation. Then she quietly emerged and went back to work as though nothing had happened. This was not unusual for JoAnn.

The man then came out of his office a little bit later, slightly red-faced, and proceeded to send out another memo, changing the ego-motivated original message to one that was honest. He came to a meeting later that day with an entirely different attitude. JoAnn knew how to speak her mind for the betterment of the organization, she didn't back down, and she took a stand for truth.

Another person who worked with JoAnn as an officer in the company told me she impacted his life in a very positive way. JoAnn told him he was discriminating against her as a female by not listening to her and discounting her in meetings. He was taken aback at first but after trying to deny it, began to slowly recognize she was telling him the truth.

She was the first woman with the courage to challenge his behavior, and though he resisted it at first, her words challenged him to change. He now holds her in great esteem, and after the confrontation she became his best confidante and trusted associate.

JoAnn became chair of the board of the local Chamber of Commerce— only the second woman in the history of the Chamber to be elected to that position. In her many activities with diverse groups, she has a natural gift for helping people move into alignment toward a higher principle.

She has an ability to step back, listen to everyone, and see the bigger picture. From that vantage point, she leads others to move to a higher level. She doesn't hesitate to ask people directly to put aside their personal agendas and seek an answer for the common good of the group. She knows how to ask the right questions to help bring clarity to the group and facilitate open communication. Without fanfare or drama, she deals with issues as they come up, always speaking from her heart.

How did JoAnn learn and develop all these leadership qualities?

I recall her acceptance speech for her chairmanship of the Chamber, given to 1,200 business and community leaders. She was describing the education and training that had prepared her for her career in business and civic affairs.

JoAnn had grown up in a family with five sisters and two brothers. She was the middle child. They were reared by her mother, who taught them responsibility and ethical values. Her mother had three rules:

- Don't whine.
- Don't fight.
- Always tell the truth.

These simple edicts from a hard-working and loving mother were pro-found lessons in living life authentically. These simple words are also the foundation of teamwork and honoring one another—a goal to which businesses and organizations everywhere aspire but rarely attain.

JoAnn is admired and liked by so many people. She never sought per-sonal glory or fame, but she has attained it in her community and region. She has earned the respect of both men and women for her sincere and dedicated leadership. I am honored that she is my friend.

Throughout history we have many examples of great leaders. They have been studied and emulated, analyzed, and worshipped. JoAnn is a quiet leader exemplifying all the qualities to which many aspire.

RODNEY EDWARD GANNON

I would like to put on center stage someone who demonstrated the qual-ities of enlightened leadership and who deeply impacted my life: Rodney Edward Gannon. Mr. Gannon, to those who worked for him, was an amazing man.

I was thirty-five years old when I went to work for a large radiology practice in my city. They had four offices and a radiology practice in the hospital, and they traveled to several outlying regions. I was hired as their marketing director.

There were seven doctors for whom I worked, but I reported most di-rectly to Mr. Gannon, the business manager. I didn't know in the begin-ning of my new job that he would forever change my life. I didn't know he would continue to be a source of inspiration and an example of what is so needed in the workplace today.

Mr. Gannon was a red-haired Catholic Irishman with thirteen children. He was not a big man, maybe 5'9" or 5'10", with a bad back. He often stood up during meetings and leaned against the wall while talking or listening.

He was the most direct man in all his conversations and yet he never seemed to intimidate or offend anyone. He was a straight shooter—take it or leave it. I often watched other men size him u p and look like they were ready to take him on. But Mr. Gannon's genuine hold-back-nothing approach always disarmed them.

When in any kind of negotiations, he would just speak frankly and put everything on the table. He would lean back in his chair and never seemed in a hurry or anxious at all. He had no strategy except to find a solution or agreement that would truly become a winning situation for both parties. He always seemed to ask them just the right question.

Coming from a sales and marketing background, I thought you always had a strategy. I noticed how others always kept an ace in the hole so they could triumph in the interaction. Not Mr. Gannon. And if the other party would start to get even slightly heated, he would lean back in his chair and chuckle in an understanding way, which would help them put down their defenses and come to a resolution.

One of the greatest things Mr. Gannon did for me was to give me his full confidence. He told me to go out and do grand things. He told me I was remarkable and capable, and he wanted me to excel. He said no matter what happened, he would always support me, even if I made a mistake.

"But if you make the same mistake twice," he said, "we'd probably have to talk about that." Still, I would learn from it.

Can you imagine how well I worked under him?

He was truly the wind beneath my wings. I excelled and achieved more than I ever thought possible. It was a wonderful time in which I grew in my own authentic power and inner confidence under his special guidance. I had no fear, and he continued to fan my spark of creativity. He expressed appreciation and always seemed delighted when I achieved new goals. If leaders and managers would convey this attitude and respect for those they lead, they would be amazed at the power and potential in others just waiting to be ignited.

Mr. Gannon was like a warm-hearted wise uncle to me, besides being a great business manager. He would often come and get me, so we could take a walk outside and talk about the business. He would share strategies and ideas for the future, and ask my opinion. I felt valued and included in the direction of the company, which gave me a real sense of contributing in a meaningful way.

One day, as we were waiting for a board meeting to get started, I naively mentioned a bill for a recent x-ray I had had done in one of our offices. I received the bill from our own company and the bill had a mistake on it.

"Let me see that," Mr. Gannon said.

He looked perplexed and the doctors laughed because the bill had such a blatant error on it, especially since I was an employee. I thought nothing more about it.

What I didn't know at the time was that this same error had gone out to over 10,000 patients. It happened because we were in a computer conversion and it turned out to be a big problem that took a lot of sorting out, and much time was wasted on it.

Mr. Gannon called me into his office right after the meeting and asked me why I would do such a thing. I had brought up a mistake for which he was responsible to the doctors and the error made him look stupid. He hadn't even known about it until I passed the bill around at the meeting.

"Why didn't you just come to me?" he asked. "I would never have done something like that to you in front of the doctors."

I was immediately devastated. I had been so ignorant and flippant about this "funny little error," not even thinking about how it affected him. I had been thoughtless, and it was at his expense—at the expense of the man I thought walked on water.

I apologized profusely, begging for forgiveness. He just looked steadily at me and then quietly asked me to leave his office.

For the first time in my career, I felt like breaking down and crying. I went to my office and closed the door. I tried to work, but I felt numb.

I kept reliving it over and over, wondering what I could do to fix things. I thought of sending flowers, writing him a long letter, going back down to his office and saying I was sorry again.

Suddenly, I had a huge shift in my own thinking. I became acutely aware I was not thinking so much about him at all—I was consumed with worry about me. I felt like I had fallen from grace, and I wanted to do something to elevate myself in his eyes once again. I wanted his benevolent light to shine on me again. I wasn't really thinking about him at all. I was concerned about my own image.

This was a startling thought. To put it in the language of this book, I was looking behind the face of my ego. I didn't like what I saw. (We rarely do like to see our ego's schemes for saving face.)

I grew up that day. I learned I didn't have to be the self-created image I liked to believe was me. And I also realized I needed to be authentic and responsible for my actions. I also understood intuitively, I needed to let him be.

I quietly worked in my office, feeling the pain but knowing I would grow through this, too. Then I heard a knock at my door. It was Mr. Gannon.

"Danna, let's take a walk."

He had a serious look on his face, but I was ready to face this conversation. I was remorseful, but also fully accountable for my lack of professionalism.

For once in my life, I completely shut up. I just let him talk. What he said endeared me to him more than words can describe. "Danna, please forgive me."

He asked me to forgive him! He said his reaction was just coming from his pride and his desire to always have a perfect business office and a smooth running organization. He realized my intention was not to embarrass him and was sorry he had gotten upset with me.

Now I could hardly hold the tears back. This great man was asking me to forgive him for what I had caused.

Mr. Gannon's words demonstrated to me, for the first time, how a truly enlightened leader is one who does not operate from false pride or a need to be superior. This wise man could say he was wrong, even though what I had done was good cause for his reaction.

I have never forgotten the lesson from that fateful day. It was an experience that shifted me deeply inside. It was like I had been digging with a shovel to move some land and then a fault in the earth just moved the land effortlessly in one fell swoop. The shift in my consciousness and understanding was that immense.

Mr. Gannon died a few years ago. His thirteen children and wife had the benefit of his loving guidance as a wonderful husband and father. I had his presence for three incredible years. He will remain forever in my heart as someone who not only encouraged me in my own growth, but unknowingly inspired in me the passion to write this book and to speak to thousands of people on how to wake up to the enlightened presence in all of us. I think he is smiling down now, too.

INNER SATISFACTION

Leading others from an open and trusting heart is so necessary in these turbulent and uncertain times.

Giving positive appreciation and recognition is an important way to help motivate others. Dominating and intimidating others will never bring about the levels of creation and success desired by everyone. Countermeasures are necessary to change this dominant style of management and it begins with each of us. The rewards are endless.

Something even deeper happens for us when we come from integrity, truth, and compassion.

It is the internal satisfaction of knowing you are making a difference. It is the inner awareness that you are contributing to the betterment of the world in a meaningful and powerful way. You are witness to universal love when you operate from compassion for others. The fulfillment you receive cannot be given to someone or handed out from another person. It is intrinsic.

My dear friend, Angelo, a brilliant radiologist, calls this "psychic income." We all strive for financial income, but genuine gratification is the inner knowledge that you are helping someone else and you are giving from your full potential endowed to you as a part of humanity.

A radiologist is a doctor's doctor. The primary care physician or specialist deals with the patients directly, and the radiologist usually doesn't even see the patients. Yet his ability to read the images from CTs, MRIs, PET scans, etc. is critical to diagnosing the patient's disease or injury.

This internal knowledge and satisfaction is all the radiologist needs.

The primary physician receives the thanks and appreciation, but the radiologist knows he helped that person without any outward recognition for it. He knows his talent and dedication is improving the health of many people, even if he never sees them. That is psychic income.

That inner essence of expression through working with your passion cannot be given—only experienced. Motivation by fear or motivation by incentives relies on something external to incite action. It will be only a temporary motivation if an underlying, overriding goal is not at the foundation.

The deep satisfaction of enriching the lives of others can only be felt within. As an enlightened leader, you can provide that opportunity for those you lead by creating an environment where people can contribute from their inner, authentic selves.

Seeing the genius in others by recognizing the spirit in them is the highest level of leadership. Indeed, it is the only leadership.

PERSONAL RESTORATION PLAN
TO PRACTICE IN YOUR WORKPLACE

1. Practice focused, deep listening this week while having a conversation with any co-worker, be it a peer, boss, or a direct report; make no distinctions. Be sure to make good eye contact and focus on their words and not your inner conversation.

- Feel the quiet centeredness and inner serenity of being present.
- Recognize the inner spiritual essence of the other. (This allows you to see past the words and actions of the ego.)
- Listen with acceptance, so the walls of the other's ego can start to come down. Treat them as if their words are golden.
- Gently ask questions that will reveal the true needs of the other.
- Ask how you can be helpful.
- Acknowledge you heard and give feedback to the real self, not the ego.
- When it is time for a response, pause and speak with honesty.
- Notice the calmness and the free energy exchange when you truly listen.

2. Pay attention to the energy you feel while in the presence of others. Focus on your own ability to invoke light, positive energy. Then practice sharing it wherever you go. If you are in a meeting, radiate it out and know it will be received on some level. Notice the response of others. Write your experiences in your journal.

CHAPTER TEN

Emancipation

To sin by silence when they should protest
makes cowards of men.

—ABRAHAM LINCOLN

*   *   *

INTEGRATION AND BECOMING WHOLE

Human beings have eternally asked the questions, "Why do I exist, who am I, and why am I here?" Without answers people are floundering. Not knowing one's destiny or purpose, a substitute is created—including a plan to obtain it. Feeling disconnected from our Source, we each develop an identity: someone we can believe in who is worthy of attention and love, someone to be admired who is safe and strong, and most of all, someone we can rely on.

We believe our identities will win respect and security and we unconsciously and sometimes very deliberately devise schemes to gain power, validation, and approval—all entrenching us in the current culture of re-action and counter-reaction. We have become so connected to these false identities that we have forgotten who we really are. Oh, we may go to church, read some books, and even express a faith in God or the Divine, but we have become so deceived by our own story we rarely allow the authentic power of our Source to emerge.

Until one can unravel the drama in his or her own psyche, he or she cannot unwind the intertwined relationships in the workplace or anywhere. What is not inside us cannot be found outside us. The person who unravels this complex web within himself or herself can finally stop replaying the same role and step out of the drama of inter-reacting egos around them. This person can be called a leader.

A leader is not a title and cannot be assigned by an organizational chart or even by an election. An enlightened leader draws from an internal authority of commitment, passion, and integrity and therefore rises above the clamor. That leader is inside you, residing beneath your false image, the self-defined identity. We can no longer suffer in silence. Those politely standing by waiting for someone else to fix the problem are part of the whole imbalance of the workplace environment. It is time to create an extraordinary workplace, and that can only happen when each of one of us has the courage to give up the grip of egoic fear. Your process has led you to this point, filled with opportunities to see reality—it is time to wake up. It is time to be restored to your inner, spiritual greatness.

More people are recognizing that the situation has become chaotic and intolerable for so many. As the workplace continues to heat up, the artificial constructs are breaking down. As the demands increase, the emotional instability and immaturity of each individual is showing up in the workplace. The false role of superiority or nonchalance used to mask unresolved issues, pains, and insecurities collapses when the pressure mounts. The child, the neuroses, and the psyche are all competing for attention. In a world of charlatans, actors, misfits, and massive confusion, staying true to your inner voice requires the faith of Job and the deepest strength of your soul. What voice you pay attention to becomes strengthened. If you find yourself being drawn into the drama, you can know you are listening to the wrong voice.

The power to lead others is possessed by those willing to look within in their own heart.

Until leaders can face their own inner doubts and fear of being over-come, all attempts at leadership will fail in the face of conflict. The masks will fail to protect and the fear will overtake all circumstances. In an at-tempt to protect the self, fearful leaders resort to the strategies they believe carried them through their stories in the past. The false roles will only result in further divisiveness, leading to larger upheavals affecting the emotional security and safety of everyone.

As pressure continues to mount, more and more people are seeking, crying out, for a way out of this confusion. At the same time, greed and corruption are being revealed daily, fracturing rigid systems that held up the previous way of life. These chain reactions are leading to the tumbling of old structures. The plastic, artificial world is collapsing, leaving behind in its wake a brand new field of potential—a new authentic way of life based on love and respect.

As you shift your perception by relying on your inner spirit, you will begin to see the wolves in sheep's clothing and children dressed as pow-erful adults. You will no longer be beguiled or intimidated. When you are awake and in the present, you are able to listen for truth behind the lies and see the spirit residing beneath their countenance. You will experience "the peace that passeth all understanding" and no longer be an object tossed around in the sea of dissension.

You will rediscover that you were born to create, evolve, serve, coop-erate, innovate, inspire, aspire, and love. But when you arrived, the drama on this planet was so believable you thought it was real. The existing cul-ture compelled you to participate and conditioned you to live a limited life of frequent suffering. But the good news is that this is not reality; it just seems like it is. It is really a dream of pain and misunderstanding that is causing you to awaken. The culture of suspicion, fear, and mistrust oc-curring in the workplace is happening throughout the country and the world. Your ability to transcend this illusion is so needed—for you and the entire world. As you remember who you are, you help amass the crit-ical proportion of those who are in alignment with the Source. You, if you so choose, will be a leader in your organization to bring about the shift in which people can be restored to their true selves. An artificial leader has no such power, regardless of the hierarchy or title.

This book and its teachings are consistent with ancient wisdom and philosophies, applied anew. I am describing how these universal truths, which have stood the test of time, still pertain to your workplace today. They are as relevant to today's business environments of individuals in pain as they were in earliest times with previous generations. Sacred books from Eastern and Western religions, ancient philosophies, mythology, literature, and historical passages of great leaders—all contain the truths and wisdom that have been a source of learning for people throughout time.

Through the centuries, there have been many changes in people and how we live. We work differently than people did hundreds of years ago. We look and dress differently. We travel and even talk differently. Technology through the ages has dramatically changed the world. Even the physical environment of our planet has gone through huge transitions. But man's search for meaning and purpose has been consistent throughout time. Human beings' need for love, families, social structure, and interaction has endured even as wars, famine, suffering, and pain have continued through the ages.

Now, here we are today, on the brink of stepping into a new consciousness. We are on a journey out of darkness to a new age for human beings. I believe the workplace stage is a vast terrain whose transformation to one of trust and compassion will impact the entire world. Rebuilding relationships where most individuals spend the majority of their waking hours will significantly shift the planet. You, as an enlightened leader, will lead others out of the dark, murky waters of human dissension into a bright and sparkling future of love and respect.

FEAR OF SACRIFICE

One of the greatest obstacles to awakening and aligning with our inner power is our fear of losing something we believe we need to survive. Our belief system and attachment to the external prevents us from relying on our true Source. Therefore, understanding what is valuable and what is not is part of the path of awakening to your inner spirit. We have been accumulating things and people that we believe are evidence of our power and strength since birth. We tightly hold and do not give up easily these pieces of evidence we think prove we are valuable.

These props are not necessary, but your ego clings desperately to them. All the attempts to have and possess people and things will never provide inner security. They are external evidence to show the world the ego is worthy; they will not satisfy the soul. Inanimate objects have no intrinsic value, but your ego assigns them a value based on your priorities. For example, a luxury car and a castle-like home can be powerful forces for the ego that believes these material objects elevate its status to king-like. How big is enough, is the question. It has been revealed that for some unethical CEOs, four or five palatial homes, private golf courses, million dollar toga birthday parties, private jets, and fleets of cars were not enough.

On the contrary, a small car and home can be symbols of modesty and evidence that you are a humble and good person to another ego. In this thought system, any display of material things is considered shallow and undesirable. None of it has any meaning at all, except that which is assigned by the individuals who desire these things. Appearing modest or very wealthy are often really two sides of the same coin.

People can even be a status symbol, seen as an accessory to bolster the ego and its appearance in society. It takes a tacit agreement on the part of both people for this to occur. An example is the selection of a partner who has an appearance or power that enhances the ego of the other partner, e.g., the young and beautiful with a rich, older person. It is an unspoken plan to elevate one's status by using each other.

Parents often use their children to elevate their status by expecting them to perform and increase the parents' self-worth. They see their children as an extension of themselves, and hope the children will materialize the dreams they failed to accomplish. The intensity of this projection can be seen when competition and even violence erupts among parents at their children's sporting events.

When you prey on others by using them for external validation, it is ultimately unsatisfying for both parties, even if they unconsciously agree to it for a while. Unspoken agreements of mutual imprisonment are so prevalent they are usually mistaken for love and commitment. When children are used for elevating the status of the parents, children have no choice except to reap the repercussions of the parents' dysfunction.

Group consciousness affects the value of things within that group, whether the group is defined by culture, gender, ethnicity, economic status, etc. Diverse groups can hold the same objects and achievements in entirely different lights. Attachment to certain objects that identify a person as being part of a special group is an example of reliance on the external for confirmation. When you feel a strong attachment to an object, then it is usually the ego using things outside itself to give you a sense of self-worth. Examples are as varied as logo clothes, fashions in clothing, sports team memorabilia, uniforms, etc. Studies have shown that men who watch their football team make a touchdown experience an increase in their own testosterone level—so identified are they with their team.

It is not wrong to have beautiful things, or prosperity, or to enjoy your associations. In fact, relationships and social activities are a human need and an opportunity for love and cooperation. It is the attachment to people and things to elevate yourself that creates the problem. If you feel you need external props and even other people to give you an identity, you may be unknowingly disempowering yourself. If all the props are so necessary to confirm your worth, it only makes sense that it would be almost impossible to give them up.

However, your fear of sacrificing these "false witnesses" can be the root of much unrecognized pain. To complicate the situation, the ego's attempt to keep you in this insane and ever-aspiring need for external objects is very seductive. The temporary high from buying and accumulating new, beautiful things can be quite alluring and exhilarating.

As you wake up, you will realize the ludicrousness of believing that an object or even an attachment to another person has anything to do with who you are. Having things for the mere pleasure of enjoying them is part of our experience. But the extreme imbalance of wealth and the insatiable
've for more things is absurd.

e more you align with your Source, the less you will be dependent
s outside yourself to make you feel secure. The fear of sacrifice
'erate grip of trying to keep these props in place will diminish.

A new freedom, lightness, and liberation will replace the empty sense of grasping for more. You will appreciate and enjoy all the prosperity you have, but it will no longer possess you.

The gift of trust in the universal power to provide and meet our needs comes as we connect more deeply with our inner spirit. Trust brings such incredible peace of mind it is wondrous we ever believe the voice of the frantic and grandiose ego. But whenever we have lack of trust in our own inner spiritual guidance, it is clear evidence we are listening to our ego. Instead of using your ego as a part of your life experience, your ego is using you.

When you truly trust in the Divine, you need do nothing. You are secure. You can relax. You live in the present. And because you have peace of mind, you have clarity. You know when to stand up and take action, coming from the intelligence of the authentic self. But relying on this Source is intolerable to the ego. Like children lost in a storm, individuals have fought the sense of separation from the Source and each other with strategies and schemes, but these are utterly hopeless attempts to be complete and happy. Instead, they have found themselves in the horrifying world of fear and doubt. And where they would seek joy, they discover empty, meaningless results with only some temporary pleasures. The lack of fulfillment leaves them always seeking more.

The world has been spinning out of control on all fronts: financial and economic downfalls, corruption in corporations and government, worldwide suffering, global warming, exploitation of natural resources, famine, and wars between countries. This causes fear, resignation, anguish, stagnation, attack, and despair. The suffering may be the threshold to an evolution like the world has never seen as people, one by one, face their fears and emotions and choose to awaken.

UNDERSTANDING EMOTIONS

Misplaced emotions occur because of the powerlessness and insecurity people feel. Some examples of misdirected anger include road rage, racial riots, sports rage, battles in the workplace, complaints about other people and the government, and political campaigns. Misdirected anger is pain within yourself that surfaces and is expressed outwardly toward other people and situations.

Emotions are often repressed, but eventually they surface, and they are often uncontrollable when they finally come out. Suppressing feelings causes them to grow in intensity. This is a sure way to create over-exaggerated emotions, interactions, and reactions. Many crimes are the result of unexpressed feelings finally coming forth in an uncontainable way.

The expression of emotions is essential to the well being of humans. Denying emotions and trying to hide your fears are the cause of conflicts everywhere. So understanding and feeling emotions is essential. Feeling emotion is the ability given to us so we can fully experience and appreciate the physical world. The many ranges of emotions provide us a variety of experiences depending on what is occurring in our world. As the energy of emotions move through us we stay balanced and healthy.

Pure love is not just an emotional sentiment. Pure love is the essence, the light, and the energy of the universe. A Course in Miracles says, "What is not love is fear." But universal love is often clouded by judgment and the constrictions of the ego. The experience of love in the physical world is an emotion. It can be experienced as compassion, empathy, joy, sentiment, understanding, friendship, romance, affinity, and familial love, to name a few. Love is expressed through words, actions, attitudes, and commitment. It is also expressed with physical touch. A human infant, for example, will not survive without physical touching and holding.

The elderly need and respond to physical touch, and often are those who receive the least. Working with the retirement industry, I watched the elderly happily receive the physical touch of family, caregivers, and even pets that were allowed to visit. They were energized and gratified by touch.

Emotion, when expressed fully, allows an exchange and free flow of energy that is not only good for the soul, but necessary. Laughing, crying, dancing, singing, writing, art, communication, and other expressions are experiences of emotions being released in a healthy and satisfying manner. Even expressing anger though aggression is healthy as long as it is not aimed at someone or causing someone harm. Sometimes by getting angry we propel ourselves into action and become refocused on who we really are—not the downtrodden.

Dreams also allow relief to the psyche from stress of unresolved issues of the day. They provide a free-flowing energy that is blocked during the waking state. Dreams can reveal to you the source of your anxiety by recreating it. Dreams also offer a glimpse into the wellspring of creativity that can be applied to your day in the waking reality.

Inspiration and understanding can occur in dreams, and it is helpful to remember and record them. I personally believe you are the best person to understand what your dreams are telling you and how they reflect your life journey. They can contain keys to solving problems in all areas of your life. They can be gentle reminders of the issues in your life that need to be addressed or loud announcements to get your attention to make changes!

I sleep with pen and paper and often wake up and write from a stream of consciousness that is wise and unfiltered by my daily activities and mental distractions. I have read about artists, inventors, writers, and other creative people describing how they received inspiration in a dream state. Many famous musicians have written amazing compositions from an altered state of consciousness or creativity that flows through them.

The universe has a natural rhythm that is soothing to our soul. Watching the waves, rocking our babies, and dancing are expressions of rhythm. Drumming, enjoying music, chanting, and even pacing are expressions of the waves of movement and energy of which we are a part. Rhythm in various forms helps balance our inner core and resets us to our natural state. Soldiers marching in formation to a compelling rhythm can incite energy and emotion to go to battle. Marching together is also an expression of unity. Look at those who march in a parade, for example.

Suppressing emotions results in blocked energy. This blocked energy can be felt physically as stress, anxiety, stomachaches and headaches, general uneasiness, irritability, crankiness, tiredness, and moodiness. Unexpressed emotions can eventually cause sickness—cancer, heart attacks, and other life- threatening diseases.

When you suppress your emotions, instead of allowing them to flow and be expressed, you are doing great damage to yourself. Denial is the tool by which the ego represses fear and anxiety to protect itself and to keep it buried so you do not have to deal with it. Denial by your ego is so powerful you do not even know you are doing it. You are missing the vital link to your freedom from this denial process. Your ego is closing a door to your soul.

Defense and resistance are techniques your ego is using because we have learned it is not okay to have emotions. We are ashamed and afraid to appear weak so we hide our feelings from others, but most tragically, we hide them from ourselves. We believe others would not approve of us, and worse, we feel vulnerable to pity, shame, and even attack. However, it takes enormous energy to keep feelings hidden and it causes pain rather than protecting us.

Recognizing and experiencing emotions is essential to understanding the issues that need attention so that you can see beyond the ego state to the enlightened state. Most often the pain is deeply imbedded in your inner psyche from experiences of long ago. Keeping the pain buried and never allowing acknowledgement is what has made it so painful. The hurting will not stop being replayed until it is extricated. There is a secret, a central belief beneath your awareness, that is self-deprecating. Looking at it squarely, once and for all, will bring forth the very origin of the belief so that you can see that it is a fictitious story from your childhood. You will be set free as you allow light to shine on it. You will be liberating yourself from the pain that is coming from you and not from an outside source.

Remind yourself that only weakness and fear need defending. Your honor stands on its own. So giving up your defense and ego protection to look behind the face of the ego will be the gateway to release. Remembering the origin of the event that is still obscured in your inner psyche is your liberation. It needs to be unearthed like a boulder imbedded in the ground. The first one is the most difficult but it prepares the way for the other smaller stones to be exposed. It can only happen when you stop fighting or fleeing.

Jerry, a multimillionaire, was the head of a large corporation with a salary and bonus system that gave him an annual income that, by most standards, was obscene. He had everything money could buy, and power and status to go with it. But because he had not healed his soul, he never had enough. His beautiful homes, his cars, his plane, his latest and greatest new toy, could not satisfy him for long. He was the perfect example of the insatiable ego: all the external validations and material attainments did not remove the inner sense of unworthiness. Jerry wielded huge power in the workplace, but could experience rejection if the grocery clerk was unfriendly. Not that he admitted it.

Jerry's ego was a great actor—an Academy Award-winning actor, in fact. He knew how to appear benevolent when necessary, jovial when it was called for, and stern and intimidating when he needed to do that role. His success in creating great deals and moving the company forward had taken him to the top. The deals were in the gray area of legality, but he and his team justified them. The accounting systems and reports that were made to look good for the shareholders—well, this was just how business was done.

Then Jerry had a heart attack. It was a serious one, and it got his attention. Lying in the hospital, Jerry began to take stock of his life. He had everything he thought he would need to be happy and more. Yet he was burdened with stress and anxiety. It all seemed so meaningless in the face of his mortality.

His family had rushed to his bedside. For the first time, he saw and felt the significance of the people who loved him. He had been so engaged in his world of business and high finance he had not valued the most meaningful parts of his life and the people who mattered. Where had the years gone?

Jerry, while quietly alone, realized that his fear of rejection and inadequacy had driven him to the height of success. It wasn't creative inspiration, but fear of failure and a need to impress the world that led him to where he was today.

He had stepped on lots of toes to get there and had made enemies along the way. The power struggles in the company had caused a lot of dissension and pain for people in the workplace. But he thought competition was the best way to motivate people and fear got them to really produce. He recalled the face of his CFO, who out of fear of losing his job, his retirement, and all financial security, agreed to do things that could cost him his license. He felt ashamed as he thought of all the compromises he asked of people, and seeing himself so clearly now was very painful.

He began to think about all the things he had missed in his life. He was now suddenly very grateful his family had stayed with him through these turbulent years. He didn't deserve this much love.

Looking back, he saw that the fear originated when he was a child, and observed how it grew and directed his life on the stage at work. His fear and inadequacy could not be hidden from himself, despite all the external attainments of the ego.

It took breaking his heart in the form of this attack to open Jerry's heart to the truth. He started to listen to his inner guidance from the eternal source. He recognized how his endless need for validation had been driving him. Now sadness, grief, and guilt about the people he had hurt along the way began to arise in him. As he allowed the unconscious feelings to surface he started to see a new way to live his life and to dramatically improve his company. He made a commitment to change everything that was not ethical and take full responsibility for any consequences. Vowing to transform the entire culture of his company, he recognized the process would start with himself and his senior administrative team. He realized others were not his opponents to be coerced and manipulated. They were not the enemies. As a team, they would be able to create a cooperative business that was based on integrity, respect, and collaboration. Fear and exploitation would no longer be used in this organization. The approach would be the synergism of all people through honor and alignment to new goals that would benefit everyone.

As he began this deep contemplation he saw that he was a person who not only caused others pain, but had, more than anyone else, tormented himself. He saw his transgressions and felt a terrible sadness. But it was at this moment that he also began forgiving himself. The release he felt, knowing he was already forgiven by the Divine, allowed him to see he needed to forgive himself. He finally saw the battle had always been with himself—his tiny but tenacious ego was his only enemy. It took a heart attack to finally get his attention. For some, even a heart attack does not do it. How far do we have to go to reach rock bottom? The key to stopping the drama is to look within ourselves as any unpleasant emotions occur. Every conflict, every subtle fear, and every angry outburst is an opportunity to learn about yourself and ultimately participate in ending the tragic drama in the workplace.

GENUINE FORGIVENESS

If giving up judgment of yourself and others is the key to freedom, then forgiveness is the release. Forgiveness of others occurs when you relinquish your claim or desire for victory over another. Forgiveness sets you free because you release the intense energy required to hold someone else responsible for your misery. The stronger the emotion, the more energy you are expending by holding onto the grievance toward another. When you truly understand that you are the only one with the power to choose your feelings, you will loosen your grip on the trigger.

What if you discovered the person who wronged you really didn't know how much they were hurting you, would you be a little less vengeful? When anyone does something you perceive as hurtful, they are playing out their role and motives based on their own needs for validation and significance. You are not the cause of their beliefs or feelings and they are not the reason of your emotions. They have projected their pain and suffering onto you and you have done the same. This is what Jesus meant when He said, "Father forgive them, for they know not what they do."

Individuals are on their path and are doing what they need to learn who they are. Your opponents are following their script just like you are. When you are able to look gently behind the fear or strongly held belief that is causing their projection onto you, your pain will be released. You will be able to see it is not personal and they are not guilty. As you see it is their pattern, you will see it isn't you. Forgiveness will release you from the grip of pain that you are holding with your grievance. When this genuinely happens, relief will flood into your heart and you will be free!

Finally, self-forgiveness occurs when you can shine the same compassion and love on your own heart, which will release the guilt and original shame residing in yourself. This is true absolution. An unhealed heart cannot experience love, peace, or joy at work or anywhere else. Therefore, forgiveness is the access to love. Forgiveness is emancipation.

At one point in my career I was the marketing consultant for a large CPA firm. As part of my job, I worked with the partners to develop and expand their individual niches. I would create a plan based on their expertise and feedback and then assist them in the implementation of their marketing strategies. I would schedule speaking opportunities, help them publish articles, work on proposals, and coach them on their sales presentations to potential clients. (Not an easy job with CPAs, by the way).

As usual, the squeaky wheel gets the grease, and some of the partners were much more inspired and interested in their personal marketing plans, so I worked with those who were most responsive. The firm was getting a lot of visibility through these combined efforts.

However, one partner, a particularly conservative person, seemed very resistant to any of my brilliant ideas and suggestions. He scoffed at me and debunked marketing in general. I began being fearful of this particular person and started avoiding him. I found myself worrying that since he was such a powerful person in the firm, he might sabotage me—possibly even suggest they fire me! And this accounting firm was a major client for me. I was a single mother and really depended on my consulting income. My anxiety grew until I was afraid to even talk to him. I was sure he didn't like me and it was causing me increasing anguish.

One evening, after immense suffering and worrying, I finally forced myself to look more deeply at what was going on. I sat on my bed, and instead of panicking, I just let the pain and fearful feelings arise in me. As I did, I started to ask myself, "In addition to the financial worry, what am I really afraid of? What do I fear this man could say about me? What is happening that is causing me to feel so disempowered around this person?"

As I asked myself these questions some feelings of inadequacy and self-blame began emerging. Instead of trying to resist or deny them, I took out a piece of paper and wrote them down. I let them spill out, and it was quite a list. When I had exhausted my negative judgments about myself, I did some soul searching. "What was I to do now? Were these self-deprecating thoughts really true?" I asked myself.

Amazingly, a new thought occurred to me. Some of my past mistakes were probably factual. I had done some things wrong in my life. I had hurt and demeaned others. I had been selfish, grandiose, and insecure throughout many experiences in my life. But I also realized many of these self-recriminations were exaggerated and I was tormenting myself with so many negative accusations. But the tightness in my heart continued and the pain was searing.

And then a miracle happened. Somewhere inside of me I heard the word *forgiveness*. And at that very moment a powerful surge of energy, combined with a beautiful sensation of relief, pulsated through me. It flowed through me like a gentle rain and I felt the grip on my heart loosen. I then started the process of self-forgiveness. I had forgiven many people in my life and I believed the Divine is forgiving of all of us. But somehow I hadn't included myself in the group worthy of forgiveness. Now I could see I was the one holding myself in a prison of condemnation. The guilt had been unconscious until I faced it, but it was unknowingly ruling my life. Fearing exposure of many faults, I had been limiting my ability to work and live with freedom. I needed to forgive myself for the mistakes of the past. They were simply part of my journey of learning.

Feeling very freed up and with a new sense of peace, I posed another question to myself. "Is it possible the client I feared might also have some hidden wounds? Maybe in some strange way he was also afraid." "No, of course not," I responded. "Take another look," I said to myself. I determined I would go in the next day and talk to him.

The following day, with great trepidation, I knocked on his office door. My heart was pounding and my hands were trembling. I asked for a few moments of time with him and with a scowl on his face he indicated I could sit down. I then told him that I would really like to highlight his expertise as a highly respected partner in the firm, and asked him if he would speak at two upcoming business events. I told him I knew he had doubts about marketing, but his knowledge would not only help our clients and potential clients, but would also help the firm grow its services. To my surprise, he accepted both of the requests to speak.

Throughout the following months I invited this man to participate in many campaigns and marketing activities. I asked his advice on projects, gained some interesting perspectives from him, but most important, built a new relationship that lasted for several years. He became a supporter of mine, and our mutual trust of one another grew through time. I realized he had felt uncomfortable with marketing and therefore blamed me. My fear of his resistance caused me to avoid him, which, in turn, caused him to feel neglected in the marketing program. Out of my willingness to boldly face the fears in myself, I was able to risk possible rejection. I also awakened to the understanding that everyone wants to be appreciated, respected, and valued—no matter where they are in the pecking order. Some are just more convincing actors.

When you can forgive another, as well as yourself, you will have a new form of communication available to you. You will talk from a place of inner serenity, rather than a reactionary and guarded position. Your spirit will recognize the spirit in others and you will know you are not separate. You will see the dynamics of conflicted relationships change dramatically. As we do this in our own heart, we contribute to the consciousness of all people.

As long as we judge others, we will continue to see the world and its people as separate from us. When we learn that everyone else is simply playing out their script and they do not owe us a part in their drama, we can forgive. As long as we see them as someone to play out our assigned role for them, we will judge their performance and hold them as wrong.

The more people you forgive, the more liberated you become. It takes a great deal of intense emotion to keep holding others responsible for our feelings and regarding them as wrong. When we can see others as the same and no longer judge them, no matter what they are doing, we free up energy for ourselves.

When we can forgive ourselves, we will find peace. It is important to see and release what we find unacceptable and unforgivable in ourselves. But we can't forgive ourselves if we can't forgive others, and we can't forgive others if we can't forgive ourselves.

When we forgive others and ourselves, genuine peace and joy emerge effortlessly.

RELIANCE ON UNIVERSAL LOVE

If you want to truly make a difference in your workplace or anywhere else, you can only do it when you are strongly rooted in authentic power stemming from the power of universal love. Again, I am not talking about the sentiment of love. I am talking about the power and source of all that is, the source of all creation. It is love. Only our judgment of ourselves and others obscures the love from shining on and through us. Love awaits us—it is in a state of suspension for each one of us who has not yet fully realized and accepted its grace and splendor. But it is our choice to do this or not to do it.

Choice is the function and the main component of free will. Unconscious choices directed by the ego rather than by the wisdom of the inner self are the source of our chaotic lives. Choice without spiritual intent can lead to pain, despair, and destruction. However, choosing differently is always an option within the time you are here. But as fair warning, the longer we wait, the more severe the consequences tend to be. We unsuspectingly bring ourselves to points in our journey where we feel pain that is often the precursor to awakening.

In the world of the ego, reliance is found with other people and things. Reliance is the act of counting on something or someone outside the self for some perceived needed support, validation, or assistance. But relying on things outside yourself will never provide security. The only reliance that will ever give you any kind of certainty is that of your inner guidance and connection with the source. Reliance on love is the straightest and purest path you can walk. Choose no other.

Choosing love over the ego requires having the experience, even if only briefly, of relying on love. Communion with spirit will allow love to expand in your heart and will lead to genuine freedom, peace, and joy. Therein lies your safety and security, because this source is constant and unchanging. It can never be reduced or taken away, except by your own choice. Who would rely on anything less than the promise of universal love? Know these two things: 1) Love asks nothing and receives everything, and 2) Pain and suffering are the result of misguided intentions that block love.

I would like to share some qualities of universal love to help you see why choosing love is the answer and how ego strategies and neediness block the very love you so desire. Universal love is the source of everything and is the power that sustains all life. When you rely on love it shines away all doubt, strengthening your resolve and confirming your intentions. Love limits nothing and controls no one, so when you find yourself trying to control people or circumstances you can know you are in the world of the ego. When you feel despair, remember that love builds hope and faith, and fortifies your strength. Love provides comfort to you and others.

In its purest form, love flourishes in spite of uncertainty and dissolves all fear. Love can move mountains and pave the way for a smooth journey. Love abandons no one but shines equally on everyone. Being both practical and masterful, it creates opportunities leading to fruition. Love does not shrink or cower in the face of obstacles; it clears all interference and amplifies all your efforts. Love is the very reason you exist. We need to envelop the world in love because love radiates peace and joy.

It is time to give up your worries and concerns and recognize that they limit your power and energy. Be patient with yourself and others. Love is enduring and can be counted on eternally. So I suggest, be joyful and what you need will follow, not the other way around. The world believes you will be happy when you get what you need, but this is not true. When you align with love, your needs and desires will be met. Trust in that.

Challenge the little voice inside that tries to distract you. Do not let it disturb your silence or allow it to perturb you. Your inner authentic voice, coming from universal love, is so powerful you can reach it at any time. It can be counted on to provide support and inner security in any situation or circumstance. The key is to be open and receptive.

THE AUTHENTIC SELF

Let's look at how the authentic, higher self lives in a world where most are still operating from the ego. The true self knows it is love and part of the Source of the ultimate creativity and intelligence. Therefore, the real self does not need to feel superior. It sees others as equal and not separate—all of one mind.

The authentic self is trusting and lives in the present, allowing events to unfold naturally, rather than trying to control outcomes for itself and others. Synchronicity and amazing coincidences are drawn into the life of the authentic self. The energy emanating from an authentic person attracts more of the same energy from others.

Decisions to take a stand for truth and to take the necessary action come from a source of wisdom that provides clarity. This clear vision is unavailable to the ego. Because the authentic self trusts in a universal force in all of us, it understands all events have a purpose and are an opportunity for learning. There is no need to judge any circumstances or other people because the true self knows the ego's opinions are from a limited point of view and they are not the truth. When we are aligned with love we accept people as they are and we don't have to fix others to meet our expectations. The authentic self honors the spirit in self and others. This causes others to be drawn to us as a natural response to our genuine sense of acceptance.

The higher self operates from inspiration and wisdom—its true source of creativity and intelligence—so it is deeply satisfied expressing its veritable wealth of abilities and talents. The authentic, higher self is an enlightened leader because the powerful qualities of a leader are a natural result of giving up the ego's artificial needs. Participating in situations with equanimity, the true self is connected to its Source and reliant on its center of tranquility.

And finally, the higher self is not afraid because it knows its natural inheritance is joy, peace, and love. Operating this way, it does not hold back or contract its energy. By being present to those qualities while living life fully, the higher self experiences all situations as natural and part of its physical life path, an opportunity to share and extend love to others. The higher self does not hold others responsible for happiness and forgives others for what they "didn't" do. The higher self is free. The higher self is at peace.

You have a choice: (1) to operate in the frenzied manner of the ego or (2) to operate in the powerful and peaceful state of the authentic self who is not disconnected from its source.

PERSONAL FREEDOM AND GLOBAL ONENESS

The pervasive ego strategy employed by the multitudes is the source of wars at all levels. The ego's effort to exonerate itself escalates the drama and discord. It is time to shatter these deadlocks of blame and persecution by seeing that all interactions are a process of reciprocity. The mutual dynamic is like a dance of pain and suffering between two people, each unwilling to stop. When it is a collective group—whether teams, organizations or nations—it produces emotional and even physical combat.

If we only understood that every pain holds the seed for freedom and peace if felt and experienced, rather than denied or projected onto another, we would feel enormous relief. What we vehemently defend holds the secret to our emancipation. When you guard yourself it intensifies the grip of fear and increases the pain. If you but knew this, you would put down your sword and shield immediately. Behind your fear of anguish and condemnation you will find the release your soul desires.

Recognize the challenges that you face are opportunities disguised as problems. They are an opening to your freedom and a threshold to a new way of being. Trust your emotions are telling you the lessons you came here to learn—they are messengers of your soul. Allow the feelings from your experiences to emerge so they can be faced and released. Stop looking for peace and love outside yourself. Discover true inner peace, love, and joy by looking at the very pain you seek to avoid.

The reason you resist is that you believe if you felt your pain fully, it would destroy you. It is as though you are running from a dreaded and impending wave of torment that you think will come crashing down on you, crushing you into oblivion. But running is exhausting and it is the origin of the pain. The huge darkness cast upon you by the relentless wave is like a cloud of suffering, blocking the light and love you want in your life. Stop, turn, and face your worst fear. When you do, you will find, to your utter relief, the foreboding wave is gently lapping against the shore.

To accelerate your growth and personal happiness, learn that any sense of fear, panic, pain, or resistance is an indicator of the parts of you that need healing. Know that your emotions are not caused by another but are coming from your own thoughts and stories of who you think you are. It is not true. Welcome your feelings and sensations instead of refusing to acknowledge them. Be gentle with yourself. And most important, give up the need to be right. It prevents your feelings from arising; it blocks your inner path to freedom and alienates your fellow human beings.

I believe we are on a journey out of darkness. I believe we are currently in an evolutionary shift like the world has never known and it will change humanity as we know it. New healing energy and vibrations are being emitted with undulating waves of light, available to those who trust and participate in the evolution. Pain and suffering, the result of misguided intentions and misalignments, can be alleviated now. Whether you believe this or not, you can be a host for an infusion of love and lightness, lifting your spirit and radiating through you. If you want rapid expansion in your awareness and consciousness you can access the energy fields that are available to you by recognizing and honoring your divine self. This will accelerate your own energy field and make you a conduit for others.

As a free and authentic person, you can pronounce truth, even when others are afraid or blind. It is time to denounce falsities, inaccurate information, platitudes, and lip service to a flawed philosophy that demeans others. As a leader, be forever in the pursuit of truth and equality for all people.

The blind faith of unthinking and unsuspecting people to a dogmatic, old system rewarding only some of the people has resulted in this turmoil and misery. Ego-driven decisions based on greed and contempt for fellow human beings have caused the confused and terrible state of the world today. Schemes devised to benefit the wealthy at the expense of others have led to inequity and imbalance. Countermeasures must be taken now to reverse the flow and shift the planet.

People work best when they have freedom and autonomy. It is our natural state to be free, and when we are not limited with constraints from others, we rise to new levels of creativity and are filled with enthusiasm. Dan Pink, in his book *Drive,* has done extensive research on what motivates people. His research has led him to state, "When it comes to motivation, there's a gap between what science knows and what business does. Our current business operating system—which is built around external, carrot-and-stick motivators—doesn't work and often does harm." He adds, "Companies that offer autonomy, sometimes in radical doses, are outperforming their competitors."

Seeing the effects of the current system and what brought about the fractures and weakening of the underpinnings is the opening to a new model. The new world model is of honor, respect, and unity—replacing aggression and competition rooted in fear. The more people who understand the source of the chaos and dissension, the faster the tidal wave of events can be reversed.

Broaden your own viewpoint and expand your scope. See the whole picture, looking beyond the mundane and limited perspective of your current view of this world. Participate in the plan to move in a new direction, redistributing wealth, feeding the hungry, healing the planet, and awakening millions. If you are reading this, your participation is needed.

As we replace fear with trust and compassion for one another, we bring rays of hope and light, uplifting the spirits of our fellow souls—our coworkers, families, and all people everywhere. A new presence is coming, sweeping the world with joy and resurrection.

The past has been shrouded in pain and fear. The curtain has lifted. The future holds the glimmering and shining possibilities for a new world—a transformation so great it will shake the foundation of the illusionary world. Trust that your part is needed. Dedicate yourself to your process of awakening and don't relinquish your inner authority.

Mastery of spiritual consciousness begins with giving up the ego's false claims of victimization. Become fully and completely accountable for your own feelings and thoughts. Own what you have imposed on yourself and stop creating enemies on whom you can blame your suffering. Give up grievances that hold you in the past and keep you locked in a self-made prison. Forgive others as you forgive yourself and see that it is all part of our learning.

Pay attention when you are in your sad story and recognize it is not true. Give up being the downtrodden because you are not the downtrodden, except by your own choice. Jesus and other teachers came here to lighten your load. Stand up; stop carrying the heavy burden and walk tall and strong. You can't help anyone or shift the culture of your workplace if you are weak, arrogant, or lost in your own drama.

Recognize a better way to interact with others on this planet. Pay attention to the opportunities to see the ego reflected back to yourself. Support your own growth and gravitate toward truth by reading books, attending seminars, meditating, and all other methods for awakening. Stay focused with the intent to wake up and enroll in this unparalleled planetary evolution. Commit to diligence against the seductive voice of the ego and don't be deceived. A deep foundation of wisdom and love is ingrained in you, awaiting your recognition.

Choose well when you see opportunities for advancement, often disguised as a problem or obstacle. Welcome options leading to a new direction and to higher possibilities. Stop feeding off addictions, which cause you to remain unconscious and numb. Wake up and realize that your very power is being denied with every choice you make to side with the ego. Stop self-suffering by identifying the thought system pulling you down, and then choose differently. And most important, quit making others responsible for your happiness and allow your true joy to arise within you. Do not seek after personal glory and attention, as it will become a stumbling block to your awakening. Flush out the impurities by being fearless, unstoppable, and undaunted by the ego's claim of triumph.

More than anything else, this is your emancipation. It is yours by your birthright. Rise up and claim your spiritual heritage, your true source, and your unlimited inner power and abilities. Now is the time of deliverance from the chains that have bound you. Freedom is first a state of mind, and what is not within us cannot be found outside us. Free will is just that—knowing that we have freedom and power within. We must avail ourselves of our inner spiritual strength. It can propel us forward or we can stay locked in our own self-defined prisons.

You are the one to prepare the way for a new generation. Place your fellow beings ahead of your tiny, helpless, demanding ego. Although the passing of time is inescapable, you choose your path, or you don't choose. And it is still a choice. Be willing to overcome your limitations and give up the beliefs that have been holding you back. Those who are politely standing by, waiting for something to happen, are part of the problem.

I believe this period in time will bring a new reality—one in which we see our fellow humans as the spiritual essences and loving beings they are. As we take off the masks of our ego-defined roles in the dramas we play, we will truly see our oneness. We will see our brothers and sisters standing there—our beloved fellow souls whom we had mistakenly identified as the enemy. What a holy day, when one by one, we give up our grievances, lay down our swords, and embrace our fellow beings.

It is time to give up divisions of all kinds: religious, political, racial, and geographical, or any positions that cause people to take sides or draw lines down the center. It is time to move to a new global level—for that is just what we are: one planet, one world, one family of diversity, beauty, and splendor. Let's take down the walls of fear and accusation. The world's stages are worn and creaking and the floorboards cannot withstand this strain much longer.

It is time to be a leader. You cannot be left behind when you are in the front, leading others to a new level of understanding, joy, and peace. Peace is what we must choose now: relentlessly, passionately and completely, in the workplace, communities, families, and the world.

You are the one to do this. Develop passageways through the thickness and heaviness of the current consciousness. Create an opening that will be the light in the darkness—that will lead others out of this cosmic, dark, thick fog of negative energy. Develop channels that are open and send energy—the delivery of which will lead others out of the deep state that has separated itself from light and life.

You can help others come out of their murky waters of negative energy and human dissension. Your willingness to arise of out of the muck, the human suffering that pulls everyone down, drowning them in a sewer of misery, is testimony to your commitment, and you will be supported with powerful spiritual energy.

Help drive away the faulty beliefs that hold people in their pain and suffering. Your courage and dedication to do this, in spite of being trapped in the same dimension, is why you are needed to help humanity. The heavens applaud and celebrate your awakening, providing support, comfort, assistance, and love in every way. You are asked only to have faith in your soul and love in your heart.

This is a restoration process—the restoration of you to your soul, your true self. It is your highest calling, what you have been waiting for all your life. Seize the opportunity. It is time to wake up and to awaken your brothers and sisters—much as a child on Christmas morning runs to her siblings sleeping in their beds and says, "Wake up! It's time to wake up. It's Christmas morning!"

Do these things and you will be restored to your authentic self. This is your spiritual assignment—to return to alignment with the power of love, not fear. It is an awesome and amazing journey. This book is intended to help you wake up. The impact it has on you is in your hands.

What is the measurement of your progress? It is very simple. The results will be evident in your life. You will feel lighter and experience a new kind of joy in your heart. You will relax more and stress less. You will feel love and receive love like you have never experienced before. Synchronicity will occur, and unexpected meetings will lead to new relationships and opportunities. You will work in cooperation with others, sharing the alignment of group will and mutual engagement, reaching exhilarating levels of creativity, productivity, and genius. You will celebrate the creativity and value of everyone and find real purpose and passion in your life. But most of all, you will have peace—deep abiding peace.

I would like to share another story about my dad, 2nd Lieutenant Daniel Wearing Gates. His story of being a prisoner demonstrates the insanity of war, an escalation of the combative attitude we see in workplaces every day. I would like to describe the day my dad, while still a POW in Stalag Luft 1, found out that World War II was over, peace had arrived, and he and the other prisoners would be released.

After nine months of being imprisoned and starved, he awoke on this day at dawn, cold and covered in lice. He heard something, and at first he thought he must be hearing things. He strained to listen because he thought he heard someone singing the American national anthem, an act punishable by death in a POW camp. He stood up and listened again, not believing what he was hearing. Only now he heard a hundred voices singing "The Star Spangled Banner." Soon it was a thousand voices, and before the song was over, he had joined as eight thousand prisoners were singing the American national anthem. That was the moment peace had come and my dad learned that World War II had ended. His imprisonment by fellow human beings on this planet was over.

The singing had erupted because the German guards had abandoned their posts and the Russians, our then allies (later to become our enemies), had marched in to release the prisoners and take them home. My dad and the other prisoners were freed, and the world celebrated the end of the war. It was time to be a nation at peace, at least for a while.

When are we going to stop the madness of war? The theme of attack and overcome that has predominated in history has not produced peace or real freedom. Fear and hatred does not beget peace or compassion. Battles between individuals or wars between nations—they are all the same. When are we going to see we are one family, on one planet, from one Source?

I would like to pose these questions: What are you doing to contribute to peace in the world? What are you doing to bring harmony and cooperation in your workplace? Please, know this. It starts with each of us, one person at a time, completing our own personal restoration with our own hearts and souls. As we transform ourselves we can express love, compassion, and respect for one another, right where we are, with the people we see every day—family, friends, co-workers, and neighbors. Where we are now is exactly where we can make a difference. If we can't see our oneness and feel love for those close to us, how can we ever have compassion for people on the other side of the world?

As Americans, I believe we can be a shining example to the world of acceptance, integrity, and belief in freedom for everyone. Acknowledging all the good that our country has done, may we also recognize the errors of our ways? May we no longer be arrogant and prejudiced, alienating other countries around the world? Let us be a peaceful nation and a paragon of hope for others.

My dad died unexpectedly on January 12, 2006, after a long and happy life. He was a devoted husband to my mother for fifty-eight years and the loving father of six children. We miss him every day but we are thankful for the wonderful memories of growing up with our dad, who was not only a war hero, but a hero in our family. I am grateful not only for his sacrifice for his country, but also because he survived his imprisonment to become a father. He fought for freedom, as so many of our troops have for decades. But I believe it is time for humanity to progress beyond this embittered, battling level of consciousness. The only remedy is to stop reacting, attacking, defending, blaming, and fearing to look at our individual and collective wounds. It is time now to forge freedom—to take a stand, wielding the swords of discernment, and cut through the entanglement of the ego.

RECOGNIZING SEVEN EGO TRAPS THAT PULL YOU BACK TO SLEEP

As you become restored to your true self, you will no longer react to the drama in the workplace. The other egos may escalate their own behavior to try to gain a reaction from you. They need your reaction to keep reinforcing their ego identities. The pressure to react, especially if the situation becomes hostile, is great because your ego is challenged. You may feel you want to defend yourself or even take the offense and attack what you believe is the source of the anxiety you are experiencing. J. Krishnamurti, a renowned writer and philosopher, stated, "Without freedom from the past, there is no freedom at all, because the mind is never new, fresh, innocent."

The ego reacts to protect the wounds from the past. But only your ego can feel this pain. Holding the calm space from within is necessary to maintain your peace during the other's attempt to increase the drama on the workplace stage. This requires a lot of practice and patience with yourself because the temptation of the ego to react is extremely strong.

Because the ego is so tenacious, recognizing some of the ego traps that can pull you back to sleep will help you not be deceived. Pay attention if you find yourself falling into any of these hidden ego behaviors. Here are seven behaviors that could prevent you from unlocking your authentic power:

- Comparing yourself with others.
  - Lack of self-esteem causes judgment and comparisons. Because the ego has no true self-worth, it will always come up short in the comparison. Practice seeing the uniqueness in each of us and celebrate our differences. It is okay to be inspired by others' accomplishments, but feeling less than someone else or trying to be superior to others is simply the ego's way of trying to validate its existence.

- Holding others responsible for your feelings, actions, and circumstances.
  - Your life is a result of your own choices and is determined by which voice you listen to. When you blame someone else for your feelings or circumstances, you are giving up your own power. Being responsible for your own life is a key ingredient of an awakened soul.

- Seeking personal glory and approval from others.
  - These behaviors will be stumbling blocks. Although it feels good to be admired and accepted, authenticity does not require the validation of others. Enlightened leaders are often called to risk rejection by taking a stand for truth. If you need personal glory and approval it will limit you and keep you playing small.

- Denying feelings and emotions.
  - When you cover your true feelings and emotions from others, but most important, from yourself, you are being dishonest. Our artificial image of strength, needing to be right, and appearing perfect builds walls and prevents others from knowing us. It takes enormous energy to be such an actor.

- Feeding your ego with external things.
  - Your ego is insatiable so it will never be satisfied. As you keep looking for new rewards and new objects to demonstrate your influence and power, you will be disappointed because things cannot satisfy your soul. Greed and the need for bigger, better props is an endless journey.

- Withholding full self-expression and creativity.
  - When you fail to take the risks of putting yourself out there and sharing your creativity, it is not humility; it is

fear. An enlightened leader shares from their Divine
Source, not limiting themselves by worrying about how
others see them.

- Resisting fear or internal pain.
  - The ego is always running for cover, distracting itself from
    looking within, and avoiding feeling pain. However, it is
    the *resistance* that is causing the pain. Allowing yourself to
    face the center of the pain lodged in the heart will bring the
    release and relief you desire. Running from the pain is the
    whole cause of the ego insanity in the first place. Feeling it
    and forgiving yourself for all your self-deprecating
    descriptions will bring you freedom—your emancipation
    from the jail sentence you have given yourself. This is true
    exoneration and absolution. The Divine has already given
    it to you; it's up to you to do the rest.

Practice bringing yourself to the place of inner serenity and presence
frequently throughout the day, every day. Be vigilant against your mind's
constant attempt to engage you in illusions and the drama of others in
your workplace, and notice when the traps try to ensnare you. As you remain true to your inner voice, you will be heavily reinforced by a new
inner confidence coming from deep within your core. You will become
aware of a difference in yourself, the stage, and the other participants.
Your perception will shift and you will see a new world. You will clearly
see that the antics, posturing, one-upsmanship, and complexities of your
workplace and the world are not reality. You will be free.

The ego's world is dependent on the reactions and re-reactions of others. When anyone then moves to stop this insane interaction, the long-
running play begins to break down. One by one, it begins to fall apart.
The engine that has been running out of control begins to run out of the
fuel that is driving it down the track. The speeding train will ultimately
come to a stop. It will take a while, depending on the speed and force with
which it is traveling and the number of cars that are attached to it. But it
will come to a stop . . . as leaders, one by one, initiate the process.

Without reactions from the ego identities, there is no drama. Without the drama being created, the performance is over. The drama will end and the players can take their final bow. The curtain will close and at long last, the actors can take off their costumes and masks. The lights will go on, and the players will finally be restored to the inner greatness intended by their Creator.

Bravo! Bravo!

It has been a very convincing performance.

PERSONAL RESTORATION PLAN
TO PRACTICE IN YOUR WORKPLACE

These two practices are essential for your emancipation, as well as that of others around you.

The next time you feel any pain or suffering, go to a place where you can be by yourself. Begin by allowing yourself to let the feelings arise. Let them come fully to the surface. It's okay if you cry, or feel rage, sadness, or pity. Feel where the pain is being experienced. It is usually right in the heart area. Then pose the following questions to yourself and *write the answers down:*

- What are the negative feelings about myself that I am covering up?
- What do I really fear people are saying about me?
- What do I think is so bad about myself?
- Are they really true? Am I really bad?

As you allow yourself to look at what you think you need to hide and that which you think is unbearable to see, you are moving toward releasing those beliefs. Even though they are unconscious, they are ruling your life and must be allowed to surface. Now say to yourself:

- Some of these things may have happened but they are just mistakes, just part of my learning.
- I am not a terrible person, I am already forgiven and I can forgive myself.
- Without these misunderstandings, I would not be who I am today.
- I forgive myself for not being perfect and for anything I perceived as terrible in my past, knowing full well I am already forgiven by the Divine.

- Continue this until you feel the release and peace of self-forgiveness.
- Commit to righting any wrongs you may have done, if it is appropriate. Sometimes just mentally asking someone's forgiveness is enough. You will know.

In your journal, list the names of anyone who has wronged you in the past and toward whom you still feel some agitation or grievance when you think about them. Then try to say to yourself the following:

- This person is not my enemy.
- He/she is simply playing out his/her script.
- This person is just like me.
- He/she wants to be loved and feel significant.
- I forgive him/her for projecting onto me.
- I thank him/her for being a mirror for me to heal my own wounds.
- I thank him/her for any pain I have experienced because it has helped me become who I am.

Now, visualize this person in your mind's eye, and look into his or her eyes. See them clearly and don't stop until you do. Now say the above words while seeing them clearly on your inner visual screen.

This might be difficult at first, but as you practice this exercise and let down your guard, you will feel a softening of your heart. As you forgive this person, you can further forgive yourself. And as you forgive yourself, you can further forgive him or her. This person is very important to you or they would not arouse such emotion. Healing the relationship will heal the world because the process radiates energy. The forgiveness will eventually transfer to all people.

Personal Freedom and Global Oneness

*   ✳   ✳

Make changes today that benefit all people. Become a part of the power that stretches the current framework and creates a new world. Give up recounting past injustices. Stop demanding others give you power. *Become* powerful. Stop being the downtrodden. Walking in suffering delays your journey and drains your power and energy. Stop carrying the heavy cross. Jesus and other teachers came to lighten your burden. Lift up and ease your load.

Give up judgment that holds others responsible for you. Stop lamenting your fate. Give up your past grievances and heal ancient wounds with forgiveness. Every time you point the finger of blame you are denying your very power.

You are not the downtrodden, except by your own choice. All people everywhere: give up the past and be in the present. Own your inner spiritual greatness. Value your heritage but don't wear it like a banner of suffering. Be proud of your heritage but don't live in the battles of the long ago past. Honor your heritage but don't wear it as a badge of supremacy.

Mastery of spiritual consciousness begins with giving up the ego's false claims of self-righteousness. It means being fully and completely accountable for your own feelings and thoughts. It means owning that which you self-imposed and no longer creating enemies on whom you can blame your suffering.

More than anything else, this passage in time is about freedom. Now is the time of deliverance from the chains that have bound you. Prepare the way for a new generation. Place your fellow beings ahead of your tiny, helpless, demanding ego. Freedom is first a state of mind. What is not within us cannot be found outside us.

The passing of time is inescapable. You choose your path, or you don't choose. And that is still a choice. Those who are politely standing by, waiting for something to happen, will be left behind. Free will is just that—knowing we have freedom and power that comes from within. We must avail ourselves of our inner spiritual strength and power. It can propel us forward or we can stay locked in our own self-defined prisons.

This passage of time will bring a new beginning of reality to others, one in which we see our fellow humans as the spiritual essences and loving beings that they are. When we can take off the masks of our ego-defined roles in the dramas we play, we will truly see our oneness. We will see our brothers and sisters standing there—our beloved fellow souls whom we had mistakenly identified as the enemy. What a holy day when, one by one, we give up our grievances, lay down our swords, and embrace our fellow beings. We are one family, of one Source, with one destiny. Why would we not want to see this?

It is time give up divisions of all kinds: religious, political, racial, and any positions that cause people to take sides or draw lines down the center. It is time to move to a new global level—for that is just what we are: one planet, one world, one family of diversity, beauty, and splendor.

We must recognize that even the slightest irritations with one another come from the ego and weaken the progress of humanity. We must refrain from attacking. We must seek a true armistice that comes from the reconciliation of ideas, not from reactionary movements.

It is time to be a leader. You cannot be left behind when you are in the front, leading others to a new level of understanding, joy, and peace. Peace is what we must choose now. We must commit relentlessly, passionately, and completely to peace.

Let us take down the walls of fear and accusation. The world stages are worn and creaking. The floorboards cannot withstand this strain much longer. The performance has played on too long. The audience and the casts have grown weary. It is time for the performance to end.

Photo: Therese Frare Photography

ABOUT THE AUTHOR

Danna Beal holds a Bachelor of Arts from Washington State University and a Master's of Education from Whitworth College. She speaks internationally, teaches at seminars, and is a business consultant.

She has been a keynote speaker and workshop leader on her model for "Leading with Spirit and Compassion" to over three hundred business groups throughout the United States and Canada. Her consulting and speaking experiences have led her to understand the issues people face in the many industries with which she has worked, including hospitals, physician practices, law firms, CPA firms, retirement communities, auto dealerships, non-profits, insurance agencies, banks and credit unions. Although their business services may differ, the fundamental human relationships and ego conflicts are the same.

Danna lives in Bellevue, Washington, and her website is www.danna beal.com.

Sentient Publications, LLC publishes books on cultural creativity, experimental education, transformative spirituality, holistic health, new science, ecology, and other topics, approached from an integral viewpoint. Our authors are intensely interested in exploring the nature of life from fresh perspectives, addressing life's great questions, and fostering the full expression of the human potential. Sentient Publications' books arise from the spirit of inquiry and the richness of the inherent dialogue between writer and reader.

Our Culture Tools series is designed to give social catalyzers and cultural entrepreneurs the essential information, technology, and inspiration to forge a sustainable, creative, and compassionate world.

We are very interested in hearing from our readers. To direct suggestions or comments to us, or to be added to our mailing list, please contact:

SENTIENT PUBLICATIONS, LLC

1113 Spruce Street
Boulder, CO 80302
303-443-2188
contact@sentientpublications.com
www.sentientpublications.com